DICTIONARY OF
HOUSEPLANTS

BRIAN WARD

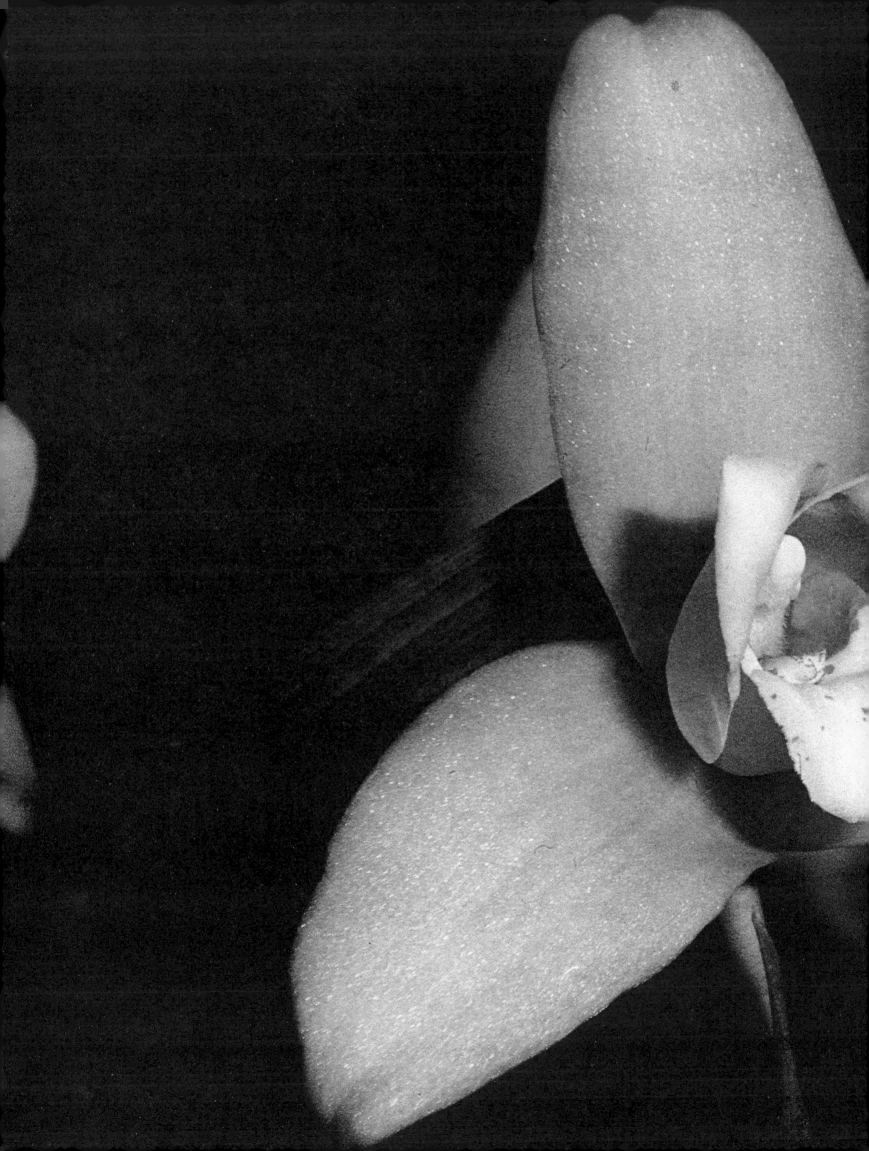

DICTIONARY OF HOUSEPLANTS

BRIAN WARD

This edition produced exclusively for

 **WHSMITH**

This edition produced exclusively
for W H Smith

This edition is © Winchmore
Publishing Services Ltd 1984

ISBN 0 907025 05 6

Designed by Roy Williams
Photographs supplied by
Stirling Macoboy
Printed in Yugoslavia

CONTENTS

INTRODUCTION

This book provides the basic information you will need to grow all the commonly available house plants, as well as some more specialised and interesting types. In addition, there are plants listed which are suitable for growing on the patio, either during warm weather or throughout the year. Large plants, such as palms, are best grown in a conservatory or cool greenhouse, but are suitable as house plants while young. Some of the more exotic types will need a heated greenhouse and continual attention if they are to thrive.

The book is laid out alphabetically, with plants listed under their Latin names. Alternative Latin names and popular names are also given and there is a cross index of Latin and English names at the end of the book. Cultivation details are provided for each entry, and brief general comments on watering, propagation, composts, etc, are given below. Specialist books are available on each major group of plants, and give further details which are outside the scope of this book.

Do not expect to find all the plants listed here in your local garden centre. Generally, those most readily available are plants that the nurseries find easiest to cultivate, and consequently are in greatest demand. If you wish to try some of the more unusual types, you will need to buy them from specialist nurseries. You will find their advertisements in the various gardening magazines.

WATERING

With very few exceptions indoor plants will rot if overwatered, and especially if the soil becomes waterlogged. The amount of water needed is dependent solely upon the plant's need for water and the rate of evaporation from the pot. However, some plants have particular needs where watering is concerned.

In general, watering is needed when the surface of the compost becomes dry, (although if disturbed, it will be found that it is still damp 1-2 cm beneath the surface). Plentiful watering means that the surface of the compost is always moist. For plants to be watered sparingly, there should never be sufficient water to spill through the drainage hole at the bottom of the pot.

For nearly all plants, underwatering is safer than overwatering. If for some reason the compost has dried right out the whole pot can be submerged, up to near the surface of the compost, and soaked for ten to fifteen minutes in tepid water. In general, drying out is more likely if clay pots are used. If in doubt, knock the plant out and check the state of roots and compost.

COMPOSTS

For the average plant, there is a choice of soil-based or peat-based composts. These are purchased ready mixed, and for the small quantities required for indoor plants, it is seldom worth mixing your own compost. Soil-based composts are messy to handle, but contain nutrients lacking in peat-based composts. Therefore, less frequent feeding will be needed if plants are grown in soil-based compost. In addition, some peat composts are very difficult to wet properly if they have been completely dried out, and they can then pack down too solidly in the pot. For special requirements other materials may be added to the basic compost such as sphagnum moss, which is normally chopped up. Ground tree bark is very useful, providing the fibrous base for composts needed for bromeliads and orchids. Perlite is a mineral material, supplied in coarse grains, which improves soil drainage and holds a certain amount of nutrients and water. Sand is used for the same purpose, and must be coarse and well washed. Baked clay pellets are also available, serving a similar purpose.

Some typical specialised composts are listed below:
Desert Cacti and Succulents
2 parts soil or peat-based compost
1 part coarse sand or perlite
Forest Cacti
2 parts soil or peat-based compost
1 part coarse sand or perlite
1 part leaf mould, well-rotted manure, or shredded and prepared tree bark
Bromeliads
1 part coarse leaf mould
1 part peat
  or
1 part soil-based compost
1 part peat
Addition of shredded tree bark may be beneficial.
Orchids
2 parts osmunda bark or shredded tree bark
1 part sphagnum moss
  or
3 parts shredded bark
1 part peat
1 part perlite
1 part charcoal

1 part sphagnum moss
Bulbs, Corms and Tubers
Soil- or peat-based compost as specified or
bulb fibre
6 parts peat
2 parts crushed shell
1 part crushed charcoal

PESTS

House plants are subject to fewer pests than
plants in the garden. Most are easily identi-
fied and easily treated. The following are the
most common.
Aphids
The common green-fly or black-fly, which
sometimes attacks new growth in very large
numbers. Easily spotted, and killed by most
aerosol insecticides.
Mealy bug/root mealy bug
Small insects covered with dense white hair,
which cluster in groups. They can affect most
plants and are especially common in cacti.
Spray affected plants with insecticide, or
sprinkle pellets of systemic insecticide into
the compost. Knock plants out of their pots to
check for root mealy bug. They can be treated
by submerging the root ball in diluted insecticide.
Red spider mites
These tiny red pests are common in dry
conditions, and cause leaves to curl or shrivel.
Spray the plant thoroughly with insecticide,
including the underside of the leaves and into
buds or leaf clusters. It may be necessary to
experiment with different insecticides to
eradicate them completely.
Scale insects
Tiny limpet-like insects protected by a waxy
scale. They are killed by dabbing with methy-
lated spirit, followed by a spray with systemic
insecticide.
White-flies
Tiny 2-mm flies which need repeated spraying for full control.

REST PERIODS

Plant growth depends on several factors, the
most important of which are adequate light
and a suitable temperature, and in winter
there is not usually enough light or warmth
for healthy growth. The plant no longer needs
nutrients at this time, so feeding becomes
unnecessary, and only sufficient water is
needed to replace that lost by evaporation
from the foliage; giving the plant more water
than it needs will lead to root rot. A few plants
need no rest period because they are used to
moist, tropical conditions and this is indicated in the text. With other plants, watering
should be restricted in winter, and the plants
stored in a cool (but not cold), light position.
Watering should be started *gradually* as
growth begins in spring. Do not let compost
dry out completely in winter because this will
damage the roots and it may be difficult to get
water to penetrate the root ball when watering begins again, especially with peat-based
compost. Bulbous plants usually die back
completely, and must be kept completely dry.
Winter rests are normally required, but in
some cases a rest is recommended after
flowering in summer. This is in order to
provide conditions approximating to those in
the plant's natural home.

PROPAGATION

A cheap propagator is invaluable for this
purpose. It is a plastic 'greenhouse', which
may be quite small. It serves to maintain high
humidity, preventing excess water loss in a
cutting or young plant. The following are the
most important techniques.
Offsets
Small plants, often with their own roots,
which are produced around the base of a
plant. These can be detached as the plant
starts active growth, and are easily grown in
normal compost.
Division
Plants producing clumps can be pulled apart,
or cut, to produce several smaller clumps.
Cuttings
Shoots or parts of stem can be cut during
active growth and rooted in a propagator. In
woody plants it is usually necessary to cut a
small section of stem (the heel) as well as the
small shoot. Rooting hormone is a powder or
liquid into which the base of the cutting is
dipped before planting. The chemical stimu-
lates the growth of roots, and is especially
valuable in woody plants.
Leaf cuttings
Fleshy leaves may sometimes be rooted by
inserting the stem, or part of the leaf into
the compost. In some cases, the leaf can
be pegged flat against the compost using
U-shaped pieces of wire.
Layering
In plants which produce long trailing stems,
these can be pinned to the compost, and
usually produce roots, after whch the stem
can be severed from the parent plant.
Air layering
This method is useful in large-leafed plants,
which are difficult to root as cuttings. The
stem is scraped or slit and dusted with

rooting hormone. This area is then surrounded with a mixture of sphagnum moss and compost and wrapped around with plastic film. When roots appear beneath the plastic, the stem can be cut below the rooting section and the whole tip of the plant is potted up. The remaining stump will usually produce several branches to replace the severed tip.

Seed

Nearly all plants can be grown from seed but this can be a very long process. With plants such as orchids it is scarcely practicable for the amateur. Specific detailed cultural instructions are given with most branded packets of seed.

General

Young plants and cuttings have insufficient roots to absorb the water they need and a propagator helps by reducing evaporation from the leaves. However, the high humidity in the propagator also encourages mould growth which easily kills young plants, and sterilised compost from sealed packs should always be used. They should not be fed at this stage, because they cannot cope with a sudden burst of rich nutrients, special seedling compost is deliberately *low* in nutrient value.

A NOTE ON PLANT NAMES

Plants are listed in alphabetical order, using the scientific or Latin names, followed by popular names, if any. The first name, such as *Ficus*, defines the genus of the plant, while the second name, e.g. *elastica*, describes the species. Thus all species of plants with the first or generic name *Ficus* are related. The popular name, in this case 'Rubber Plant', could be applied to any member of the *Ficus* genus, so could not be used safely when ordering a plant. In a few cases, such as the Swiss Cheese Plant (*Monstera deliciosa*), the popular name is not at all ambiguous and would not be easily mistaken, but names such as 'Firecracker Plant' could refer to many quite unrelated plants. However, to help the reader who is unfamiliar with Latin names, an extensive index of popular names is also included.

Unfortunately, many nurserymen do not label their stock with the proper name, and this can make it difficult to identify the plant and establish any special treatment or care it might need.

Another problem with plant names is that even the scientists have second thoughts, and quite frequently change the names. In this book, alternative names are given in brackets, any of which may be used.

COLOUR PLATES

Facing page: Achimenes longiflora

This page
Right: Acacia podalyriifolia
Below: Abutilon hybridum 'Boule de Neige'
Centre right: Acer Palmatum 'Disectum Aureum'
Centre left: Acalypha Wilkesiana 'Macrophylla'
Bottom right: Acokanthera spectabilis
Bottom left: Acalypha hispida

Facing page
Top left: Acorus gramineus
Top centre: Adiantum trapeziforme
Top right: Aechmea dichlamydea
Centre left: Adenium obesum
Bottom left: Aechmea fasciata
Bottom right: Aeonium arboreum

This page
Left: Aerides mitratum
Below: Aeschynanthus speciosus

Facing page
Top left: Agave filifera
Top right: Agave americana
'Marginata'
Bottom: Albizzia julibrissin
'Rosea'

This page
Top left: Aglaonema sp
Below left: Aglaonema ×
'Silver King'
Far left: Aglaonema treubii
Below: Agapanthus praecox
orientalis

Facing page: Amaryllis
belladonna

This page
Right: Allamanda nerifolia
Far right: Alternanthera
amoena
Below left: Alocasia odora
Below centre: Aloe speciosa
Below right: Aloe brevifolia
Bottom left: Alocasia
macrorrhiza
Bottom right:
Amorphophallus bulbifer

Facing page
Top right: Anigosanthos
flavida 'Rubra'
Top left: Angraecum
superbum
Bottom right: Anigozanthos
manglesii
Bottom centre: Anthurium
scherzeranum

This page
Top right: Ananas bracteatus
Top left: Ananas comosus
Right: Anthurium andreanum
Below: Anthurium
andreanum 'Rubrum'

Right: Aphelandra ×
'Rembrandt'
Far right: Araucaria
heterophylla
Below: Aporocactus
flagelliformis

Left: Arthropodium cirrhatum
Far left: Araujia sp
Below: Ardisia sp (bonsai)
Bottom left: Arum italicum
Bottom right: Aristolochia grandiflora

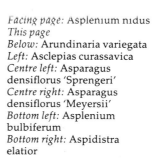

Facing page: Asplenium nidus
This page
Below: Arundinaria variegata
Left: Asclepias curassavica
Centre left: Asparagus
densiflorus 'Sprengeri'
Centre right: Asparagus
densiflorus 'Meyersii'
Bottom left: Asplenium
bulbiferum
Bottom right: Aspidistra
elatior

Facing page
Top left: Azalea kurume 'flora' (Bonsai)
Top right: Azalea × 'Elsa Karga' Belgian Hybrid
Bottom: Astrophytum myriostigma

This page
Top left: Babiana stricta
Top right: Barleria micans
Centre: Barleria cristata
Bottom left: Aucuba japonica

Facing page
Top left: Begonia × 'gypsy'
Top right: Begonia scaptrum
Centre right: Beaumontia
grandiflora
Bottom left: Begonia
tuberhybrida 'Tahiti'
Bottom right: Beaucarnea
recurvata

This page
Right: Bauhinia blakeana
Centre right: Bauhinia
variegata
Bottom right: Bauhinia
scandens
Below: Bauhinia galpini

Facing page
Top left: Bougainvillea
'Hawaiian Gold'
Top right: Bomarea
shuttleworthii
Bottom: Bougainvillea blabra
'common purple'

This page
Right: Billbergia pyramidalis
Below: Blechnum brasiliense
Bottom left: Bifrenaria
harrisoniae
Bottom right: Billbergia
nutans

Facing page
Top left: Browallia speciosa
Top right: Bryophyllum tubiflorum
Bottom left: Brugmansia cornigera
Bottom right: Brunfelsia brasiliensis v. acuminatia

This page
Right: Bouvardia longiflora (Syn B. humboldtii)
Far right: Breynia nivosa
Below: Brassolaeliacattleya 'Crispu Royale'

Facing page
Top left: Calathea cylindrica
Top right: Calceolaria
'monarch grandiflora'
Bottom: Calceolaria
crenatiflora

This page
Top left: Buxus Sempervirens
Top right: Calanthe vestita
Above: Bulbophyllum
Right: Caladium 'Rose Bud'

Facing page
Top: Campanula muralis
Bottom left: Canna indica
Bottom right: Canna indica

This page
Right: Camellia japonica
'kokuryu' (Bonsai)
Below: Camellia × 'Donation
Seedling'
Bottom left: Campelia zanonia
Bottom right: Callistemon
viminalis

Facing page: Cattleya
bowringiana

This page
Right: Capsicum sp
Far right: Celosia cristata
plumosa
Below: Cattleya aurantiaca
Below centre: Cantua
buxifolia
Bottom left: Caryota fishtail
palm
Bottom right: Cedrus (Bonsai)

Facing page
Top left: Chrysanthemum
Top right: Chlorophytum
comosum
Bottom: Chrysanthemum
'Thumbelina'

This page
Top left: Cissus rhombifolia
'Grape Ivy'
Top right: Cibotium scheidii
Above: Cissus discolor
'Begonia Treebine'
Right: Chrysalidocarpus

Facing page
Top left: Clerodendron nutans
Top right: Clerodendron
thomsoniae
Bottom: Clematis 'Twilight'

This page
Top left: Cleistocactus strausii
Top right: Clerodendron
speciosissimum
Above: Citrus aurantium
myrtifolia (Chinotto)
Right: Citrus Limonia
'meyeri' (Meyer lemon)

Facing page
Top left: Columnea 'Yellow Dancer'
Top right: Columnea banksii
Bottom: Columnea gloriosa

This page
Right: Collinia elegans
Above: Coleus
Top left: Coleus rehneltianus
Top right: Coffea arabica

Facing page
Top left: Codiaeum
variegatum Var pictum
Top right: Clivia miniata
Bottom left: Coelogyne
rossiana
Bottom right: Codiaeum
variegatum × 'Appleleaf'

This page
Above: Clivia miniata
Above centre: Clivia nobilis
Top left: Codiaeum × 'Ducks
foot'
Top right: Cobea scandens
Right: Clytostoma
callistegioides
Far right: Coelogyne cristata

Facing page
Top left: Crassula × 'Hummel
Sunset'
Top right: Crassula falcata
Bottom: Crinum asiaticum

This page
Above: Cotyledon macrantha
Above centre: Crinum moorei
Above top: Costus speciosus
'Crepe or Malay Ginger'
Top right: Cordyline
terminalis
Top centre: Cordyline
terminalis
Right: Cordyline terminalis
'Baby Ti'

Facing page
Top left: Cyclamen persicum
Top right: Cymbidium ×
'Tommy'
Bottom left: Cymbidium
Bottom right: Cyperus
alternifolius

This page
Top left: Cymbidium ×
'Prince Charles'
Top right: Cyclamen persicum
Above: Cymbidium
Right: Cyperus papyrus

Facing page
Top: Dendrobium
jamesianum
Bottom left: Dendrobium
eburneum
Bottom right: Dichorisandra
thyrsiflora

This page:
Top left: Darlingtonia
californica
Top right: Davallia fejeensis
Above: Dieffenbachia picta
Right: Dicksonia antarctica
Far right: Cyrtomium
falcatum

Facing page
Top left: Echeveria elegans
Top right: Echinocereus subinermis
Bottom: Echeveria meridian

This page
Above: Echinocactus grusonii
Above centre: Echeveria sp
Top left: Dracaena × 'Tricolor'
Top right: Dionaea muscipula
Top centre: Dracaena fragrans victoriae
Right: Echinopsis 'Darley Queen'

Facing page
Top left: Epidendrum 'Cream Puff'
Top right: Epiphyllum ackermanii
Bottom: Epiphyllum oxypetalum

This page
Top left: Epidendrum radicans
Top right: Erica cenerea 'C.D. Eason'
Right: Episcia dianthiflora
Above: Episcia reptans

Facing page
Top left: Eucomis comosus
Top right: Euphorbia
pulcherrima
Far right centre: Euphorbia
splendens
Bottom left: Eupatorium
megalophyllum
Bottom right: Euphorbia
pulcherrima

This page
Left: Eucalyptus juvenile
foliage 'florist's bluegum'
Far left: Eucalyptus calophylla
Below: Eucharis amazonica

Facing page: Ficus elastica

This page
Right: Fittonia verschaffeltii
         (top)
         Fittonia Argyroneura
Below: Ficus retusa
Below centre: Ficus radicans
Bottom left: Ficus pumila hillii
Bottom centre: Ficus lyrata
Bottom right: Ficus
wildemanniana

Facing page
Top left: Fuchsia magellanica tricolor
Top right: Fuchsia 'a bit of red'
Bottom: Fuchsia × 'Alice Hoffman'

This page
Right: Fortunella japonica
Far right: Fortunella marginata
Below: Freesia
Below right: Freesia × 'Flame'
Bottom: Fuchsia (in basket)

Facing page
Top left: Gasteria verrucosa
Top right: Gloriosa
rothschildiana 'Gloriosa Lily'
Below: Gloriosa
rothschildiana

This page
Right: Gardenia augusta
Below: Geogenanthus
Below centre: Gardenia ×
'Professor Pucci'
Bottom left: Bonsai, Gardenia
florida
Bottom right: Gardenia
tahitiensis

Facing page
Top left: Gymnocalycium sp
Top right: Gynura ovrantiaea
Bottom left: Gymnocalycium
Bottom right: Guzmania
gloriosa

This page
Right: Grevillea juniperina
Far right: Grevillea robusta
Below: Greville × Coochin
Hills'
Bottom: Grevillea hookerana
(fine leaf)

Facing page
Top left: Hedera
Centre left: Hedera helix
'Needlepoint'
Top centre: Haemanthus
katherinae
Top right: Hamatocactus
setispinus
Below: Haemanthus
nataliensis

This page
Top left: Haworthia
margaritifera
Top right: Hedychium
cronarium
Above: Hedychium
coccineum
Left: Hedychium coronarium
× gardnerianum

Facing page
Top left: Hippeastrum (White form)
Top right: Hippeastrum
Centre left: Hippeastrum pardalinum
Bottom left: Hosta fortunei 'Aureo-maculata'
Bottom right: Hippeastrum amaryllis

This page
Right: Heliotropium arborescens 'Aureum'
Far right: Helxine soleirolii
Below: Heliocereus mallisonii

Facing page
Top left: Hydrangea
macrophylla
Top right: Howea
Bottom: Hydrangea

This page
Right: Hoya bella
Below: Hyacinthus
'Hollyhock'
Top right: Hoya multiflora
Centre right: Hyacinthus
'Violet Beauty'
Bottom right: Hyacinthus
orientalis

Facing page: Impatiens ×
'Pawnee'

This page
Right: Hymenocallis littoralis
Below: Hylocereus undatus
Below left: Hypocyrta sp
Below right: Hypoestes
phyllostachys 'Splash'
Right centre: Hypoestes
aristata
Bottom left: Hymenocallis
festalis
Bottom centre: Impatiens
repens 'Golden Dragon'
Bottom right: Impatiens ×
'Fanfare'

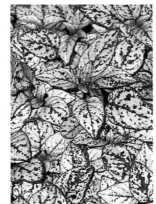

Facing page
Top left: Ixora chinensis
'Prince of Orange'
Top right: Ixora coccinea
Bottom: Ipomoea tricolor

This page
Left: Jasminum azoricum
Bottom left: Iresine lindenii
Below: Jasminum
polyanthum
Below centre: Jasminum
fruticosum
Bottom: Jacaranda
mimosifolia

Facing page: Justicia carnea

This page
Top left: Justicia aurea
Top right: Kohleria × eriantha
Centre left: Juniperus
chinensis (Bonsai)
Centre right: Juniperus
chinensis 'Aurea'
Bottom left: Kalanchoe
orgyalis
Bottom right: Kalanchoe
blossfeldiana

This page
Left: Lantana 'Chelsea Gem'
Below: Lantana
montevidensis
Bottom left: Laelia purpurata
Bottom right: Laeliocattleya ×
'Florence Patterson'
Centre right: Laeliocattleya
'Chit chat'

Facing page
Top left. Lilium speciosum
Top right: Lilium × 'Wildfire'
Bottom: Lilium ×
'Enchantment'

This page
Top left: Lilium longiflorum
Top right: Lilium × 'Mimosa
Star'
Above: Laurus nobilis
Above right: Laurus nobilis
Right: Linospadix
monostachya

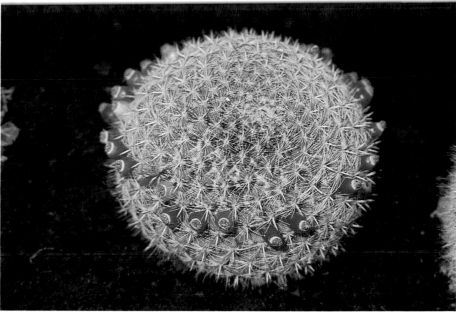

Facing page
Top left: Lithops lesleyi
Top right: Lithops glesinae
Centre left: Lycaste aromatica
Bottom left: Lobivia huascha
Bottom right: Livistona

This page
Top left: Mamillaria bocasana
Top right: Mamillaria hahniana
Left: Manettia bicolor
Above: Maranta leuconeura var erythrophylla

Facing page
Top left: Monstera variegata
Top right: Monstera obliqua
expilata
Centre left: Marraya exotica
Centre right: Marraya exotica
Bottom left: Musa coccinea
Bottom right: Musa ×
paradisiaca (fruit)

This page
Right: Miltonia irma × 'Lyath
Blue'
Far right: Mimosa pudica
Below: Medinilla magnifica

Facing page: Neoregelia
concentrica marginata

This page
Right: Myrtus communis
Far right: Narcissus poetaz
Below: Narcissus 'Silver
Chimes'
Bottom left: Neoregelia sp
Bottom right: Neoregelia

Above: Nidularium
bilbergioides citrinum
Above right: Odontoglossum
sp
Right: Oncidium
haematochilum
Far right: Ochna serrulata

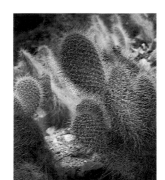

Facing page: Paphiopedilum
insigne
This page
Right: Pachyphytum
oviferum
Far right: Paphiopedilum
insigne sanderae
Below: Palisota barteri
Centre left: Oxypetalum
caeruleum
Centre right: Parodia 'St
Pienna'
Bottom left: Pachystachys
lutea
Bottom right: Pandanus
odoratissimus

Facing page
Top right: Pelargonium
domesticum 'Lavender grand
slam'
Centre right: Pelargonium
zonale 'Henri Joignot'
Bottom right: Pelargonium
zonale

This page
Main picture: Pelargonium
peltatum 'Ville de Paris'
Right: Pelargonium
domesticum
Below: Pelargonium
tomentosum
Bottom: Pedilanthus
tithymaloides Variegatus

Facing page
Top left: Pereskia aculeata
Top right: Peperomia caperata
'Emerald ripples'
Centre right: Peperomia
obtusifolia Tricolor
Bottom right: Double Petunias

This page
Right: Passiflora
quadrangularis
Far right: Pentas lanceolata
Below: Passiflora coccinea
Main picture: Petunia 'Blue
Jay'

Facing page
Top: Phoenix roebelenii
Bottom: Phalaenopsis
amboinensis
Main picture: Philodendron ×
'Red wings'

This page
Top left: Philodendron
bipinnatifidum
Top right: Philodendron
andreanum
Centre left: Phyllitis
scolopendrium
Centre right: Philodendron
sagittifolium
Above: Philodendron
bipinnatifidum

Facing page
Top left: Pilea mollis 'Moon Valley'
Top right: Picea (Bonsai)
Centre right: Pilea cadierii
Bottom left: Pilea nummulariifolia
Bottom right: Pinguicula caudata

This page
Top left: Pittosporum tobira
Top right: Pittosporum tobira
Above: Piper ornatum
Left: Platycerium grande

Facing page: Plumeria
acuminata

This page
Right: Plumeria rubra
Far right: Plumeria sp (Cairns
rose scented)
Below: Podocarpus sp
Centre left: Plectranthus
australis
Centre: Podocarpus falcatus
Centre right: Plumbago sp
Bottom left: Pleione
formosana
Bottom right: Pleomele
augustifolia

Facing page
Top left: Primula polyantha
Top right: Primula malacoides
Bottom: Primula polyantha

This page
Top left: Primula auricula
'Douglas blue alpine'
Top right: Primula obconica
Above left: Polypodium
aureum
Above right: Polyscias ficifolia
(Bonsai)
Right: Polyscias scutellaria
'Pennockii'

Facing page
Top: Rhododendron
yakushimianum 'Gertie'
Centre: Rhododendron
augustinii
Bottom: Rhododendron
fragrantissimum

This page
Main picture: Rhododendron
lochae
Right: Ricinocarpus pinifolius
Below: Rhoicissus
rhomboidea
Below centre: Rhoeo discolor
Bottom: Rhoeo spathacea
Vittata

Facing page: Ruellia
macrantha

This page
Right: Saintpaulia sp
Far right top: Saintpaulia sp
Far right upper centre:
Saintpaulia 'red rhapsodie'
Far right lower centre:
Sarracenia × chelsonii
Bottom left: Sanchezia nobilis
Bottom centre: Sansevieria
trifasciata
Bottom right: Sarracenia flava

Facing page
Top left: Scilla adlami
Top right: Saxifraga stolonifera
Centre right: Saxifraga caespitosa
Bottom left: Scilla peruviana
Bottom right: Scindapsus pictus

This page
Right above: Schefflera actinophylla Variegata
Right below: Schefflera polybotrya
Far right: Schefflera arboricola
Below: Schlumbergera 'Lilac bouquet'

Facing page
Top left: Selaginella uncinata
Top centre: Sedum
morganianum
Far right top: Senecio
macroglossus
Far right bottom: Sedum
pachyphyllum
Main picture: Selenicereus
grandiflorus

This page
Right: Senecio maritima
Far right: Senecio jacobsenii
Below: Senecio cruenta

Right: Sonerila margaritacea
Below: Sinningia sp
Bottom right: Solanum
pseudocapsicum
Bottom left: Spathiphyllum

Left: Smithiantha hybrida 'Compacta'
Far left: Sobralia fragrans
Below: Sophronitis coccinea
Bottom: Siderasis fuscata

Facing page
Top left: Streptocalyx sp
Top right: Streptocarpus
Bottom left: Strobilanthes
gossipiinus
Bottom right: Stromanthe
sanguinea

This page
Right: Streptosolen jamesonii
Bottom left: Streptocarpus sp
Bottom right: Strobilanthes
dyerianus

Facing page
Top left: Thunbergia fragrans
Top right: Thunbergia
mysorensis
Centre left: Syngonium sp
Bottom left: Syzygium
floribundum
Bottom right: Thunbergia
alata

This page
Left: Tillandsia lindenii
Above: Tetrastigma sp
Above centre: Tigridia
Top: Tillandsia fasciculata

Facing page
Top left: Trachycarpus
fortunei
Top right: ursinia anethoides
Centre left: Tradescantia
fluminensis
Bottom left: Tradescantia
virginiana
Bottom right: Tradescantia
blossfeldiana

This page
Right: Vallota purpurea
Bottom left: Trichocereus
thelagonus
Bottom right: Tulipa 'Royal
Splendour'

Facing page
Top left: Wistaria floribunda
Violacea Plena
Top right: Vriesia
Bottom: Bonsai Wistaria
chinensis

This page
Above top: Vriesia fenestralis
Above centre: Vanda teres
Above: Vriesia carinata
Above right: Wistaria sinensis
Top right: Vanda ×
rothschildiana
Top far right: Veltheimia capensis
Right: Vanda sanderiana

Facing page
Top left: Zantedeschia
elliottiana
Top centre: Zantedeschia
aethiopica
Top right: Zantedeschia
'Green goddess'
Bottom: Zygocactus

This page
Above: Zebrina pendula
(hanging plant)
Top: Zebrina pendula
Top centre: Zygocactus
truncatus
Top right: Zebrina sp
Right: Zantedeschia
rehmannii

DICTIONARY

ABUTILON
(Flowering Maple, Parlour Maple)
Group of trees, shrubs and herbs, related to HIBISCUS. Grown for their attractive mottled or variegated foliage, and for their bell-shaped flowers. Some species are very large, and only suitable for the cool greenhouse.

They need good light, either direct or indirect, and a minimum temperature of 10°C (50°F), living well under normal conditions. Water well during active growth, but allow surface of compost to dry before watering. Feed frequently during growing phase. Pot in loam or soil-based compost. Propagate from tip cuttings in spring and summer, rooted with aid of hormone rooting powder. Prune well to prevent spindly growth. All tolerate outdoor conditions in summer.

A. hybridum *Chinese Lantern*
Large group of hybrids, which can grow to 1.5 metres in height, with a similar spread. Pendant flowers, 5 cm long, with five petals. Pink, white and yellow varieties are available. Foliage splashed with creamy white.

A. megapotamicum
Slender shrub, which may need supporting on sticks. Bright red and yellow flowers with red stamens, appearing from spring to October.

A. pictum (A. striatum) *Thompsonii Flowering Maple*
Rich variegation of leaves, caused by a harmless virus. Salmon-coloured 4 cm flowers. Grows rapidly and may need cutting back.

ACACIA
Acacia armata *Kangaroo Thorn, Hedge Wattle*
Only a single species of **Acacia** is commonly kept as a house plant. *A. armata* is a fast-growing shrub, which thrives in good light and temperatures of 13°-18°C (55°-65°F). Produces fluffy yellow flowers resembling MIMOSA. Requires frequent watering and feeding in spring and summer. Cease feeding and reduce watering in winter. Prune in spring to keep size within reasonable limits, and to prevent straggly growth. Pot in soil-based compost.

ACALYPHA
Large group of plants generally grown for their showy, bright-coloured foliage. One species, A. hispida, is grown for its flowers; the others have small, inconspicuous flowers. They are fast growing, and prefer hot, humid conditions; minimum 16°C (60°F), and preferably at least 21°C (70°F). Need strong indirect light and should be stood on a tray of wet gravel or moss to provide high humidity, together with frequent mist-spraying. Water frequently during active growth. Pot in loam or peat-based compost. Prune to encourage side shoots, and propagate from tip cuttings in early spring. Most indoor gardeners discard old plants and renew each year from cuttings.

A. hispida *Chenille plant, Red-Hot Cat's Tail*
Foliage is unremarkable, but produces 30 cm bright red drooping flower spikes in late summer and autumn, which persist for many weeks.

A. wilkesiana *Copperleaf, Beefsteak Plant*
Large shrub which can be kept down to about 75 cm by yearly pruning. Large oval leaves, coloured copper, red and purple, with mottling. Requires good light to maintain leaf colour. There are numerous colour varieties, including forms with white-edged leaves.

ACER
(Japanese Maple)
Large group of hardy trees, normally grown outdoors. Smaller species are ideal as patio plants, grown in tubs, and are quite hardy, provided they are not exposed to strong wind and early frosts, which damage the tender foliage. Acers grow slowly and can live for many years in a container, in normal loam or peat-based compost.

A. palmatum 'Dissectum atropurpureum'
Small spreading tree, with feathery divided leaves which turn a rich red in the autumn. Seldom grows to more than 2 metres in height. Suitable for Bonsai cultivation. Many similarly decorative species are available.

ACHIMENES
(Hot Water Plant, Magic Flower, Cupid's Bower)
A group of popular and attractive flowering plants growing from clusters of small rhizomes, each of which produces a single stem. Leaves are dark green, velvety, and saw-edged. Flowers are tubular flaring out into five lobes, and are short-lived, but produced throughout the summer. Achimenes require a minimum temperature of about 13°C (55°F), and prefer strong, indirect light. Keep out of direct sunlight. The name 'Hot Water Plant' comes from the practice of starting rhizomes into growth by plunging them into hot water. Water plentifully when growth starts in spring, as even brief drying out will cause the plant to become dormant. Feed regularly as soon as buds appear. Allow to dry out after flowering, and store rhizomes over winter in a warm place after plant has withered. Restart

at a temperature of 16°C (60°F) in spring. Pot in peat-based compost, with added moss or perlite. Propagate by dividing rhizomes.

A. erecta (A. coccinea)
Long, trailing, reddish stems and whorls of deep green leaves. Brilliant red flowers, 2 cm long and 2 cm wide.

A. grandiflora
Upright hairy stems, 35 cm in height. Large leaves are rust-coloured underneath. Flowers purple-red, with a conspicuous white eye, 4 cm long.

A. longiflora
Long trailing stems, with saw-toothed leaves. Flowers are 7 cm in length, usually blue, but sometimes white or pink. Many hybrid forms of Achimenes are available.

ACOKANTHERA

Acokanthera spectabilis *Winter-sweet*
Large shrub for the conservatory or greenhouse, reaching 2 metres or more. Large leathery leaves, oval in shape, and glossy. Glossy white flowers develop in clusters in spring. Grow in soil-based compost in humid conditions, in indirect light.

ACORUS

Acorus gramineus 'Variegatus' *Sweet Flag*
Small grassy plant, up to 30 cm in height, growing in a dense tuft from a rhizome lying just beneath the surface of the compost. Attractive cream-and-green variegated leaves, and insignificant flowers. Prefers medium or strong indirect light, and a temperature of 7°-13°C (45°-55°F), and must be kept moist. Grows slowly, and is ideal for bottle gardens. Easily propagated by dividing the rhizome, and thrives in a small pot. Use soil-based compost. Keep moist at all times, or stand pot in shallow dish of water. Feed during summer months.

ADENIUM

Adenium obesum 'multiflorum' *Desert Rose, Impala Lily*
A flowering succulent, which needs a high temperature of 13°-30°C (55°-86°F) to succeed. Requires full sunlight and complete absence of draughts. Thick, gnarled stems serve as water-storage organs, and carry clusters of glossy leaves which usually fall in winter. Produces masses of pink or red flowers in spring or summer, when it needs frequent watering and feeding. Allow to dry out almost completely in winter. Pot in soil- or peat-based compost. Propagate from cuttings taken from fresh growth in summer.

ADIANTUM
(Maidenhair Fern)
The most popular genus of fern for indoor use, but quite difficult to keep healthy in the home. Adiantums all have extremely dainty fronds, and wiry, black stems. They grow from rhizomes. The thin fronds quickly shrivel in dry atmospheres and seldom withstand central heating. They prefer shaded conditions and a temperature of 18°-21°C (65°-70°F). Stand the pot on a tray containing wet gravel or peat, and spray foliage regularly. Leaves will be scorched by insecticides or leaf-cleaning sprays. Pot in peat or loam-based compost, and repot only when black roots appear on soil surface. Propagate by dividing rhizome in spring, and water new plants sparingly to avoid rotting. Feed occasionally throughout summer.

A. capillus-veneris *Common Maidenhair*
Graceful fern, growing up to 30 cm in height. Many small fan-shaped leaflets. A British native, but hardy only in very sheltered areas.

A. hispidulum *Australian Maidenhair*
Small species, with finger-like fronds which are reddish brown when young.

A. raddianum *Delta Maidenhair*
Triangular fronds, up to 45 cm in height, with very finely divided leaflets. Graceful arching growth. Available in several varieties.

AECHMEA

Large group of bromeliad plants, all having their leathery leaves arranged in rosettes, and many being epiphytes capable of living on rocks or tree branches. All have a vase-like centre which holds water and should not be allowed to dry out. The flower arises from this central vase. Aechmeas like a high humidity, so compost should be kept damp, as well as 'topping up' water in the vase. Allow compost partly to dry out in winter. Good indirect light is required and temperatures of 13°-18°C (55°-65°F), although Aechmeas can tolerate temperatures as low as 10°C (50°F).

Keep in a small pot, in a porous, sandy compost. Propagate by separating sideshoots after flowering. Do not overwater young plants.

A. chantinii *Urn Plant, Amazon Zebra Plant, Queen of Bromeliads*
Large (45 cm), tough plant, with viciously barbed edges to the silver and green banded leaves. In mature plants, spiky orange-pink bracts appear on a short stem in the summer, provided temperatures are sufficiently high. This 'flower' persists for several months.

A. fasciata *Silver Vase, Urn Plant*

Arched, silvery-grey leaves, with a powdery covering. Produces pink bracts containing small blue flowers. Variegated forms exist.

A. fulgens *Coral Berry*

Large, flattish growth, with deep green leaves, with purple undersides dusted with white powder. Deep reddish-purple flowers, followed by scarlet berries which persist for several months.

AEONIUM

Group of succulents which produce tight rosettes of fleshy leaves, usually carried on a woody stem. The lower leaves are continually shed, leaving characteristic scars on the stem. Clusters of small, cream, star-shaped flowers may be produced, after which the rosette dies.

Aeoniums require direct sunlight, and temperatures of 5°-30°C (41°-86°F). Keep in a cool place while they are resting in winter. Water moderately in spring and summer, but allow to dry out between waterings. Feed during active growth. Pot in porous, sandy compost, and propagate by severing and rooting a complete rosette, after drying out for a few days. Water cuttings sparingly.

A. arboreum 'Schwarzkopf' *Black Tree Aeonium*

Tree-like form, growing up to 1 metre in height. The large (20 cm) rosettes are almost black in colour (var. 'Atropurpureum' is purple). Requires strong sunlight to maintain its colour.

A. haworthii *Pin-Wheel*

Up to 60 cm in height, with blue-grey rosettes. Leaves are edged with red. Cream or pink flowers.

A. tabuliforme

Flat rosettes on very short stem. Should be grown with the rosette at an angle to allow water to run off. Rosette may contain more than 150 leaves, and reach 30 cm in diameter.

A. undulatum

Tall, thick stem (1 metre) topped by a 30 cm rosette of dark leaves. Produces sideshoots from base of woody 'trunk'.

AERANGIS

See ANGRAECUM

AERIDES

(Fox-tail Orchid)

Group of Asian epiphytic orchids which grow well under basket culture in the warm or moderately warm greenhouse. Temperatures from 13°C-18°C (55°-65°F). Leaves are strap-shaped and fleshy. Drooping flower spikes up to 60 cm in length, in spring or summer. Waxy fragrant flowers grow in cylindrical clusters. Grow in baskets or special perforated orchid pots, in mixture of shredded bark or osmunda fibre, and sphagnum moss. Spray frequently in summer to maintain humidity, and water well during growth phase. Propagate by removing and potting small plants produced at base of plant.

A. fieldingii *Free-flowering orchid*

Fairly easy to grow. Flowers 2.5 cm across, pale pink with mauve blush, and very long lasting. Numerous other species available, in various colours.

AESCHYNANTHUS

Large genus of rather temperamental trailing plants with paired leathery leaves, and showy flowers which are produced either singly along the stem, or in clusters at the tip. Flowers are tubular in shape, opening into five lobes.

Requires continuous warmth, with a minimum temperature of 13°C (55°F), and indirect lighting. Best grown in hanging baskets or trained over a frame, and may require spraying in summer to maintain humidity. Allow to dry out slightly in winter. Pot in peat-based compost, and propagate with cuttings taken in spring or summer. Rooted cuttings need continuous high humidity.

A. lobbianus (A. radicans) *Lipstick Plant*

Purple-edged leaves, and flowers coloured bright crimson inside, and with creamy-white throat. Flowers from May to July.

A. marmoratus *Zebra Basket Vine*

Grown more for its foliage than the green and brown flowers. Leaves have brown markings on upper side, and are reddish underneath.

A. speciosus

The most spectacular species, trailing to 60 cm. Flowers are up to 7 cm in length, orange with a yellow throat and scarlet markings.

AGAPANTHUS

(African Lily)

Often grown in the garden, but only hardy in protected areas. Can be overwintered in the house or greenhouse, or grown on the patio in tubs. Very long, strap-shaped leaves, and large rounded clusters of flowers carried on a long stem. Grow in tubs, in soil-based compost. Keep cool in winter, but protect from frost.

A. africanus

Grows to 70 cm in height, with enormous clusters of deep blue flowers in June to September. Grow in full sun, but needs protection in winter.

A. praecox

Most common species of Agapanthus, producing pale blue or white flowers in dense clusters. Half hardy. The most commonly available species.

AGAVE
(Century Plant)

Large family of tough, spiky succulents, which are mostly too large for indoor use. Many are viciously spined, and most are variegated. Leaves are hard and fleshy, and are arranged in a whorl around the central shoot. Most are slow-growing, and tolerate a wide range of temperatures, with a minimum of 5°C (40°F) in winter. Require good light, and moderate watering in summer, partly drying out between waterings. Keep relatively dry in winter. Pot in ordinary soil-based compost, and propagate by detaching and potting offsets produced around the base.

A. americana

The most common species, which eventually grows to enormous size, with 2-metre leaves. Loose rosette of blue-green leaves, edged with crimson. Flower stem may be up to 8 metres! Suitable for indoor cultivation when young. Variegated forms are available, which grow slowly.

A. filifera

Slow-growing Agave, forming a rosette 65 cm across. Tough green leaves are edged with loose white fibres. May occasionally produce a 2-metre spike with purple flowers, after which the main plant dies (like other Agaves), although new plantlets soon appear.

A. paniflora

Small (17 cm) Agave with dark green leaves edged with white threads. Forms a very dense leaf rosette. Older plants occasionally produce yellow flowers.

A. victoria-reginae

The most attractive of the Agaves. Produces a dense globular cluster of spines, up to 40 cm across. Leaves are fleshy and triangular in section with brilliant white edges and a fierce spine at the tip. Very slow growing, hence large plants are expensive. Needs to be put in the garden in summer to develop its best colouring.

AGLAONEMA
(Chinese Evergreens)

Large group of attractive foliage plants, having large leathery leaves, and mostly silvery or variegated. May occasionally develop a short 'trunk' as the lower leaves fall. Requires temperature of 18°-21°C (65°-70°F), and light shade. Aglaonemas need to be kept moist (some are completely aquatic) and require a high humidity to prevent leaf damage. In winter give only enough water to prevent complete drying out. Grow in a sandy soil-based compost, and propagate by detaching and rooting offsets produced from the base.

A. commutatum 'Silver Spear'

Grows up to 30 cm in height. This variety has silvery bars splashed across its spear-shaped leaves.

A. crispum 'Silver Queen'

Leaves are silvery-cream with green speckling only on the borders and along the veins. Due to its excessive variegation needs strong but indirect light if it is to thrive.

A. pseudobracteum

A large but more delicate plant which cannot tolerate low temperatures and is especially sensitive to cold draughts. Green-edged leaves, with yellow centres. Grows up to 1 metre in height.

ALLAMANDA
(Golden Trumpet)

A. cathartica

Climber which does best in a conservatory or cool greenhouse. Large oval leaves carried on sprawling stems, and enormous (10 cm) trumpet-shaped brilliant yellow flowers, produced throughout the summer. Needs a temperature of 16°-21°C (60°-70°F) and strong light (but shade from direct sun). Needs heavy pruning to keep under control. Feed fortnightly during active growth, and water sparingly in winter. Grow in soil-based compost and propagate with cuttings.

ALOCASIA

A group of exotic and attractive, though temperamental plants related to the Arum lily. All are really suited to the warm greenhouse, but can survive in the house with care. They grow from tubers and have arrow-head-shaped velvety leaves in various colours. Temperature range 18°-24°C (65°-75°F), and a high humidity which must be maintained by standing pot on a tray of wet gravel or peat. Do not allow the plant to become waterlogged. Allow to dry out in autumn and leave in the pot until spring. Propagate by dividing tubers in dormant phase.

A. indica

Relatively tough species with large, waxy, deep-green leaves. Grows up to 65 cm in height.

A. macrorrhiza   *Giant Elephant's Ear*

Enormous tree-like form for the greenhouse or conservatory, with 60 cm leaves growing on 1 metre stalks, eventually resembling a small tree.

A. sanderiana *Kris Plant*
Toughest species of Alocasia with metallic green leaves with white veins and margins. Undersides of leaves are purple. Grows to about 65 cm.

ALOE
Enormous group of succulents with thick leaves usually arranged in rosettes and often heavily spined. Some have stems and others may sprawl untidily and trail from the pot. Many have variegations or attractively marked leaves. Flowers are produced on spikes and are tubular and usually orange or red. Can withstand a wide range of temperatures 5°-30°C (41°-86°F), and need good light. Heavily spined species can usually withstand direct sunlight. Water well during spring and summer and allow to become nearly dry through the winter. Grow in sandy, soil-based compost. Propagate by potting rosettes developed at the plant base, or cut from the shoots.

A. arborescens *Candelabra Plant, Tree Aloe*
Large and often untidy looking Aloe, which can grow to 2 metres or more, but usually remains smaller in the home. Long, narrow-toothed leaves, growing in a rosette on a bare woody stem.

A. aristata *Lace Aloe, Torch Plant*
Small stemless Aloe with dark grey-green leaves in a globular rosette. Small spikes all over leaves, and a thread at the leaf tip. Does not tolerate direct sunlight.

A. jacunda *Dwarf Aloe*
Small form, producing rosettes only 8 cm across. Forms a dense clump of rosettes. Leaves are mottled with cream, and have spined edges.

A. variegata *Partridge-breasted Aloe, Tiger Aloe*
The most popular dwarf species. Produces upright clusters of leaves which gradually spiral as the plant grows. Leaves are dark green, with white mottles and bands. Grows up to 30 cm, but very slowly. May flop over side of pot or form untidy clusters. Frequently flowers in late winter. Very tolerant of dry conditions.

ALTERNANTHERA
A. amoena *Parrot Leaf*
Small evergreen foliage plant noted for its brilliant colouration. Leaves are blotched orange and red, with bright-green borders. Suitable for cool greenhouse or conservatory, grown in peat-based compost, and protected from direct sunlight.

AMARYLLIS
A. belladonna *Belladonna Lily*
Often confused with HIPPEASTRUM which it closely resembles. Grows from a large bulb, producing trumpet-shaped flowers 8 cm across, and coloured red, pink or white. Flowers in autumn or winter, before strap-shaped leaves appear. Plant in normal soil-based compost in summer. Allow to dry out when leaves yellow. Can be grown outside in good weather, or will thrive in conservatory or on a window-sill.

AMORPHOPHALLUS
Small group of lily-like plants for the warm greenhouse. Require moist, shady conditions. All have fleshy spathes which are interesting looking, rather than attractive. Allow to dry off when foliage yellows in winter.

A. bulbifer
Large three-lobed leaves on 1 metre stalks. 12 cm spathes, coloured greenish-red with pink spots, surrounding a long pink spadix.

A. rivieri *Voodoo Plant, Devil's Tongue*
Very large plant with leaves up to 1 metre across. Purplish-green spathe surrounds a blue spadix, and smells revolting.

ANANAS
(Pineapple)
These bromeliad plants have long slender leaves edged with sharp spines and arranged in a rosette. Flowers arise on a stalk carrying pink bracts and blue flowers, followed some months later by the familiar pineapple, which is also topped by saw-toothed leaves. Require good indirect light and a temperature of 13°-18°C (55°-65°F). They prefer high humidity, but do not need excessive watering. Grow in a peaty compost, and propagate from the small offsets produced around the base of the plant.

A. bracteatus 'Striatus' *Red Pineapple*
Variegated form of the pineapple, with cream-striped leaves and growing slowly to a 1 metre spread. Very sharp leaf spines. Leaves become pink as the red fruit begins to develop.

Acomosus 'Variegatus'
Smaller variegated form of the common pineapple. Leaves develop pink colouration in adequate light. May fruit when about six years old.

ANCHUSA

A. capensis

Usually grown as a garden annual, but a suitable house plant for cultivation on a sunny window-sill. Prefer well-drained peat-based compost. Grow from seed sown in January, and do not overwater. They grow to about 45 cm, producing sprays of blue flowers resembling the Forget-me-not.

ANGRAECUM

Group of spectacular orchids for the warm greenhouse, and unsuitable as house plants. Produce typical orchid strap-like leaves, and have an epiphytic growth necessitating basket culture. Require temperature of 18°C (65°F), high humidity and indirect light. Produce spectacular waxy flowers during the winter. Do not have a winter rest period, and need feeding throughout most of the year. Cultivate in special orchid compost and propagate from cuttings taken from shoots. Given the right conditions, Angraecum are easy to grow and flower prolifically.

A. eburneum

An upright-growing species with 45 cm leaves. Flowers are produced on a 1 metre stem, and are green and white, and fragrant. Flowers are spider-like, and appear to be growing upside-down.

A. sesquipedale *Star of Bethlehem Orchid*

One of the most spectacular of all orchids. A large plant, producing enormous 17 cm flowers from the leaf axils. Flowers are star-shaped, creamy white, and have a pale green spur which trails for 30 cm. Flowers persist for a long while on the plant. Highly recommended for greenhouse cultivation.

ANIGOZANTHOS

A. manglesii *Kangaroo Paw, Sword Lily*

Fans of sword-like leaves and stiff flowering stems covered with red downy hairs. Flowers are produced on 1 metre stems, and are hairy and tubular, with reddish-blue base and spidery petals. Grow in a cool greenhouse in soil-based compost. Flowers from May to July.

ANTHURIUM

Large group of lily-like plants grown for their foliage and for their spectacular flowers. Foliage types are relatively difficult to grow in the home, while the flowering types are much easier. All have large arrow-head-shaped leaves carried on long stems. Require light shade, and a temperature of 18°-24°C (65°-75°F). Need frequent feeding during active growth, and must also be kept moist. Reduce watering in the winter. Propagate by division of clumps in spring, or grow from seed in a propagator. Cultivate in a mixture of moss and peaty compost.

A. andreanum *Oilcloth Plant, Flamingo Flower, Painter's Palette*

Deep-green, arrow-shaped leaves, height 60 cm or more. Blooms are a flat plate-like spathe containing a spike of tiny flowers, as a yellow spadix. Shiny flowers are red, pink or white, and are produced between spring and autumn. Flowers persist for six weeks or more, but are produced only on mature plants.

A. crystallinum *Crystal Anthurium, Strap Flower*

Grown for its attractive foliage, but rather temperamental. Very large deep-green leaves (up to 60 cm in length) which are purple when young, and develop prominent white veins as they mature. Large leaves may require some support. Requires a moss stick for support as aerial roots are developed. Hates dry conditions, and will not tolerate chemical sprays on the leaves.

A. scherzeranum *Flamingo Flower, Pigtail Plant*

The most common and the toughest Anthurium. Has lance-shaped arched leaves up to 60 cm in height. Flowers consist of a crinkled red spathe (smaller than that of **A. andreanum**), with a long, curled, yellow spadix. There are varieties with orange, pink or mottled spathes. Relatively easy to grow.

ANTIGON

A. leptopus *Coral Vine*

Tropical vine suitable for the warm greenhouse. Produces large clusters of small pink flowers, each having a darker centre. Clings to a support by means of tendrils. Needs high humidity in summer, and strong light if flowers are to be produced.

APHELANDRA

(Zebra Plant, Saffron Spike)

Two species of Aphelandra are commonly grown as house plants. They grow up to 60 cm in height, and require temperatures of 16°-21°C (60°-70°F), and light shade. Require rich peat or soil-based composts and heavy feeding every week during active growth. Keep moist during growth, and allow partly to dry out during winter, watering just enough to prevent leaf droop. Propagate from tip cuttings in late spring.

A. chamissoniana
Uncommon form with closely set leaves, and slim pointed flower bracts, yellow in colour.

A. squarrosa
Very large, dark-green leaves striped along the veins and mid-rib with creamy silver. Brilliant yellow flower spike. Many colour varieties exist, usually with differing leaf colouring. Most are more hardy than the original form.

APOROCACTUS
(Rat Tail Cactus)

Desert cacti with long trailing stems which can reach a length of 2 metres, thus best grown in a hanging basket. Stems are covered with clusters of small brown spines. Flower profusely in spring, producing clusters of flowers which continue for several weeks. Require a temperature of 5°-30°C (41°-86°F), and ideally should be hung in a sunny window. Keep moist all year round, but avoid overwatering in winter, and feed during the summer. Cultivate in a soil- or peat-based compost, and repot annually. To propagate, take 15 cm cuttings in late spring, allow them to dry for three days, then insert them into the compost.

A. flagelliformis
Produces bright pinkish-mauve flowers (4 cm long by 3 cm across), in April and May. Sometimes sold grafted onto a tall cactus stem to make a self-supporting standard.

A. mallisonii (Heliaporus smithii)
Actually a hybrid between **H. flagelliformis** and **Heliocereus speciosus**. Shorter and stouter than the other species, but still trailing. Large, brilliant-red flowers are produced in profusion.

ARALIA
See FATSIA

ARAUCARIA

A. excelsa (A. heterophylla) *Norfolk Island Pine, House Pine*
A large tree from New Zealand, suitable as a house plant while small, but becoming coarse and unwieldly as it grows. Should remain below 1.5 metres for several years. Grow in light shade, and temperatures of 13°-18°C (55°-65°F). At higher temperatures it may droop and shed its needles. Upright growth with ferny branches covered with soft needles. Does not respond well to pruning. Keep moist, but not waterlogged. Cultivate in soil-based compost and repot only when pot-bound. Difficult to propagate.

ARAUJIA

A. sericofera *Bladder Flower*
Rampant climber for the conservatory or cool greenhouse. Tough woody stems with green leaves covered with white down on their undersides. Produces clusters of white, flattened, sticky flowers. Requires protection from direct sun. Grow in soil-based compost.

ARDISIA

A. crispa (A. crenata) *Coralberry, Spiceberry*
There are two species which are difficult to distinguish and are frequently confused. Attractive plant eventually reaching a height of 1 metre, grown for its glossy foliage and long-lasting scarlet berries. Pink or white flowers are inconspicuous. Berries are produced in winter and may persist to next flowering season. Grow in bright indirect light at a temperature of 16°-21°C (60°-70°F). Do not water excessively or overfeed. Cultivate in a small pot, in soil-based compost. Does not appreciate peat compost. Propagate from cuttings of young shoots taken in spring.

ARISTOLOCHIA
(Dutchman's Pipe)

Spectacular flowering climbers for the conservatory or cool greenhouse. They produce odd, drooping flowers with a hood and a curved lip, like an old-fashioned tobacco pipe. Cultivate in soil-based compost in good indirect light. Propagate by cuttings.

A. altissima (A. sempervirens)
Large plant with shiny, bright green leaves. Flowers are yellow with red stripes, produced from June to August.

A. elegans *Calico Plant*
Kidney-shaped leaves and 10 cm flowers, coloured yellow and mottled brown. May need heated greenhouse conditions.

ARTHROPODIUM

A. cirrhatum *Rock Lily*
Lily suited to growth indoors or in the cool greenhouse. Spreading light green leaves with semi-transparent edges. Produces large clusters of white flowers with large masses of stamens. Keep out of direct sunlight, water well during growing season. Cultivate in soil-based compost. Propagate by division of clumps.

ARUNDINARIA spp
(Dwarf Bamboo)

Extensive group of plants, most of which are

very large. Dwarf bamboos, however, are ideal for indoor cultivation or for growing in tubs on the patio. They withstand temperatures of up to 18°C (65°F) or more, provided they are kept moist and fed adequately. Most are hardy out of doors in sheltered areas. They require good indirect light. Bamboos grow slowly, but will eventually fill their pot completely. Grow in soil- or peat-based compost and propagate by separating the clump. Small variegated varieties are preferable as they grow relatively slowly.

ASCLEPIAS

A. curassavica
Small shrub for the conservatory or cool greenhouse. Glossy dark-green foliage and masses of orange flowers in October. Requires moist conditions and peat-based compost.

ASPARAGUS
These foliage plants (including the edible asparagus) are often mistakenly referred to as ferns, but are actually related to lilies. All have dainty fern-like foliage, which actually consists of flattened stems rather than leaves. Their flowers are inconspicuous, and are followed by attractive red or orange berries. Asparagus likes bright indirect light, but will not tolerate direct sunlight. They require a temperature of 13°-18°C (55°-65°F), thus are excellent for a cool room. They need to be kept moist but not waterlogged during active growth. Feed every two weeks through the summer. Grow in a soil-based compost, and repot as necessary. The vigorous root system may force compost up out of the pot. Propagate by dividing the tuberous roots in spring. Spray foliage with water every day in warm weather.

A. asparagoides (A. medeoloides) *Smilax*
Vigorous climbing plant with zigzag stems and shiny branchlets. Scrambles up any convenient support to a maximum height of 3 metres.

A. densiflorus 'Sprengeri' *Emerald Fern*
The basic plant is seldom cultivated but the variety 'Sprengeri' is very popular. This has slender drooping stems 1 metre in length and covered in 2 cm branchlets. It is ideally suited for hanging baskets or can be trained up supports. Vigorous growth.

A. densiflorus 'Myersii' *Foxtail Fern*
Elegant variety with stiff erect foxtail-shaped branches up to 60 cm in length. The most handsome member of the group.

A. setaceus (A. plumosus) *Asparagus Fern*
Widely used by florists, has fine needle-like growth on erect wiry stems 35 cm or more in length.

ASPIDISTRA
(Cast Iron Plant, Bar-room Plant)

A. eliator
The only member of the genus commonly grown, **A. eliator** is an immensely tough house plant, which is legendary for its ability to withstand such insults as drying out, smoke, paint fumes, etc. However, it does appreciate better care and this is rewarded by much more rapid growth than usual. Prefers shade, and temperatures of 13°-18°C (55°-65°F). Water moderately throughout the year: overwatering produces brown patches on the leaves. Pot in soil-based composts and allow roots to fill pot thoroughly before repotting. Propagate by dividing the creeping rhizome in spring.

Two forms are available. The basic green aspidistra produces spear-like leaves growing directly from the rhizome without a central stem. May produce tiny purple flowers at soil level. Grows up to 60 cm in height. The variegated form is striped with creamy white and is slightly less tough than the true species, needing more light and warmth. Both forms are scorched by direct sunlight.

ASPLENIUM
(Spleenwort)
The genus Asplenium contains many ferns which are popular as house plants. Like nearly all ferns Aspleniums are delicate, requiring warm temperatures of 18°-24°C (65°-75°F) and constant moisture. The delicate fronds dry out very easily and are scorched by dry atmospheres and draughts. Foliage must be sprayed daily with warm water and plants should be stood in damp gravel or peat to maintain a high humidity. Do not use insecticides or leaf dressings of any sort. Grow in a loose peaty compost, and do not repot until the mass of black roots has completely filled the existing pot. Propagate **A. bulbiferum** and **A. nidus** by removing the small bulbils which develop on the frond tips, once they have produced two or three fronds of their own. Plant in fibrous compost and keep moist.

A. bulbiferum *Hen and Chicken Fern, Mother Spleenwort*
Typical fern fronds that resemble Asparagus or carrot foliage, growing up to 60 cm long

and carried on a wiry black stalk. Small plants develop from bulbils on the frond tips.

A. daucifolium (A. viviparum)
Similar to **A. bulbiferum** but has arching, dark green fronds carried on green stalks. Produces bulbils and plantlets on the frond tips.

A. nidus *Bird's Nest Fern*
So called because it produces a large bowl-shaped plant. Very large, undivided fronds, up to 1 metre in length in mature plants. Fronds unroll from the central core of the plant and are pale lettuce-green in colour with a brown central rib. Fronds are extremely delicate and should not be handled. This fern can only be propagated from spores which is a specialist technique for the expert.

ASTROPHYTUM
A group of desert cacti with globular unbranched stems and deep longitudinal ridges. Cup-shaped flowers are produced on mature plants in summer. These cacti require direct sunlight and temperatures of 5°-30°C (41°-86°F). They should be watered lightly in summer and while flowering, and scarcely at all in winter. Pot in normal cactus compost; soil-based compost with 50 per cent sharp sand. Repotting is seldom necessary, but feed occasionally in summer. Can be propagated only from seed.

A. asterias *Sea Urchin Cactus, Sand Dollar Cactus*
Resembles a sea urchin shell. Forms a spineless, flattened globe up to 10 cm in diameter. It is covered with raised white spots. Produces fragrant yellow flowers with red throats.

A. myriostigma *Bishop's Hood, Monk's Hood*
Slowly grows to a cylindrical shape, 20 cm in diameter. Dark green, and covered with tiny tufts of white hair, looking like scales. Small notches edge the ribs on the stem. Flowers profusely, with yellow flowers having a red base.

A. ornatum
Flowers only when it reaches maturity, at about ten years, by which time it is about 15 cm in diameter. A globular cactus, with eight deep ribs carrying clusters of tough 2.4 cm spines. The stem is banded with silvery scales. Produces pale yellow, fragrant flowers.

AUCUBA
A. japonica 'Variegata' *Japanese Laurel*
The so-called 'laurel' was used in the garden by Victorian gardeners because it is almost indestructable, tolerating the worst atmospheric pollution. Indoors, they are just as tolerant, surviving even in draughty passages. Grown indoors Aucubas seldom exceed 1 metre in height. They are tree-like with large, paired oval leaves, speckled with gold, and with toothed edges. They tolerate temperatures of 7°-13°C (45°-55°F) or higher, and need to be kept moist throughout the year. Good light is needed for the colourful leaf speckles to develop. Grow in loam-based compost, and use a relatively small pot. Propagate from 10 cm cuttings taken in spring. Aucubas make ideal patio plants, but should be overwintered indoors.

AZALEA
See RHODODENDRON

Left: Azalea 'Paul Schame'
Far left: Astrophytum asterias

BABIANA

A group of flowering plants growing from corms, having sword-shaped leaves and very brightly coloured flowers. Best grown in the cool greenhouse or conservatory, in soil-based compost. Plant corms in October and water sparingly until growth commences, after which continue watering as required. Allow to dry out after leaves have yellowed, and leave corms in pots until next season. Propagate by removing cormlets in spring and potting separately.

B. stricta *Baboon Flower*
Large fragrant blue and white flowers carried on 30 cm stems.

BARLERIA

B. lupina
60 cm evergreen shrub for the warm greenhouse. Has tough spear-shaped leaves with spines in the leaf axils. 2.5 cm yellow-pink flowers growing in a spike in August. Grow in peat or loam-based compost, in strong indirect light. Propagate from stem cuttings.

BAUHINIA

B. variegata (purpurea) *Purple Orchid Tree*
Small deciduous bush for the cool greenhouse or conservatory. Has slim, tough leaves and 7 cm purple and crimson flowers in June, which resemble orchid flowers. Requires sun if it is to flower.

BEAUCARNEA

B. recurvata (Nolea recurvata) *Bottle Palm, Ponytail Plant, Elephant Foot Tree*
Sometimes described as a walking stick growing out of a turnip, this plant has an elusive charm. It grows slowly to a height of 2 metres, with a woody trunk arising from a knobbly, swollen base. Foliage consists of a tuft of tough, strap-like leaves which droop gracefully. Grows well in light shade, at temperatures of 10°-21°C (50°-70°F) and is very tolerant of central heating. Cultivate in soil-based compost, and do not overwater. Propagate from bulbils developing around the base, or grow from seed.

BEAUMONTIA

B. grandiflora *Herald's Trumpet*
An untidy rambling plant for the warm greenhouse. Large glossy leaves, hairy underneath. Large trumpet-shaped white flowers in winter, although some may be produced at other times. Grow in soil-based compost, and support with canes. Needs humid conditions.

BEGONIA

Huge group of plants grown for their foliage or their flowers. Their most obvious characteristic is that the leaves are asymmetric or lopsided, and produced alternately along the stems. Flowers are produced from the leaf axils, and male and female flowers are produced separately. There are three major groups of Begonia:

1 Fibrous rooted – having the normal branched root system
2 Rhizomatous rooted – growing from a creeping rhizome
3 Tuberous rooted – growing from a fleshy tuber

The fibrous and rhizomatous types are similar in their needs and their growth, and are usually considered together.

Fibrous-rooted and Rhizomatous Begonias

This group is very varied, including types with woody stems, fleshy stems, and dwarf forms. All need bright indirect light, although the flowering types need some direct sunlight each day. Keep warm, with a minimum temperature of 13°C (55°F), and maintain in humid conditions with a gravel or peat tray. Keep relatively dry in winter, and keep moist throughout the active growth phase, feeding every two weeks. Grow in a rich soil-based compost, with added sand, perlite or clay pot fragments for better drainage. Propagate fibrous-rooted forms by cuttings from non-flowering stems in spring or summer. Rhizomatous forms are propagated by dividing the rhizome, or by taking leaf cuttings. A leaf stalk should be detached complete with leaf and inserted in peaty compost at an angle of 45° to the soil surface, with the whole placed in a propagator. Plantlets are developed from the leaf after several weeks, and may be detached and planted out in the propagator.

B. boweri *Eyelash Begonia*
Grows to 15 cm, with a spread of 30 cm. Large leaves are mottled green and deep purple, and are edged with white hairs: the 'eyelashes'. Produces white 2.5 cm flowers.

B. 'Cleopatrea'
Similar size to **B. boweri**, but has heavily lobed leaves mottled with bronze. Needs strong light to develop its colour. Good in hanging baskets. Pink or white flowers on 10 cm stems.

B. 'Lucerna'
Large, vigorous plant growing to 1.5 metres, having jointed bamboo-like stems. Large

glossy leaves are speckled with silver above and coloured maroon beneath. Produces large clusters of small pink flowers.

B. maculata
Tall slim form growing up to 1 metre in height. Leaves are speckled with silver-grey, and are a rich crimson below. Has branching bamboo-like stems. Small flowers carried in sprays on drooping red stalks.

B. masonica *Iron Cross Begonia*
Handsome rhizomatous begonia with large warty leaves, covered with fine bristles. Leaves are pale green, with central blackish area resembling an Iron Cross. Needs a large pot to accommodate the rhizome, which grows on the surface. Needs light shade.

B. rex hybrids *Painted Leaf Begonias*
Grown for their decorative foliage, which comes in every conceivable colour and pattern. There are an enormous number of hybrids, some with unusually shaped leaves. Plants are available with red, purple, silver or white colouration. These rhizomatous forms are difficult to keep for more than two or three years and are then best discarded. Easily propagated by leaf cuttings or rhizome division.

B. semperflorens hybrids
Another very large group of fibrous-rooted begonias. Warty stem and leaves, growing up to 30 cm in height. Flowers most prolifically throughout almost all the year. Flowers are white, pink, yellow or red, and are single or double. Grows equally well indoors, or outdoors in hanging basket or tub.

Tuberous Begonias
Grown for their attractive flowers, this group tends to die back in winter, or at least to become dormant. Tuberous begonias need bright indirect light during their growing period. Start tubers into growth, planted in peaty compost, at a temperature of around 15°C (60°F). Keep growing plants humid and at a constant temperature to avoid leaf drop. Feed fortnightly with a high-potash fertilizer. Make sure tubers are planted the right way up, with the hollow side uppermost! Propagate from the bulbils produced from leaf axils in the autumn.

B. hiemalis hybrids
Winter flowering plants, large glossy rounded leaves on red stems, growing to 45 cm. Flowers are 4.5 cm across, bright red with a yellow centre.

B. tuberhybrida
Best of the flowering begonias, growing up to 60 cm and carrying flowers up to 12 cm in size, which may be white, yellow, orange, pink or red. Thick fleshy stems and leaves die back completely in winter.

Note There are many species and hybrid forms of Begonia, too many to be described in a book of this nature. Consult a specialised reference work for more details.

BELOPERONE

B. guttata (Drejella guttata) *Shrimp Plant*
The popular name derives from its drooping, shrimp-like flowers, which are produced almost continuously. The plant is a rather straggly shrub growing up to 1 metre, unless properly pruned and trained. Foliage is nondescript, but the flowers are extremely attractive. Grow in light shade at a temperature of 16°-21°C (60°-70°F), and keep moist and well fed. Unlike most house plants, Beloperone resents a small pot and becomes pot-bound very easily. Pot on into soil-based compost with added chopped sphagnum moss. Propagate from tip cuttings taken in spring. Colour varieties with yellow and with dark red flowers are also available.

BERTOLONIA

Small group of creeping evergreen plants with handsome metallic foliage. Heart-shaped leaves are hairy and coloured maroon beneath. Prefer indirect light, normal room temperatures, and high humidity which can be maintained by standing them on wet gravel. Avoid wetting the leaves as this causes limey deposits. Keep moist through growing period: drier in winter. Grow in rich, well-drained compost and repot when plants begin to trail out of the pot. Propagate from tip cuttings taken in spring.

B. maculata
Leaves are olive green, with lighter markings, red edges and silvery spots. Pink 1 cm flowers at intervals through summer.

B. marmorata
More pointed leaves of vivid green, with satiny finish and silvery lines running lengthwise along them. Pink 1 cm flowers throughout summer.

BIFRENARIA

B. harrisonii
One of the easiest orchids to grow in the house, but difficult to persuade to flower. Bifrenaria is an epiphyte, usually grown in a basket in normal orchid compost, but can be grown in a clay pot. Needs temperatures of minimum 11°C (52°F) in winter, when it needs a complete rest with no water until new

growth appears. Flowers are creamy-white, up to 7.5 cm across and produced sparingly in summer on short stems. Propagation is difficult and is a specialist process.

BILLBERGIA

Group of easily grown bromeliads, suitable for the home or conservatory. They have slim, stiff leaves arranged in narrow rosettes, and flaring out gracefully. The showy flowers are tubular, with petals turned back towards the stem, and are backed with papery bracts. They may flower in almost any season. Undemanding plants which survive in temperatures down to 13°C (55°F), but like some direct sunlight if they are to flower. They grow well in a mixture of soil-based compost and leaf mould. Water only when soil surface feels dry. Propagate by removing and potting offsets, once they have reached 10 cm in length. Many species are available, and those with central cups should have these kept topped up with clean water. This does not apply to the two species discussed below.

B. nutans *Queen's Tears, Angel's Tears, Indoor Oats*
Most popular of the Billbergias. Has erect grey-green leaves growing to 45 cm, which may become reddish in strong light. Spectacular flowers are produced in spikes from glowing pink spathes. Flowers are multicoloured: green, yellow, blue and pink. Remove each flower as it dies off.

B. × windii
Hybrid form with broader leaves than **B. nutans**. Both leaves and flower stems are more arching than the preceding type, and the plant is slightly less hardy.

BLECHNUM

This genus includes several handsome ferns of very varied form and habit, including some that grow tree-like trunks. Unlike most ferns they thrive in warm room conditions and can tolerate some dry conditions, although they prefer high humidities. They withstand temperatures ranging between 13°-24°C (55°-75°F) but prefer more moderate conditions. Spray regularly to maintain humidity, or stand on trays of moist gravel. Water well, but do not allow to become waterlogged. Grow in a mixture of soil-based compost and leaf mould. Difficult to propagate, as they are usually grown from spores.

B. brasiliense *Brazilian Tree Fern, Rib Fern*
Grows slowly to produce a tree-like form topped with fronds up to 1 metre in length. A smaller form, B.b. 'Crispum' has reddish fronds.

B. gibbum
Tidy rosette of fronds up to 1 metre long and 30 cm wide, growing on a short black trunk. Fronds droop attractively.

BOUGAINVILLEA

Well-known group of vigorous subtropical climbers, familiar to those who have visited warmer climates. Foliage is uninteresting, and the plant is grown only for its highly decorative papery bracts, which are produced in large clusters in a wide range of vivid colours. Grown indoors, they can be pruned to remain bushy, or dwarf forms may be grown. Bougainvilleas demand several hours of bright sunlight each day, and temperatures of 13°-18°C (55°-65°F). Keep relatively dry at all times, watering only when soil surface feels dry. Allow to dry out almost completely during winter, resuming watering when new growth appears. Grow in a soil-based compost with added peat. Propagation by cuttings requires a heated propagator. Prune severely in the autumn to keep the plant bushy.

B. × buttiana
Vigorous spiky climbers which can be trained and pruned into a shrub form. Most forms are crimson or magenta. Several named hybrids are available.

B. glabra *Paper Flower*
Smaller and more free-flowering. Flowers in both spring and autumn. Variegated varieties are available.

BOUVARDIA

B. × domestica *Trompetilla*
Small evergreen shrub with tubular pink or scarlet flowers on drooping branches. Likes light shade, and temperatures of 13°-18°C (55°-65°F). Water freely in summer, and feed regularly. Stop feeding and reduce watering in winter. Larger plants (60 cm) can be put outdoors in a sheltered position in the summer. Grow in soil-based compost. Propagate by cuttings or by dividing clumps.

BRASSOLAELIACATTLEYA

B. hybrids
This group of robust hybrid orchids have enormous flowers up to 23 cm across. Most are pink or magenta, although other colours are available. They will grow indoors provided they have strong but indirect light, and a minimum temperature of 13°C (55°F). A high humidity is essential. Grow in orchid compost in perforated pots or baskets. Most

flower in autumn or winter, and must be allowed to rest and partly dry out after flowering. Water if pseudo-bulbs show signs of shrivelling, and when plants begin to grow once more.

BREYNIA

B. nivosa *Snow Bush*
Small greenhouse shrub, suitable for house cultivation while small. Finely branched stems carry small leaves marbled with white. Grow in peat compost, out of direct sun, and maintain a high humidity.

BROWALLIA

(Bush Violets)
Small bushy annuals, grown for their brilliant blue flowers. Sprawling growth makes them ideal for basket cultivation. Browallias need bright light, and tolerate direct sun. They thrive at 13°-18°C (55°-65°F) and dislike higher temperatures. Water well, but allow soil surface to dry between waterings. Grow from seed in early spring, in soil-based compost. Plants will flower in early autumn. Discard after flowering. Susceptible to greenfly. Nip out tips to keep bushy.

B. speciosa
Usually grown as a named variety. Blue or white flowers 4.5 cm across, and drooping 50 cm stems. Flowers usually have a white throat and blue veins.

B. viscosa
Smaller and more compact than **B. speciosa**, with rounded leaves and 3 cm blue flowers with white throats.

BRUGMANSIA

See DATURA

BRUNFELSIA

B. pauciflora (B. calycina) *Yesterday-Today-and-Tomorrow*
Small evergreen shrub growing up to 60 cm, with glossy, leathery leaves. Popular name derives from the colour changes in the flowers, which are violet when they open, fade to pale blue, then white, and are dead by the fourth day. Flowers are up to 5 cm across, and are flattened, with five lobes. Flowers are produced in clusters from June to October. Cultivate in the conservatory or a large airy room, in minimum temperatures of 10°C (50°F). Avoid draughts, and water well in summer, allowing plant to dry out almost completely in winter. Grow in a relatively small pot, in soil-based compost. Maintain humidity by spraying with water, and stand

in damp gravel. Keep in bright light; some sunlight is essential for flower development. Prune drastically to maintain attractive shape. Propagate from stem cuttings.

BRYOPHYLLUM

Sometimes included under KALANCHOE, but universally known as Bryophyllums. These succulent plants are notable for their production of tiny plantlets on the leaves, complete with roots. These drop off and root spontaneously. Grow in bright light or direct sun, maintaining a minimum temperature of 10°C (50°F). Grow in a mixture of soil-based compost and sharp sand. Water sparingly.

B. daigremontianum *Devil's Backbone, Mexican Hat*
Grows up to 70 cm high, with a single stem and widely spaced, paired leaves. The large leaves are bluish-green, mottled purple beneath. Plantlets are produced between the notches on the leaf edges.

B. tubiflora *Chandelier Plant*
Up to 1 metre tall, with a single slender stem. Leaves are tubular and marked with purplish blotches, and plantlets are produced in clusters on the leaf tips.

BULBOPHYLLUM

B. × hybrids
The largest orchid genus, containing at least 2,000 species. Bulbophyllums are epiphytic orchids which can be grown in pots or hanging baskets, in normal orchid compost. They are relatively easy to grow and flower freely. Keep at a minimum temperature of 13°C (55°F). Flowers are very varied, but all are large and spectacular, and many have a long trailing lip.

BUXUS

B. sempervirens *Common Box*
This is the familiar garden box, which is ideally suited for cultivation in tubs on the patio. It grows very slowly, and retains a compact, neat shape. Very undemanding and hardy, but does not tolerate drying out.

CALADIUM

Caladium × hortulanum *Angel Wings, Elephant Ears*

Beautiful but delicate foliage plants, producing 30-50 cm leaves on a slim stalk rising from a tuber. Leaves are paper-thin and coloured green, pink, red, white, or purple, often richly veined or marbled. The thin leaves are easily damaged by direct sunlight, dryness, or chemical sprays. Caladiums require a temperature of 18°-24°C (65°-75°F) and bright indirect light. Maintain high humidity with frequent water sprays, and stand on wet gravel. These plants die back in winter. Plant rhizomes just below the surface in peat-based compost, which must be very well drained. Feed fortnightly during active growth. When leaves begin to deteriorate in autumn, let compost dry out. Overwinter tubers in their pot, and start into growth in spring, with sparing watering. Propagate by detaching and planting small tubers when repotting in spring. Remove flowers to stimulate leaf growth – they are unattractive.

CALANTHE

C. vestita

Handsome orchid for the warm greenhouse. Cultivate in minimum temperature of 18°C (65°F), in soil-based compost. These orchids are deciduous and have a rest period when watering should be withheld to allow the plant to dry off. Flowers are produced in winter on long stems, and are white to pink. There are many cultivated varieties, and other species of Calanthe are also available.

CALATHEA

Group of foliage plants often confused with MARANTA to which they are closely related. The large leaves are carried on long stems rising from a short shoot. Leaves may be as much as 60 cm long, with striped upper surfaces and reddish colour beneath. Calatheas require a temperature of 16°-25°C (60°-75°F) and should be grown in light shade. Grow in peat-based compost and feed regularly throughout the summer. Calatheas require humid conditions, and do best with water sprays and a damp gravel bed for the pot. Do not allow compost to become saturated, and water with soft water or rainwater. Propagate by dividing clumps in spring.

C. bachemiana

The 25 cm leaves are held at right angles to the stem, thus the plant is low growing. Leaves have feathery, fan-shaped, dark-green markings and are purple beneath.

C. insignis (C. lancifolia) *Rattlesnake Plant*

Slim lance-like leaves up to 45 cm long. Leaves have wavy edges and the upper surfaces are marked with a dark blotchy herring-bone pattern. Undersides are purple.

C. makoyana *Cathedral Windows, Peacock Plant*

Probably the showiest of the group. Has large silvery leaves with a dainty tracery of green lines and larger blotches on the upper surface of the leaves.

C. ornata

Long, narrow leaves, coloured dark green, with a fine herring-bone pattern of paired pink or white lines.

C. picturata

15 cm leaves, on short stalks, producing a bushy plant. Leaves have emerald-green edges and silvery-white centre.

C. zebrina *Zebra Plant*

30 cm leaves with velvety green upper surface, overlaid with purplish patches. Very beautiful, but extremely temperamental. Rapidly scorched by direct sun.

CALCEOLARIA

C. × herbeohybrida *Pouch Flower, Slipper Flower, Slipperwort*

Undemanding and colourful flowering plants for the home, which should be kept only for one season. Calceolarias need bright light but not direct sunlight. They grow well at temperatures of 10°-16°C (50°-60°F), and must be kept moist and well fed. Spray plants with water frequently in summer. They grow up to 30 cm high, with uninteresting foliage, but have large, bladder-like flowers in a range of white, pink, yellow or red, and spotted mixtures of these colours. Check that plants do not become pot bound, and if necessary, pot on in soil-based compost. Very susceptible to aphids. Discard plants after flowering.

CALLISIA

See TRADESCANTIA

CALLISTEMON

C. citrinus *Bottle-brush*

Several other species of Callistemon are grown outdoors, but **C. citrinus** is the only type generally suitable as a house plant. Slow-growing, woody shrub which reaches 1.5 metres if not pruned back. Has grey-green, spiky leaves, and fluffy flower spikes, usually crimson in colour, produced in summer. Requires direct sunlight, and temperatures of 13°-16°C (55°-60°F). They require a cool (but not too cool) rest in winter. Keep moist, but not waterlogged. Grow in soil-based compost, and propagate with cuttings taken from non-flowering side-shoots in spring. Appreciate being stood outdoors in mild summer weather.

CAMELLIA
C. japonica (many varieties)
Magnificent stately flowering shrub or tree for the conservatory or patio. Produces beautiful flowers in many colours, in early spring. Foliage is glossy, deep green, on woody stems. Best cultivated in large tubs, in lime-free, soil-based compost. Will not tolerate hard water or limey soils. Protect from cold wind or frosts if grown outdoors. Less satisfactory as a house plant, where it seldom flowers and dislikes warm temperatures. Does best at 10°-16°C (50°-60°F), and will need frequent water spraying if grown in the house. Not practical for indoor propagation.

CAMPANULA
C. isophylla *Star of Bethlehem, Italian Bell-flower*
The only member of the genus commonly grown indoors, as a flowering trailer. Produces attractive pale blue or white flowers from spring right through to autumn. Needs good indirect light, and temperatures of 10°-16°C (50°-60°F), and should be kept moist and well fed while flowering. Allow to become almost dry in winter, when the long stems should be cut back almost to soil level. Grow in hanging baskets or pots, in soil-based compost. Propagate by cuttings or by division of established plants.

CAMPELIA
See DICHORISANDRA

CANNA
C. × hybrida *Indian Shot*
Grows from fleshy tubers to produce large plant, 1-2 metres high, with spectacular orchid-like flowers and broad, ribbed leaves. Slim, erect plant, best suited to the conservatory, cool greenhouse or tubs on the patio in summer. Plant in spring in peat or soil-based compost, and feed and water freely as growth commences. Flowers in late summer (earlier indoors). Allow to dry off after flowering is finished, and store rhizomes in a warm place over the winter. Propagate by dividing the tubers in spring. Many colour varieties exist, some with reddish foliage.

CANTUA
C. buxifolia
Climbing shrub for the cool greenhouse or conservatory. Uninteresting foliage, but large tubular, trumpet-shaped flowers, mauvish-red with yellow tube, which appears in April. Grow in soil-based compost and provide climbing supports.

CAPSICUM
(Red Pepper, Christmas Pepper)
C. anuun
Capsicums are grown for their attractive red, orange fruit produced in early winter. They are usually regarded as temporary plants, to be purchased while in fruit and discarded shortly afterwards. Capsicums can, however, be grown in the house or the cool greenhouse, with a little care. Most grow only to 40 cm and are spreading, shrubby plants. They produce a great deal of fruit which may be round or elongated. Capsicums require a temperature of 10°-16°C (50°-60°F) and bright light, including a few hours of direct sunlight each day. Leaf drop will occur in insufficient light. Water copiously, but do not allow to become waterlogged. Can be grown from seed, planted in spring, and raised in a warm propagator. Not easy to bring to fruiting in the house.

CAREX
C. morrowii 'Variegata' *Japanese Sedge Grass*
The only member of this group of sedges grown indoors. 30 cm grass-like leaves, striped white and green, and growing in a tuft from a creeping rhizome. Grows slowly but steadily to fill the pot. Carex will grow outdoors, and appreciates being put outside in mild weather. Indoors, grow in bright indirect light at a maximum 16°-21°C (60°-70°F), and keep humid by standing pot in damp gravel. Do not overwater, and feed once a month during the growing season. Pot in soil-based compost and propagate by dividing the rhizome in spring.

CARPOBROTUS
C. edulis *Hottentot Fig*
Shrubby prostrate succulent which can be grown outdoors in mild weather, or throughout the year in sheltered areas. It is best grown indoors, however, in full sun. Produces 90 cm branches with thick cylindrical leaves. Can be trained up a wall or allowed to trail. Produces 10 cm fluffy flowers, coloured bright magenta, orange or yellow, throughout the summer. Grow in well-drained soil-based

compost, and water well in hot weather. Propagate from stem cuttings.

CRYOTA
(Fishtail Palms)
Palms with very unusual leaves which are triangular, with rough edges looking as though they are torn from paper. They grow large, but very slowly, so they can be kept in the home for many years. Prefer bright indirect light, and temperatures about 13°C (55°F). They require reasonably humid conditions and more watering than most palms, although they do not have a well-defined rest period. Feed monthly throughout the summer. Grow in soil-based compost, and keep in a small pot until obviously pot-bound. **C. mitis** can be propagated from suckers or offsets.

C. mitis *Burmese or Tufted Fishtail Palm*
Eventually grows to 2 metres or more, producing its characteristic leaves in a tuft on its bare stems. Produces another cluster of leaves at the base of the stems.

C. uris *Jaggery Palm, Sago Palm*
Grows to 2 metres or more. Produces drooping fronds, and leaves are more triangular and less jagged than **C. mitis.**

CATHARANTHUS
C. roseus *Madagascar or Rose Periwinkle, Old Maid*
Pretty shrub for indoor cultivation, very easy to grow. Has attractive glossy foliage but is grown for its 4 cm flowers, which are usually pink or white, with a deeper-coloured centre. Prefers a sunny window-sill, and temperatures of 13°-18°C (55°-65°F). Must be kept well watered and fed fortnightly during the growing season. Grow in a soil-based compost. Can be propagated from stem cuttings or seeds. Best treated as an annual, to be discarded after flowering ends in the autumn.

CATTLEYA
Large group of magnificent orchids, mainly for the warm greenhouse. In the home need great care to protect from effects of dry air. Cattleyas are epiphytic orchids, growing from pseudo-bulbs. Produces flowers as large as 25 cm in some species, either singly or in sprays on a short stalk. Grow in orchid compost, in bright indirect light, at temperatures of about 13°C (55°F). Stand pot in damp gravel during active growth. Allow to dry out partly between waterings. After flowering water only enough to prevent shrivelling of the pseudo-bulbs. Depending on the species,

flowers may be produced at any time of year. Propagate by dividing the rhizome from which the pseudo-bulbs grow. Many hybrids exist.

C. aurantiaca
Small summer flowering species with 7 to 10 cm orange flowers, growing in small sprays. A small species, suitable for the home, but susceptible to excess drying out after flowering.

C. bowringiana *Cluster Cattleya*
Autumn flowering species noted for producing a very large number of purple-pink flowers, up to 8 cm across, and marked with golden yellow. Fairly small plant often recommended for the beginner to orchid growing. Easy to propagate.

C. intermedia *Cocktail Orchid*
Large cylindrical psuedo-bulbs and large rose-pink flowers, which remain fresh for five to six weeks.

C. labiata *Autumn Cattleya*
Club-shaped pseudo-bulbs, and large fragrant flowers, produced in autumn. Flowers are up to 15 cm across, pale pink and waxy, with a frilled maroon lip and yellow throat.

C. triannaei *Christmas Orchid, Winter Cattleya*
Winter flowering species with large flowers in clusters. The 18 cm flowers are pink or lilac, with a crimson lip and yellow throat. Flowers are very long lasting.

CELOSIA
C. argentia (C. plumosa, C. cristata) *Cockscomb*
Popular name derives from the dense 'cockscomb' of tightly packed flowers, although a looser pyramidal form is also available. Grows to 60 cm with flowers coloured red, orange or yellow. Requires good light and prefers a little sunlight. Prefers coolish conditions of 10°-16°C (50°-60°F), and should be kept moist and well fed. If too wet Celosias will rot. Treat as an annual, to be grown from seed in peat or soil-based compost, and discarded after flowering. Can be stood outside in mild weather. Many hybrids exist, some with very strange, contorted plumes of flowers.

CEPHALOCEREUS
C. senilis *Old Man Cactus*
The only species commonly grown indoors. This desert cactus is completely swathed with long white hairs covering the 3 cm yellow spines. So hairy that it needs occasional shampooing with detergent and warm water

(which should not be allowed to soak into the compost). May live to 200 years and grow to 12 metres in a single column – fortunately, very slowly! Grow in a mixture of soil-based compost and sand, and water moderately during the active growth phase. Allow to dry out in winter, watering just enough to prevent shrivelling. Requires full sun, and a temperature of 7°-30°C (45°-86°F). Can be grown from seed, or from a stem cutting (which irreparably damages the parent plant).

CEREUS

Another group of giant desert cacti, which produce elegant columns when grown indoors. Grow relatively fast for cacti, and produce flowers up to 30 cm in size which are fragrant and open at night. Needs full sunlight and temperatures of 5°-30°C (41°-86°F). Can be forced to branch by cutting off the tip, which can be dried out for three days, and then potted as a stem cutting. Grow in a mixture of soil-based compost and sharp sand. Cereus are often used as a base on which other cacti are grafted, to produce a standard shape. Water well in summer; keep relatively dry in winter.

C. jamacaru
Greenish-blue columnar form, deeply notched and with white areoles containing clusters of yellowish 2 cm spines.

C. peruvianus
Very similar to **C. jamacaru**, but usually grown as a naturally occurring variety 'Monstrosus', which is distorted and knobbly, and very slow growing. 'Monstrosus' is less hardy than the basic **C. peruvianus**, and prone to rot if overwatered.

CEROPEGIA
C. woodi
Hearts-on-a-String, Rosary Vine, Hearts Entangled
Unusual trailing plant growing from a tough potato-like tuber. Produces pairs of heart-shaped 2 cm leaves, mottled grey and green. Stems trail for as much as 1 metre. Flowers are pink and tubular. Grow in a hanging basket or trailing from a shelf, in good light. Will tolerate some sunlight. Requires temperatures of 13°-18°C (55°-65°F) and should be watered sparingly in the growth phase, and even less in winter. Feed occasionally in summer. Grow in well-drained, soil-based compost, and propagate from stem cuttings, or from small tubers produced along the stems. Water the young plants very sparingly.

CHAMAECEREUS
C. silvestrii *Peanut Cactus*
Produces finger-like stems, with young shoots vaguely resembling unshelled peanuts. Covered with clusters of small white spines. Tends to sprawl and become prostrate, with stems about 15 cm long. Stems break off easily, and root spontaneously in the compost. Produces brilliant red 4 cm flowers in spring and summer, which are short lived but produced continually. Hybrids exist, producing yellow, orange or mauve flowers. The variety **C. sylvestrii** 'Lutea' has no chlorophyll and is coloured bright yellow. It cannot be grown on its own roots and is sold grafted on to a cactus such as CEREUS. Grow all types in full sun, at 0°-30°C (32°-86°F), watering moderately and keeping almost completely dry in winter (the colder the temperature the drier the plant). Pot in a mixture of soil-based compost and sharp sand. Almost too easy to propagate from snapped-off pieces of stem.

CHAMAECYPARIS
Conifers available in an almost limitless range of species, varieties and hybrids. To be grown outdoors as patio plants, or in the cool greenhouse or conservatory as a bonsai. Select a slow-growing or dwarf type for either purpose, as many form very large trees. Grow in well-drained peat-based compost, and feed well with bonemeal if grown on the patio. Popularly but incorrectly known as 'Cypress'.

CHAMAEDOREA
Large group of palms, of which only a few are small enough for indoor cultivation. Have erect woody stems and arched fronds. Small yellow flowers are produced in sprays on older plants. Grow in light shade, and keep moist but well drained. Can tolerate dry atmospheres, but prefer more humid conditions. Keep at temperatures of 16°-21°C (60°-70°F), and spray fronds with water regularly in summer. Grow in well-drained, soil-based compost with added chopped sphagnum moss or leaf mould. Difficult to propagate.
C. elegans (Neanthe bella, Collinia elegans)
Parlour Palm
Grows slowly to a height of 1 metre. Has a short stubby trunk and graceful arching fronds, with leaflets arranged in pairs. May produce yellow fruits. Good in a bottle garden, where it grows quite slowly.
C. erumpeus *Bamboo Palm*
Produces tall, jointed stems like bamboo, topped with clusters of upright leaves, leav-

ing the stems bare. Grows to 2 metres or more.

CHAMAEROPS

C. humilis *European Fan Palm, Dwarf Fan Palm, Hair Palm*

The only native European palm. Produces fan-shaped upright fronds 40 cm long, on 1 metre stalks. Produces an elegant plant when given sufficient room for the wide fronds to spread out. Several varieties are available, growing taller, shorter, or more bushy than the basic form. Needs some direct sunlight and normal room temperatures. Water plentifully during active growth. Water sparingly in winter. Feed every two weeks during active growth period. Grow in soil-based compost and propagate from suckers produced at the base of the plant. Seldom produces fruit indoors, but can be grown from seed.

CHLOROPHYTUM

C. comosum (C. elatum, C. capense) (many varieties) *Spider Plant, Ribbon Plant, St Bernard's Lily*

One of the most familiar indoor plants, very easy to grow if fed adequately. Produces clumps of arching, strap-like leaves. Flowers are produced on 60 cm stems, and are succeeded by small plantlets which weigh the stem down, and often take root in adjacent pots. Prefers good light, and temperatures of 10°-16°C (50°-60°F). Grow in soil-based compost and feed at least every two weeks throughout the year if the plant is to thrive. Water plentifully except during the rest period when it can still be watered moderately. Propagate from plantlets on stems, either treated as cuttings, or stood in water while they develop roots. Alternatively, bend down the shoot complete with plantlets and pin them to the compost. Sever the shoot once the plantlets are rooted. Several varieties exist, all basically with striped green and yellow-white leaves.

CHRYSALIDOCARPUS

C. lutescens (Areca lutescens) *Areca Palm, Yellow Palm, Butterfly Palm*

Graceful palm with clusters of yellowish stems carrying large arching fronds divided into dainty leaflets. Grows slowly, producing a stubby trunk. Produces suckers from the base which can be used for propagation. Prefers strong light, with some direct sun. Normal room temperatures are adequate with a minimum of 13°C (55°F). Grow in a soil-based compost, and keep moist during grow-

ing season. Keep drier in winter. Feed every two weeks during active growth phase. Can be grown from seed (very slowly!) or propagated from well-developed suckers, which must have some root growth before being detached from the parent plant.

CHRYSANTHEMUM

Although there are more than 200 species of Chrysanthemum, those cultivated indoors are varieties or hybrids derived from just two species. Chrysanthemums are temporary plants in the home, and are normally discarded or planted out in the garden after flowering. They are bushy plants with slightly woody stems, requiring strong light and moderate temperatures of 13°-18°C (55°-65°F). Excess temperature greatly shortens the life of the flower. Modern growing techniques allow Chrysanthemums to be forced into flower at any time of year, and the normally tall-growing types are usually dwarfed by chemical treatments. Chrysanthemums need to be kept moist during the growing phase. Feeding and repotting are not normally required as plants cannot be usefully retained after flowering. Be sure the flower buds show signs of opening before purchasing a plant for indoor flowering.

C. frutescens

Normally grows up to 1 metre in height but is usually artificially dwarfed or 'pinched out' to be about 45 cm high. Flowers are 6-8 cm across. This type of Chrysanthemum requires some direct sunlight if flower buds are to open.

C. × morifolium

Smaller plant, usually up to 30 cm high when sold. Requires strong light, but not direct sunlight.

CIBOTIUM

C. shiedei *Treefern*

Very large, palm-like ferns, which eventually produce a trunk. Fronds are carried on long stalks and are divided into narrow 30 cm leaflets, which are again divided. Suitable for the home when young. Grow in peat-based compost in indirect light. Propagate from offsets.

CINERARIA

× hybrids **(Senecio hybridus, S. cruentus)**

Wide range of flowering hybrids suitable for temporary growth in the home. Cinerarias have large coarse leaves and grow to around 30-60 cm in height. They are typically plants of late winter/early spring, and remain in flower for several weeks, after which they should be discarded. Grow in strong, indirect light, at temperatures of 13°-18°C (55°-65°F), and keep moist and well fed. Particularly prone to collapse if dried out. If the plant shows signs of wilting, submerge pot in luke-warm water to allow it to recover. Also highly prone to attack by insect pests. Feeding and repotting is unnecessary during the short time the plant is retained. Flowers are daisy-like, often with a white centre, and of every conceivable colour. Flowers are produced in broad clusters.

CISSUS

One of the most popular types of plant grown indoors in the early days of the post-war boom in house plants. Cissus are climbing or scrambling plants, which can be allowed to climb or trail. Most produce tendrils with which they cling to any suitable support. Most types tolerate poor or strong light, although they are scorched by direct sunlight. They prefer normal house temperatures of 18°-24°C (65°-75°F) and should be kept moist and well fed, except for a brief rest period in winter when they can be left unfed, cooler and drier. Grow in a soil-based compost and repot only when roots fill the existing pot. Propagate from tip cuttings or by layering. Very easy to root from either method.

C. antartica *Kangaroo Vine*
Tall and rather spindly scrambling plant that must be trained up supports. Large heart-shaped leaves with deeply toothed edges. Can be encouraged to bush out by 'pinching out' the growing tips.

C. discolor *Rex-Begonia Vine*
Oddly and inaccurately named, this climbing vine has beautiful foliage. The heart-shaped leaves have purple undersides, while the upper surfaces have silver and purple markings. Not an easy plant to grow. Overwatering causes the leaves to drop. It needs constant warm temperatures, absence from draughts, and a high humidity. Probably best grown in the cool greenhouse or conservatory.

C. striatus *Miniature Grape Ivy*
The smallest type of Cissus. A dainty climber with red stems and clinging tendrils. Leaves are divided into five finger-like sections coloured greeny-bronze. Excellent in hanging baskets or as a climber.

CITRUS

Group of small evergreen trees and shubs, including the orange, lemon, lime and grapefruit. Young plants of all types make good house plants with their glossy dark-green foliage. Small types will produce fragrant flowers and fruit indoors or in the conservatory. Most have prickly stems. Flowers are white, and produced in spring or summer, although some types flower almost continuously. Fruit ripens very slowly. Grow in direct sunlight and place outdoors during the day in summer. Grow in normal room temperatures of 13°-18°C (55°-65°F) and water moderately during active growth. Feed with high-potassium (tomato type) fertiliser during active growth, and if leaf yellowing is noticed, feed with sequestered iron (normally used on Rhododendrons and Camellias). Grow in large pots or tubs, in soil-based compost. Tip cuttings can be rooted in propagator, or plants can be grown from seed. Nip out tips to encourage bushy growth. Susceptible to red spider mite when grown indoors.

C. limon *Lemon*
Good ornamental species with red-tinged flowers. Some dwarf (1 metre) forms are available, which still produce large fruit.

C. mitis *Calamondin Orange, Panama Orange*
Charming plant which freely produces large numbers of 3 cm oranges, even while very small. Small and compact, seldom growing to more than 1 metre, and producing flowers and fruit intermittently throughout the year.

C. sinensis *Sweet Orange*
The only 'indoor' type to produce sweet fruit. Heavily spined and rapid growing, up to about 1.5 metres. Fruit are about 4 cm in diameter.

CLEISTOCACTUS

C. straussii *Silver torch*
The only member of this group of desert cacti to be commonly cultivated. A slender columnar cactus, growing slowly up to 1.5 metres. Green stem is covered with short whitish spines, making it look blue-grey. Generally unbranched, but may produce upright growing shoots, from near the base. Ten to twelve-year-old plants flower, producing tubular, deep-red flowers which last for only a few days. Needs as much sun as possible, and temperatures of 5°-30°C (41°-86°F). Grows rapidly, therefore in growth phase needs plenty of water and feeding with high-potassium (tomato-type) fertiliser. Grow in a soil-based compost and propagate from shoots removed from the base, or grow from seed.

CLEMATIS

Beautiful climbing plant for outdoor cultivation on the patio. Grow in large tubs in normal soil, and keep roots cool by covering soil with large stones or tiles. Grow in full sun and provide supports for the plant to climb up. All types except **C. montana** should be pruned almost to ground level each winter. Very many cultivated forms are available, as well as several interesting species.

CLERODENDRON

C. thomsoniae *Bleeding-Heart Vine, Glory Bower*

Large twining shrub best suited to the conservatory or cool greenhouse, as it grows rapidly to 3 metres. Can be kept shorter by careful pruning. Has large heart-shaped leaves with deeper indented veins. Large clusters of flowers produced in spring, each consisting of a 2 cm white calyx with a protruding scarlet, star-shaped flower. Other colour varieties are available. Grow at temperatures of 16°-21°C (60°-70°F) in strong indirect light. Needs a winter rest period of 10°C (50°F) for a few weeks. Water plentifully and spray foliage with water during active growth, feeding every two weeks. Grow in soil-based compost, and propagate from shoot cuttings taken in spring and raised in a propagator. Prune well before growth starts in spring.

CLEYERA

C. japonica 'Tricolor' **(C. fortunei)**

Small shrub grown for its attractive foliage. 8 cm leaves are marbled with light- and dark-green and edged with creamy-yellow, sometimes with a pink tinge. Grows up to 75 cm in height and does well at normal room temperatures. Prefers to be kept at about 10°C (50°F) in winter, during the rest period. Prone to dry out easily, so needs frequent watering in summer. Feed every two weeks. Grow in soil-based compost and propagate from tip cuttings taken in early spring. May require mist spraying of foliage if kept in very dry room.

CLIVIA

C. miniata *Kaffir Lily*

Large and spectacular plants producing strap-like leaves in a heavy fan. Thick 60 cm flower stalks are produced in late winter, carrying up to 15 large trumpet-shaped orange flowers. Other colour varieties are available. Usually flowers freely only when thoroughly pot-bound. Requires bright light, but will not tolerate direct sun. Thrives at temperatures of 16°-21°C (60°-70°F) during the growth phase. During the winter they should be rested at about 10°C (50°F) or slightly less. Water well through the summer and allow to become almost dry over the winter rest period. Feed only during active growth, and cultivate in soil-based compost. Repot only if really necessary, and propagate by separating offsets from the plant, complete with roots. The thick roots are easily snapped off and should be handled very carefully. Remove flowers as they fade, so plant does not waste its strength in producing fruit.

COBAEA

C. scandens *Cathedral Bells, Cup and Saucer Vine*

Rampant growing vine, usually grown outdoors as a half-hardy perennial. Grows large and fast in the conservatory or cool greenhouse, producing large bell-shaped flowers which are at first pale green, then becoming violet. A white form 'Alba', is also available. Grow in soil-based compost and pinch out to prevent excessive growth.

COCOS

C. wedelliana (Microcoelium wedelliana)

Slow growing palm which eventually produces a stout trunk. Finely divided fronds. Requires indirect light and temperatures of 16°-21°C (60°-70°F). Requires feeding during the spring and summer, and needs a rest period in winter.

CODIAEUM

C. variegatum pictum *Croton, Joseph's Coat*

Colourful and spectacular foliage, but difficult to keep in good condition for long. Codiaeums are densely branching shrubs seldom exceeding 1 metre in height, and with large leaves of very diverse shape, veined or blotched with red, yellow or orange in almost any combination. Almost all are hybrids, although they can look so different that they may appear quite unrelated. Codiaeums need good indirect light, preferably with some direct sunlight. Grow in a temperature of 16°-21°C (60°-70°F), and keep moist but not waterlogged throughout the year. There is no true resting period. Stand in damp gravel tray to maintain high humidity. In dry atmosphere the lower leaves will drop. Grow in well-drained, soil-based compost and feed fortnightly from spring to autumn. Propagate from stem cuttings. These exude milky latex when cut, and must be sealed by wetting the cut end to coagulate the latex. Grow on in a propagator. Similarly, stems cut during pruning or shaping should be sealed by water spraying. Very prone to attack by red spider mites.

COELOGYNE

Large group of attractive epiphytic orchids, most of which are suitable for cultivation in the home. They grow from large pseudobulbs and are noted for their prolific flowering. Coelogynes are rather large and untidy plants but are well worth cultivating for their blossom. They prefer bright, indirect light and require minimum temperatures of about 10°C (50°F), with a maximum at around normal room temperature. Most require a winter rest and should otherwise be kept moist. Do not let water remain on the pseudobulbs, which might rot. Water with a foliar feed every two weeks during active growth, and cultivate in normal orchid compost. Do not disturb the roots unnecessarily. Propagate by division of the rhizome complete with several pseudo-bulbs.

C. cristata

Most common species for home cultivation, producing a dense cluster of egg-shaped pseudo-bulbs, up to 6 cm high, becoming wrinkled after flowering. Flowers are carried on 30 cm stems and are up to 8 cm across. They are white, with orange blotches and lines on the lip. Winter flowering.

C. ochracea

Large summer flowering species which is one of the easiest to grow and flower. White flowers are extremely fragrant, 3 cm across, and have lip blotched with bright yellow.

C. pandurata *Black Orchid*

Largest flowers of the group, up to 10 cm across, coloured green with black speckles and black hairs on the lip. Flowers are carried in long sprays. Requires warmer temperatures than other Coelogynes; minimum of 16°C (60°F).

COFFEA
(Coffee)
C. arabica

This shrub is the normal source of coffee beans. It seldom grows taller than 1 metre indoors but will grow much larger in the greenhouse. A dwarf form, **c. arabica 'nana'**, is sometimes available. Produces willow-like branches with dark green glossy leaves. Mature plants produce small fragrant white flowers in summer, sometimes followed by the 1 cm red fruits, each containing two coffee 'beans' or seeds. Prefers indirect light, and tolerates winter temperatures as low as 13°C (55°F). Grow in well-drained soil-based compost, standing pot in a damp gravel tray in summer to maintain the humidity. Allow to become almost dry during winter. Difficult to propagate from cuttings, but can be grown from *unroasted* coffee beans. Susceptible to scale insects and mealy bugs.

COLEUS
(Flame Nettle, Painted Leaves)
C. blumei

Coleus are cheap and cheerful plants; that is, they are inexpensive, and as colourful as it is possible to be with foliage in green, brown, red, magenta, yellow or orange. They are perennials, but are usually discarded after a year's growth, being replaced with cuttings. Coleus have fleshy stems growing to around 45 cm, and kept bushy by pinching out the growing tips. The soft velvety leaves have saw-toothed edges. Coleus prefer bright light, including some sunlight and temperatures of 10°-16°C (50°-60°F). They must be kept moist at all times, otherwise they will wilt spectacularly. Although they will recover after such a drying out, leaf drop is common. Feed at two-weekly intervals and grow in soil-based compost. Roots very easily from cuttings taken in summer and autumn, and these grow rapidly to replace the original plant next spring. Prone to attack from red spider mites, especially in dry room conditions.

COLLINIA

See CHAMAEDOREA

COLUMNEA
(Goldfish Vine)

Columneas produce either trailing or arching stems, with small fleshy leaves and attractive flowers which can be produced right through spring, summer and autumn. Flowers are tubular, flaring out into five lobes. They are long lasting, and may be produced in very large numbers. Grow Columneas in bright indirect light, at temperatures of 16°-21°C (60°-70°F), keeping moist throughout the growing period, and drier in winter. Feed during active growth with high-potash (tomato-type) fertiliser. May be grown in moss or peat-based compost in hanging baskets, or in soil- or peat-based compost in normal pots. Repot if pot-bound, trimming away excess roots. Propagate from tip cuttings. Susceptible to aphid attack.
C. × 'Banksii'

Long trailing stems, with 5 cm long scarlet flowers, with yellow streaks. Prolific flowering hybrid form. Also available as 'variegata', which is slower growing and more difficult to propagate.

C. gloriosa
Trailing species with leaves covered with purple hairs. 7 cm scarlet flowers with yellow throat, followed by attractive white berries.

C. linearis
Upright species growing to 45 cm, and having deep pink flowers throughout the growing season.

C. microphylla
Spectacular but temperamental species with 2 metre trailing stems, covered with small reddish hairy leaves. 7 cm long flowers are scarlet with yellow throat.

Numerous other hybrids and varieties are available.

CONOPHYTUM
(Cone Plant)

Small cactus-like succulent plants, consisting of a pair of fleshy leaves separated by a slit through which flowers grow. They resemble a heart when seen in profile. These odd little plants need a definite winter rest. When watering ceases they gradually shrivel and appear completely dead. Eventually new shoots appear from inside the husk of the original leaves and watering can be commenced. Grow in direct sunlight, at a temperature of 5°-30°C (41°-86°F), and pot in normal cactus or succulent compost. Propagate from seed sown in mid-summer.

C. bilobum
Leaves are grey-green, tinged with red. Flowers are lemon-yellow, appearing in autumn. A very small, low-growing plant.

C. frutesceus (C. salmonicolor)
Leaves are covered with pale speckles and are about 3 cm in height. With age the plant develops short stems, producing a 15 cm clump. Portions can then be removed and treated as cuttings. Produces very attractive salmon-pink flowers in mid-summer.

CORDYLINE
Large group of shrubs or trees, often confused with DRACAENA. Leaves are produced in rosettes, and as outer leaves age and drop off, a woody trunk may be produced. Leaves are usually long and spear-shaped. Cordylines grow well in well-lit, spacious rooms, in direct sunlight where possible. They require temperatures of 10°C (50°F) minimum, and larger types do well if put outdoors during mild weather. Grow in a rich open compost, preferably containing leaf-mould, and keep well watered, though not waterlogged, throughout the active growth period when they should be fed fortnightly. Can be grown (very slowly) from seed, or from tip cuttings or shoots from the base of the plant. Old plants can be cut into short lengths of stem, each containing one or more buds (seen as a small swelling), which are treated as cuttings.

C. australis (Draecaena australis) *Giant Dracaena, Cabbage Tree*
Very long slim arching leaves up to 70 cm in length. Grows up to 1.5 metres high in a graceful 'palm' shape. Side branches may be produced on mature plants. Varieties are available with cream or purple stripes.

C. indivisa (Draecaena indivisa) *Mountain Cabbage Tree*
Another large Cordyline, with even larger leaves up to 1.5 metres in length. Best suited to the conservatory or cool greenhouse.

C. terminalis (Draecaena terminalis) *Good-luck Plant, Polynesian Ti Plant*
Moderate-sized Cordyline grown for its magnificent colouring which is crimson to coppery-green. Many varieties exist, some of which are brilliant crimson with cream striping, or with darker stripes. Less tolerant of cold conditions than the other species and requires spraying to maintain humidity. Needs strong light to develop its full colour, but is scorched by direct summer sunlight.

COTYLEDON
Large group of succulents. Those suitable for indoor cultivation have fleshy, grey-tinged leaves and may produce bell-shaped flowers. The leaves are covered with a powdery 'bloom'. Cotyledons grow very slowly, and only flower after several years, producing flower clusters on thin 40 cm stems. 3 cm flowers are produced in summer. They thrive at normal room temperatures, in full sun. Water moderately in growth phase and give short rest in winter with only minimal watering. Pot in well-drained, soil-based compost and propagate from tip cuttings.

C. orbiculata
Grows to 30-40 cm, with branched stems. Leaves grow in rosettes, and are fleshy, powdery, and with a fine red border. The 2 cm flowers are orange in colour.

C. undulata *Silver Crown*
Branched stems with erect 4 cm leaves, widening to a wavy top edge which appears to have been crimped. Do not wet or touch leaves as this mars the powdery bloom.

Flowers are orange.

CRASSULA

Widely varying group of succulents easy to grow indoors provided they are given adequate direct sunlight. They tolerate temperatures of 5°-30°C (41°-86°F) and unlike many desert plants should be kept slightly moist throughout the year, with fortnightly feeding during the growth phase. Keep cool during winter (below 13°C/55°F). Grow in well-drained soil-based compost with added sharp sand. Propagates easily from stem cuttings or from mature leaves which are pulled off, allowed to dry for two days, then potted up as cuttings.

C. arborescens *Silver Jade, Chinese Jade, Silver Urn Plant*
Tree-like plant with a stocky 'trunk' and many branches, sometimes growing to 1.5 metres. Fleshy leaves are grey-green with red edges. Flowers are occasionally produced.

C. argentea (C. portulacea) *Jade Plant*
Similar to **C. arborescens** but with more rounded leaves of shiny jade-green colour, often with red edges. Mature plants produce clusters of tiny pink flowers. Grows up to 1 metre tall, but is very slow growing. Variegated forms are available.

C. deceptrix (C. deceptor)
Miniature plant growing only 6 cm high, with the whitish-grey leaves very tightly packed around the stems. Grows during the winter and produces small white flowers on slim stems. Needs warmer temperatures than the other types and should be generally treated like a cactus.

C. falcata (Rochea falcata) *Aeroplane Propeller Plant, Scarlet Paintbrush*
Long sickle-shaped blue-grey leaves on sprawling stems, eventually forming an untidy clump 15 cm high. Produces spectacular scarlet or orange flowers in a large cluster in summer. Many colour varieties are available. Very easy to grow.

C. lycopodioides *Toy Cypress, Moss Crassula*
Small delicately branched plant with erect stems completely covered by tiny triangular leaves. Grows up to 10 cm in height. Ideal for the bottle garden.

C. rupestris *Buttons-on-a-String, Rosary Plant*
Small sprawling form with plump blue-grey leaves through which the stems appear to pass. Produces small pink flowers.

CRINUM
(Spider Lilies)
C. × 'Powelli'
Large plants growing from enormous 12 cm bulbs. They produce clusters of large trumpet-shaped flowers on 60 to 90 cm stalks in autumn. Flowers are up to 12 cm across and are usually pink or red. Leaves are coarse and strap-like. Need several hours of direct sun every day and grow well at normal room temperatures. Foliage dies back in winter when the plants should be rested. Plant the bulb in soil-based compost in a relatively small pot, and do not disturb unnecessarily. Feed at three-week intervals during active growth. Propagate by dividing clumps carefully and potting the new bulbs separately. Cut away leaves as they yellow.

CROCUS
Crocus grow well indoors but are only temporary inhabitants, being returned to the garden after flowering. They need as much light as possible, growing only in the winter. Corms must be planted in soil-based compost in the autumn and left outdoors in a cool dark place until the shoots appear. They can be brought indoors for flowering. Without this cool treatment flowering will not take place. Keep cool once indoors and plant outdoors as soon as flowering is finished.

CROSSANDRA
C. infundibuliformis (C. undulifolia) *Firecracker Flower*
A 40 cm plant with attractive glossy leaves. Produces sprays of orange flowers, tubular and flared out into five lobes. Flowers are produced in spring and at intervals throughout the summer. Several other colour varieties exist. Grow in indirect light, at 16°-21°C (60°-70°F), and keep moist and fed throughout the growing period. Keep relatively dry in winter. Grow in soil-based compost and propagate from cuttings. Maintain humidity by standing pot in moist gravel.

CRYPTANTHUS
(Earth Star, Starfish Plant)
Group of small bromeliad plants which unlike most of their relatives, grow on the ground. Most are flattened and spreading in form, with attractive mottled or striped leaves, which may also have an undulating surface. Some types have a whitish 'bloom' on the leaves. They are easy to grow in light shade, at temperatures of 16°-21°C (60°-70°F), in peat-based compost, or compost containing leaf mould. They require only sparing watering and can be fed occasionally with a foliar feed.

C. acaulis
Small flattened rosettes up to 15 cm across. Leaves have undulating surface with grey scurf and serrated edges. Pink tinged varieties are available.

C. bivittatus
10-12 cm rosettes with undulating leaves having a dark background with two cream or pink stripes.

C. bromeloides (C. terminalis var. 'tricolor') *Rainbow Star, Colour Band*
The most attractive species. More erect than most. Rosettes are up to 30 cm across but difficult to grow as they tend to rot. Avoid overwatering. Leaves are striped in cream and green with bright red edges.

C. fosterianus *Pheasant Leaf*
Large plant with rosettes up to 60 cm across. Leaves are coppery-purple with irregular cross-banding.

C. zonatus *Zebra Plant*
Rosettes are up to 30 cm diameter. Leaves are green with cross-banding in white and brown, and have white scurf beneath. Var. 'Zebrinus' (Pheasant Leaf) has brighter colouring.

CTENANTHE

Related to CALATHEA and MARANTA, but producing more compact plants with narrower leaves. These are large plants growing up to 1 metre in height. The leaves are lance-shaped with a velvety surface, and are carried on long stems. Many have coloured bars in a herring-bone pattern. Ctenanthes require bright but indirect light and will not tolerate draughts or temperatures below 13°C (55°F). Stand pots on damp gravel to maintain humidity. Water moderately during active growth, and only sparingly in winter. Grow in soil-based compost and propagate from stem cuttings or offsets taken in summer.

C. lubbersiana
Large and fast-growing species. Upper leaf surface is deep green, mottled with yellow and pale green undersurface.

C. oppenheimiana *Never-Never Plant*
Usually available as the variety 'Tricolor', which has slim pointed leaves splashed with creamy yellow and a deep pink underside.

CUPHEA
(Firecracker Plant)

Small shrubs which flower almost continuously from spring to autumn. They grow in a straggly form to above 60 cm, and have leathery leaves. Cupheas require bright light, including some direct sunlight, and can be kept at normal room temperature. They should be kept moist and fed at fortnightly intervals during the growth phase and rested at 10°-13°C (50°-55°F) over the winter, when they should also be kept relatively dry. Grow in soil-based compost and propagate from shoot cuttings taken in late summer or seed sown in the spring. Many people prefer to discard them after flowering.

C. hyssopifolia *Elfin Herb, False Heather*
Small plant with uninteresting dark green foliage. Attractive bell-shaped flowers coloured white, pink or mauve.

C. ignea (C. platycentra) *Cigar Flower, Red-White-and-Blue-Flower*
Large leaves turning reddish in good light. Flowers are 2 cm long – bright red tubes with black and white markings at the tip, hence the popular name. Flowers are produced in great profusion. A variegated leaf form is available, with speckled yellow leaves.

CYANOTIS

Group of semi-succulent creeping or trailing plants, related to TRADESCANTIA. They need strong light if they are not to become straggly, and are at their best in hanging baskets. Cyanotis thrive at normal room temperatures, provided humidity is reasonably high. Unlike many similar plants they have no rest period, so must be kept moist throughout the year. Stand in moist gravel and spray frequently to maintain humidity. Feeding is necessary only infrequently. Grow in a mixture of sand and soil-based compost and propagate from tip cuttings taken in spring. These plants are relatively short lived and are normally discarded after two years.

C. kewensis *Teddy-Bear Plant*
Small fleshy leaves are triangular, coloured purple underneath. The entire plant is densely covered with rusty-brown hair.

C. somaliensis *Pussy-Ears*
Slim 4 cm leaves are hairy all over, and edged with especially long white hairs.

CYCAS

C. revoluta *Sago Palm*
One of the oldest genera of flowering plants, the Cycas looks very like a palm. Although it can grow into a large tree, it is one of the slowest growing plants, seldom producing more than one leaf each year, so it is unlikely to outgrow the home. The 1 metre leaves are feathery-looking, but are actually very stiff and tough. The leaves spread from a stubby trunk resembling a gnarled pineapple, which is actually a water-storage organ.

Needs bright light, with or without direct sun, and a minimum temperature of 13°C (55°F). Can tolerate very low humidity and grows slowly throughout the year. Water moderately from spring to autumn and during winter water only enough to stop the compost drying out completely. Feed at monthly intervals during active growth. Repot only if obviously pot-bound, using soil-based compost mixed with sharp sand. Propagation is not feasible in the home.

CYCLAMEN
C. persicum (C. indicum)
Cyclamen are tuberous-rooted plants grown for their attractive foliage, but mainly for their delicate flowers. The large, leathery heart-shaped leaves are marbled or edged with silver. Flowers are produced at various times of year, depending on previous treatment of the plant, for these are usually temporary house plants, artificially forced into flower around Christmas time. Flowers are carried on separate slender stalks and are butterfly-like, coloured white, pink or red. Many varieties exist, some with ruffled or frilled flowers. Cyclamen need indirect light, and must be kept cool at all times, preferring a temperature of 10°-16°C (50°-60°F). They must be kept moist, and allowed to dry out gradually after flowering. All leaves should have withered by June, and the tubers are left dormant in their pot until autumn, when watering can recommence as signs of re-growth are seen. Cyclamen are best watered from beneath, by part-submerging the pot in water. They dislike water being poured over the part-exposed tuber. Grow in soil-based compost and feed fortnightly during active growth.

CYMBIDIUM
Large genus of easily grown orchids, all suitable for the cool greenhouse or conservatory, and some suitable for home cultivation. Those suitable for home cultivation are epiphytic. Many are very large, but there are numerous miniature varieties which are comparatively easy to keep. Cymbidiums produce slim upright pseudo-bulbs, and typical strap-like orchid leaves. Flowers are carried either erect or on drooping stems. The miniature varieties produce 7 cm flowers in a wide range of colours; red, pink, yellow, green or white, and many flowers may be carried on each stem. Most flower in late spring to early summer, the flowers lasting for several weeks. Cymbidiums should be grown in strong indirect light at about 16°C (60°F). They should be kept moist throughout the year, possibly with a brief winter rest. Feed every two weeks during active growth, and grow in normal fibrous orchid compost. Old plants can be propagated by division of the rhizome complete with pseudo-bulbs, just after flowering.

CYPERUS
(Umbrella Sedge)
Cyperus are a group of rush-like plants which are essentially aquatic. Thus they are among the few house plants which can cope with excess water. In fact, they do best when standing in a bowl of water. Cyperus have thin grass-like leaves and flowering stems surmounted by umbrella-shaped leafy bracts. The flowers are brown or green, and are insignificant. Grow in full sun or indirect light, at temperatures of 13°-18°C (55°-65°F). Remember to keep the plant wet at all times. Browning of the tips of leaves is a sign of too-dry conditions, and is corrected by standing the plants in water. Grow in soil-based compost and repot frequently as the plant grows. Feed monthly with liquid fertilizer through the growing phase. Propagate by division of large clumps in spring, cutting through the root ball with a sharp knife and prising the clump apart. **C. alternifolius** may be propagated by treating the flowering head as a cutting, with the stem trimmed off within 1 cm of the head.
C. alternifolius   Umbrella Palm
Grows up to 1 metre in height with narrow ribbed stems and drooping bracts on the flowering heads. Dwarf and variegated forms are also available.
C. papyrus   Egyptian Paper Plant, Papyrus
The true papyrus plant of the Nile. This is a very large plant, growing up to 2 metres in height with small, drooping, brown flowers surrounded by arched bracts. This species needs greater humidity and is less tolerant of low temperatures than **C. alternifolius**. Needs a minimum temperature of 18°C (65°F) and prefers it even warmer. Probably best grown in the greenhouse or conservatory. A dwarf form 'Nanus' or **C. isocladus** is also available.

CYRTOMIUM
C. falcatum   Fish-Tail Fern, Holly Fern
The only species of this genus of fern which is commonly grown as a house plant. It has large holly-like 'leaves' rather than the usual dainty fern foliage. As ferns go, this is a relatively

tough plant, and even survives outdoors in some sheltered areas. Cyrtomiums grow well in light shade, and will not tolerate any sunlight. It will live in a normal cool room, but may need standing in a damp tray in dry atmospheres. Should be kept moist through- out the year, and fed fortnightly while in active growth. Grow in mixture of soil-based compost and leaf mould or coarse peat. Propagate by pulling apart the creeping rhi- zome, complete with several fronds. Prone to attack by scale insects and mealy bugs.

Cymbidium X

DARLINGTONIA

D. californica *Californian Pitcher Plant, Cobra Lily*

A curious insectivorous plant only available from specialist nurseries. Produces bright yellow-green tubular leaves from 8 cm to 80 cm in height, swelling towards the tip into a hood with sinister-looking red veins. Flies are attracted into the hollow leaf trap, where they drown, and their decaying remains nourish the plant. Red globular flowers are produced in late spring. Can be grown in the cool greenhouse in a live sphagnum moss, kept very moist and watered with soft water. Propagate from seed or by division.

DATURA

(syn. Brugmansia)

Genus of shrubby plants for the cool greenhouse or conservatory. Their foliage is undistinguished, but all produce enormous and spectacular flowers. Grow in normal soil-based compost, and cut back flowering shoots severely during winter. Propagate from cuttings or seed.

D. cornigera (Brugmansia knightii)

Large oval leaves. Produce 15 cm trumpet-shaped creamy-white flowers in mid-summer. Var. 'Grand Marnier' produces flowers up to 20 cm long, with pointed filaments edging the trumpet-shaped blossom.

D. sanguinea (Brugmansia sanguinea)

Smaller (2 metre) species, which produces scarlet 18 cm tubular flowers with orange bases, appearing in mid-summer.

D. suaveolens

One of the largest flowers available for indoor cultivation. This large shrub produces wide bell-shaped fragrant white flowers which are up to 30 cm in length.

DAVALLIA

Genus of ferns having finely divided fronds, and very suitable for hanging baskets. Grows from a creeping hairy rhizome, from which spring slim stalks carrying the large fronds. Grows well in light shade, and normal room temperatures. More tolerant of dry atmospheres than are most ferns and should be watered lightly throughout the year. Feed mature plants every two weeks when in active growth. Grow in peat-based compost or a mixture of soil-based compost and leaf mould. Propagate by severing sections of rhizome with fronds attached and pinning these down on the compost surface in a propagator.

D. canariensis *Deersfoot Fern, Hare's Foot Fern*

Popular species named after the hairy creeping rhizome which often hangs out of the pot. Large feathery fronds up to 45 cm in length, rather resembling carrot leaves.

D. trichomanoides (D. bullata, D. mariesii) *Ball Fern, Squirrel's Foot*

Feathery, light-green fronds but chiefly grown for its rhizome, which is covered with reddish-brown fur and long silvery hairs. The rhizome can be trained into a ball shape.

DENDROBIUM

(Rock Lily)

Epiphytic orchids for the cool greenhouse, conservatory or the home. Has long stem-like pseudo-bulbs from which the flowers grow on short stalks. Most types thrive in normal room temperatures and tolerate temperatures as low as 10°C (50°F) during the winter rest period, when in some species the leaves turn yellow and drop off. Otherwise, treat as a typical orchid growing in fibrous compost and feeding during the growth phase. Do not let water spray rest on new growth, which is prone to rot.

D. infundibulum

Spring flowering evergreen orchid, producing 10 cm white flowers with bright yellow throats. May need some watering during the rest period to prevent shrivelling. Can be grown outdoors in mild summer weather.

D. kingianum

Small orchid growing to about 30 cm and with white-lipped purple flowers, 3 cm across. Spring flowering.

D. nobile

Very large plant growing to 1 metre or more, producing purple and maroon blossom from leafless pseudo-bulbs in spring. Leaves fall prior to flowering. High temperatures may prevent flowering. The most popular Dendrobium and the easiest to flower.

DICHORISANDRA

D. reginae (Campelia zanonia albo-marginata) *Queen's Spiderwort*

A relative of TRADESCANTIA, this is a sprawling plant which can be trained upright. Has large spear-shaped leaves arranged in pairs and grows to height of 60 cm or more. Leaves are bright green with silvery stripes and patches, and are coloured maroon beneath. Grows best in good indirect light at temperatures of 16°-21°C (60°-70°F), with no rest period. Dislikes dry air, and is best kept well watered and stood on a damp gravel bed to maintain humidity. Feed fortnightly during active growth. Woody stems tend to shed lower leaves, so old plants are best discarded and replaced with young plants grown from tip cuttings rooted in a propagator. Grow in normal soil-based compost.

DIEFFENBACHIA
(Dumb Cane)

Dieffenbachia are a large family of showy foliage plants with large variegated leaves and fleshy stems. Many grow to 1.5 metres or more, and the stems often become bare as the lower leaves dry up and fall off. The leaves arch downwards to hide the bare stems, but it is always preferable to purchase specimens which already carry bushy side shoots. Alternatively the growing tip can be removed to encourage bushy growth. Dieffenbachias require good indirect light, and temperatures of around 16°-21°C (60°-70°F). At temperatures below 16°C (60°F) leaf damage will occur, as it will also in draughts, or in too-dry atmospheres. High humidity can be maintained by standing the plant on damp gravel. Grow in soil-based compost and water moderately throughout the year. Dieffenbachias continue to grow all through the year and have no real rest period. Propagate by tip cuttings taken in spring or summer. Alternatively, take short sections of stem, each containing at least one growth bud. These are secured horizontally on the compost surface and the developing plant maintained in a propagator. A further alternative is air layering, in which a packet of moss/compost mixture is secured around the stem, just below the crown of the plant. When roots penetrate the bundle, the stem is severed just below and the rooted section is potted. Dieffenbachia stems invariably produce side shoots once the top of the plant is removed.

Caution: Dieffenbachias contain poisonous sap (hence the name 'Dumb Cane'). Wash the hands well after handling leaves, and especially after cutting stems. Keep these plants away from very young children.

D. amoena
One of the largest Dieffenbachias, with leaves up to 45 cm long by 30 cm wide coloured deep green and splashed with white and cream markings. Reaches a height of 1.5 metres.

D. camilla
A small (60 cm) species with a leaf almost entirely white and having only a narrow band of green around the edges. Naturally bushy, with many small shoots being produced from the base. Prefers strong indirect light.

D. exotica
The most popular, and the most hardy type of Dieffenbachia. Grows to 60 cm, and is naturally bushy in form. Leaves are marked with light green and cream, in an irregular herringbone pattern. May be a hybrid form rather than a true species.

D. picta (D. maculata) *Spotted Dumb Cane*
Large and robust plant with large dark-green leaves, speckled with cream along the ribs. This is one of the earliest conservatory plants, introduced by the Victorians, and by modern standards is rather delicate.

DIONAEA
D. muscipula *Venus' Fly Trap*
Fascinating insectivorous plant, very difficult to cultivate but worthwhile if only for a brief time. Usually purchased in dormant form. Produces flat rosette up to 25 cm across, with the flattened leaves crowned by the insect trap. This looks rather like an opened oyster shell, with its edges lined by long tooth-like bristles. When brushed by a fly, the two sections slam shut, trapping the fly, which is slowly digested. In its bog habitat this is the plant's only source of nitrogen. Must be grown in a pot covered with a glass or plastic dome to maintain high humidity. Alternatively can be grown in a fern case or covered, empty aquarium. Requires temperatures of 18°-27°C (65°-80°F), and light shade. Cultivate in a mixture of peat and coarse sand, and stand the pot in a shallow dish of water. Will not tolerate hard water, and *does not* require feeding. Propagate by division.

DIOSCOREA
D. discolor *Ornamental Yam*
Attractive climbing plant, growing from a large potato-like tuber. Produces many slim twining stems which can grow to 3 metres in a single season. Leaves are heart-shaped, and up to 18 cm long. They are coloured rich dark green, with a silver midrib and irregular yellowish marbling, and are purple underneath. This plant dies back completely in autumn, recommencing its growth in early spring. Grow in good light, with some direct sunlight, at a minimum temperature of 13°C (55°F). Water sparingly when growth starts in spring and increase watering as the plant develops. Pinch out growing tips to encourage bushy growth and provide support with canes or a climbing frame. Feed every two weeks until the autumn. Allow tuber to dry out completely over winter. Propagate from small tubers developed on the roots.

DIPLADENIA
D. splendens (Mandevilla splendens)
Large woody-stemmed climber for the green-house or conservatory. They require bright indirect light and temperatures of around 16°-21°C (60°-70°F). Produces glossy pointed leaves, and even while small, carries masses of trumpet-shaped pink flowers up to 7 cm across. Flowers are produced in clusters throughout the summer. Prune excess growth severely after flowering. Grow in well-drained soil-based compost and provide wire climbing supports. Feed fortnightly only during active growth. Propagate from tip cuttings in a heated propagator; minimum temperature 27°C (80°F).

DIZYGOTHECA
D. elegantissima *False Aralia*
Delicate-looking foliage plant having leaves divided into approximately eight slender leaflets, with saw-toothed edges. Leaf colour is at first coppery, darkening almost to black. Grows slowly into a small but elegant tree, but may need pinching out to achieve bushy growth. Can eventually reach a height of 3 metres, but seldom survives that long in the home. Grow in light shade, at a temperature of 18°-21°C (65°-75°F), and avoid sudden drops in temperature. Maintain humidity by frequent water spraying, and stand pot in damp gravel. Keep compost moist at all times, but do not overwater, especially in winter. Feed only during active growth. Grow in soil-based compost and propagate from seed in a propagator.

DRACAENA
(Dragon Tree)
Large groups of shrubs and trees which have a generally palm-like appearance. They are frequently confused with CORDYLINE. Most Dracaenas develop a woody trunk with age and all have lance- or spear-shaped leaves growing in rosettes. Most thrive in good indirect light at normal room temperatures. Variegated types prefer a minimum temperature of 16°C (60°F), otherwise their leaves will be damaged. Maintain high humidity with a damp gravel bed around the pot, especially in centrally heated homes. Water and feed plentifully throughout the growth period, and water sparingly during winter. Grow in soil-based compost and propagate from either tip cuttings or short sections of the woody stem, containing at least one growth bud. Make sure you plant them the right way up! Raise young plants in a propagator.

D. deremensis
Produce long (45 cm) glossy leaves with two silver stripes. The variety 'Bausei' has a single broad white stripe, and still more coloured varieties exist. Grows to about 1.5 metres, slowly shedding its lower leaves to produce a woody trunk.
D. draco *Dragon Tree*
A large tree which seldom exceeds 1 metre in the home, this Dracaena eventually forms a gnarled trunk with dense rosettes of blue-grey leaves, with a clear or red margin. Rosettes are at first developed at soil level before the trunk grows. Prefers more light than most species and can tolerate temperatures as low as 10°C (50°F).
D. fragrans *Corn Plant, Cornstalk Plant*
Produces broad, arched leaves, which are prone to damage in dry atmospheres. The basic plant is striped in bright green and gold and colour varieties are available with creamy stripes. Gradually sheds its lower leaves to produce a long trunk.
D. marginata *Madagascar Dragon Tree*
One of the easiest Dracaenas, which can eventually develop into a tree. Develops slowly into a long slim stem, topped with a rosette of slim arching leaves, coloured dark green with a purple margin. Usually sold as the variety 'Tricolor' which is striped in green, pink and cream.
D. sanderana *Belgian Evergreen, Ribbon Plant*
Produces a stiff stem carrying 20 cm leaves boldly striped in grey-green and white. Retains its leaves and the woody stem is not as apparent as in other Dracaenas. Seldom produces side branches.
D. succulosa (D. godseffiana) *Gold-Dust Dracaena*
An untypical species, slow growing and much branched. Leaves are broad and laurel-like speckled with gold. Colour varieties exist with very large areas of variegation. Occasionally produces small yellow flowers, followed by red berries.

DREJERELLA
See BELOPERONE

DROSERA
(Sundew)
Insectivorous plant which produces flat rosettes. The upper surface of the leaves is covered with reddish hairs, each tipped with a drop of sticky nectar. Flies become entangled in the nectar, and the leaves fold over and digest them. Cultivation and care are exactly as DIONAEA.

ECHEVERIA

Large group of succulents producing fleshy leaves in rosettes. The plant may produce small flat rosettes, or large shrubby forms. Several forms are hardy enough for outdoor cultivation in summer. Most have an easily damaged waxy bloom and some are hairy. Leaves are easily broken off and can be used for propagation. Grow easily in full sun at temperatures of 5°-30°C (41°-86°F), watering sparingly during the growth period, and scarcely at all in winter. Do not allow water to mark the foliage. Feed sparingly during the summer and pot in a mixture of soil-based compost and sharp sand. Propagate from leaf cuttings, offsets, stem cuttings, or from seed. Rather prone to attack by mealy bugs. There are many available species including numerous hybrids. They produce bell-shaped flowers on short stems in summer.

E. agavoides (Cotyledon agavoides)

Very fleshy leaves up to 6 cm long growing in an elongated rosette up to a height of 30 cm. Unlike most species, leaves do not have a powdery bloom and are coloured pale green with brownish tips, becoming flushed with pink in good light. Flowers are produced in mid-summer, and are coloured red and yellow.

E. derenbergii   *Painted Lady, Baby Echeveria*

Forms a cushion-like clump of tightly packed 7 cm rosettes, coloured blue-grey and with red tips to the leaves. Has a delicate waxy bloom. Produces orange-yellow flowers on short stems in mid-summer. An easy, undemanding plant.

E. gibbiflora

Large plant, up to 45 cm tall and producing its rosette at the top of a stout stem. Large (20 cm) leaves are spoon-shaped and coloured pinkish-grey. A cultivated variety 'Carunculata' has patches of blister-like bumps on the leaves; other varieties have wavy leaf margins, or bronze coloration. Occasionally produces red flowers in winter.

E. harmsii (E. elegans)

Looser, tree-like form, with much-branched stems carrying loose rosettes. Usually grown for its flowers rather than foliage. Leaves are covered with dense soft hairs. Flowers appear in early summer and are 2.5 cm long, they are scarlet with a yellow interior.

E. setosa   *Mexican Firecracker*

Produces flat rosettes up to 15 cm in diameter. Leaves are thickly coated with soft white hairs. The shape of the rosettes is spoiled by developing offsets, which should be pulled off and planted. Produces pink flowers on 30 cm stems in early summer.

Below right:
Epidendrum radicans
Crucifix Orchid
Below left:
Epiphyllum 'Pink Nymph'

ECHINOCACTUS

Classic barrel-shaped cacti; either globular or cylindrical. They grow very slowly and are unlikely to reach more than 20 cm in diameter. Echinocactus require full sun, and temperatures of 7°-30°C (45°-86°F). It will take many years for these cacti to reach 15 cm diameter, and they seldom flower until they are even larger. Give a winter rest period in a cool place, with little or no watering. Feed with high potash (tomato type) fertiliser once a month in the summer. Grow in well-drained soil-based compost with added coarse sand, and allow to dry out between waterings. Can be propagated only from seed, but when young, grow quite rapidly. Prone to attack by mealy bugs, especially in the roots.

E. grusonii *Golden Ball Cactus, Barrel Cactus*
Forms an almost perfect ball, growing up to 1 metre across (but only after 100 years or more). Covered with about thirty ribs, divided by deep grooves. Densely covered by white areoles, from which grow the long golden yellow spines. Areoles and spines are so tightly packed at the top of the plant that it looks woolly. 4 cm yellow flowers are produced on very large plants.

E. horizonthalonius
Smaller type growing as a flattened sphere, with a maximum height of about 25 cm and diameter of 35 cm. About ten pronounced ribs, and bluish-grey stem coloration. Spines are long, curved and grey coloured. Flowers fairly readily, producing pink flowers in a ring around the top of the plant. Not quite as hardy as **E. grusonii**.

ECHINOCEREUS
(Hedgehog Cactus)

Large group of cacti grown both for their interesting appearance, and for their flowers, which are produced readily. They are barrel-shaped or cylindrical, and some grow in clusters or as sprawling prostrate forms. Grow in full sun, at temperatures of 5°-30°C (41°-86°F), ensuring a winter rest at a cool temperature. They can withstand even freezing temperatures if kept completely dry in winter. Require moderate watering during active growth, and little or none during winter. Grow in a mixture of sand and soil-based compost, feeding every two weeks in summer with a high-potash (tomato type) fertiliser. Propagate by severing a shoot in summer, drying it for three days, then potting in the normal cactus compost. Can also be raised from seed.

E. knippelianus

Small dark-green cactus, nearly globular, and about 7 cm high. After several years it begins to branch, forming a tight clump. Stem has five ribs, and small areoles carrying from one to three short soft white spines. Flowers are produced in late spring or summer, and are violet-pink.

E. pectinatus
More columnar cactus, slowly growing to 25 cm tall and 7 cm across. Stem has about thirty ribs, and the short white spines are neatly fanned out. Large cerise flowers are produced in mid-summer.

E. pentalophus procumbens
Produces a tangled mass of sprawling stems up to 12 cm long and 2 cm thick, densely branching and covered by soft white and brown spines. An untidy plant which does not tolerate overwatering, and which produces a mass of 8 cm violet-pink flowers in summer.

ECHINOPSIS
(Sea Urchin Cactus, Thistle Globe)

Small cacti which start as perfect spheres, gradually elongating as they become older. Flowers open in the evening and remain open for several days. Flowers are very large and freely produced and continue through most of the summer. Grow in full sun, at temperatures of 5°-30°C (41°-86°F). A winter rest at low temperature is essential to promote flower bud development. Water plentifully during active growth, and feed every two weeks. Allow to become relatively dry in the winter rest period. Grow in sand/soil-based compost mixture. Propagate by detaching and potting the offsets, which are usually produced in great numbers. Can also be grown from seed. Squeeze out seeds from fleshy berries, dry them, and sow in early spring. Many hybrids are obtained inadvertently in this way. Numerous cultivated hybrids and colour varieties are available.

E. eyriesii
Most types now available are hybrid forms. Twelve ribs with reddish brown spines. Very large flowers, up to 18 cm long, in various colours.

E. multiplex
Very similar to **E. eyriesii**, with night-blooming pink flowers, 18 cm long. There are many hybrids most of which are day-blooming and may be coloured white, red, yellow or orange. Do not expose night-blooming types to artificial light once the buds have formed. **E. multiplex** tends to branch freely, forming dense clumps of offsets.

ELETTARIA
E. cardamomum *Cardamom*
A rather uninteresting plant grown purely for its ability to survive in very poor light. It has lance-shaped, mid-green leaves carried on short stalks, and grows about 60 cm high in a dense clump. Leaves are produced from a large creeping rhizome. Grows at normal room temperatures, with a minimum of 13°C (55°F), and tolerates all light except direct sun. Keep moderately damp during active growth, but allow to part dry out between waterings. Feed at fortnightly intervals during the summer, and allow to become fairly dry during winter. Grow in soil-based compost and propagate by prising apart the clumps.

EPIDENDRUM
A large group of very diverse orchids. Most are epiphytes with fleshy pseudo-bulbs, but others develop like long canes. Flowers are generally small and brightly coloured. Grow in bright, indirect light, in normal fibrous orchid compost. Temperatures should be carefully controlled, with a minimum of 13°C (55°F) at night, and a steady 21°C (70°F) by day; thus these plants are best kept in the greenhouse or conservatory. Maintain high humidity with trays of moist gravel. Water moderately, and keep fairly dry during the winter rest period.
Note Individual species may require slightly different treatment. Propagate by separating pseudo-bulbs and rhizome in spring.
E. ibaguense (E. radicans)
A reed-like species, producing canes up to 1.5 metres in height, with rounded leaves. 2.5 cm flowers are orange or red. This species is more tolerant of cooler conditions than other Epidendrums, and is an evergreen with no winter rest period.
E. pentotis
Long club-shaped pseudo-bulbs up to 30 cm high, and carrying two 12 cm leaves. Flower stems each carry two cream-and-purple flowers.
E. vitellinum
Plump blue-grey pseudo-bulbs, 7 cm high, and carrying a few 10 cm leaves. Flowers are freely produced on 30 cm stems in summer, and are orange and yellow.

Many other species are available in diverse shapes and colours.

EPIPHYLLUM
(Orchid Cactus)
Large forest cacti, noted for their beautiful flowers. Almost all those available are hybrid types. Most have elongated fleshy stems with notched edges, and small clumps of spines arising from areoles in the notches. They usually require some support to prevent sprawling growth, and reach a height of 60 cm or more. The flowers are very large, up to 15 cm or more and in almost any colour except blue. Some are night-blooming and highly fragrant. Flowers are usually produced in spring. Epiphyllums do well in the conservatory, and in the home, occasional water spraying may be necessary. They will not tolerate direct sunlight, and require temperatures of 5°-27°C (41°-86°F). Keep them fairly dry during winter, and water well in spring and summer, feeding with high-potash (tomato type) fertiliser every two weeks until the buds begin to open. Grow in a mixture of sand and peat-based compost, preferably with some added leaf mould. They do not tolerate limey soil. Propagate from cuttings taken in summer. Grown from seed, odd hybrids often result.

EPISCIA
(Carpet Plant)
Small creeping plants with attractive foliage and flowers. Most form a dense carpet covering their pot. They spread by means of a thick, creeping stolon, which roots along its length. Leaves are oval, hairy and puckered. They flower from spring through to autumn. Ideal plants for the bottle garden or hanging basket. Grow in bright, indirect light, at temperatures of 13°-18°C (55°-65°F). They are damaged by dry atmospheres, and best grown with the pot standing in damp gravel. Keep well watered and only lightly fed in summer, and fairly dry in winter. Grow in rich peat-based compost containing chopped sphagnum moss. Propagates easily by separation of sections of the creeping stolon. Prone to attack by aphids.
E. cupreata *Flame Violet*
Coppery-green leaves with silvery outlines over the leaf veins. The leaf surface may be smooth or deeply embossed. The stolons are usually red. Flowers are crimson with a yellow throat, lined with silvery hairs.
E. dianthiflora *Lace Flower*
Small, velvety, rounded leaves, sometimes with red veins. The 3 cm flowers are white with a purple-spotted throat, and have remarkable frilled edges. Flowers for only a short period during the summer.
E. reptans (E. fulgea)
Large bronze-green leaves with silvery markings along the veins. The leaves are heavily

embossed. Produces flame-red flowers in mid-summer, having fringed petals and long hairs lining the throat.

ERICA
(Heath, Heather)
Popular plants which only thrive in the home when soft water is available for watering. They are best treated as temporary plants. They prefer cool conditions, and may not survive centrally heated conditions. Grow in bright, indirect light, at temperatures below 16°C (60°F), and mist spray with water daily to maintain the humidity, otherwise they will suffer leaf drop. Keep moist and never allow the plants to dry out. Water with soft water, rainwater, or water obtained from the drip tray when defrosting the refrigerator. Grow in peat-based compost and do not feed. Put the plant in the garden or discard after flowering. Difficult to propagate by stem cuttings.

E. canaliculata (E. melanthera) *Christmas Heather*
Large (60 cm) shrub, flowering in winter. Produces clusters of white or pink bell-shaped flowers with conspicuous brown anthers.

E. × hyemalis *French Heather*
45 cm high, with abundant tubular white flowers in winter. Soft needle-like foliage.

EUCALYPTUS
(Gum Tree, Iron-Bark Tree)
Fast-growing Australian trees which can be kept in the home for a year or so. The juvenile foliage is very attractive, being oddly shaped and covered with a powdery bloom. Grow in full sunlight at temperatures of 7°-16°C (45°-60°F) and water sparingly. Feed every ten days while in active growth, and cultivate in soil-based compost. Propagate by seed.

E. globulus *Tasmanian Blue Gum*
Juvenile leaves are heart-shaped and grow in pairs so that the stems look like strings of beads, up to 7 cm across. Grows very rapidly.

E. gunnii *Cider Gum*
Paired leaves wrap right round the stems, and are pink-tinged when grown in good light. Slower growing than **E. globulus**, and can be further restricted with a small pot.

EUCHARIS
E. grandiflora (E. amazonica) *Amazon Lily, Eucharist Lily*
Large bulbous plant resembling HIPPEASTRUM. Produces broad 20 cm leaves from its large bulb. Flowers are produced on 60 cm stems in summer and resemble enormous white daffo-dils up to 12 cm across. Requires light shade, and warm temperatures of 13°-18°C (55°-65°F), with a high humidity. Stand pot on moist gravel tray during active growth, and feed every two weeks. Must be allowed to dry out completely after flowering, and is stored in a cool, dry place until growth restarts. Grow in soil-based compost and propagate from offsets produced on the bulb in spring.

EUCOMIS
(Pineapple Flower, Amazon Lily)
Large bulbous plant suitable for growing indoors or on the patio. Produces rosettes of slim leaves and dense flower spikes resembling a pineapple. Thrives in normal room conditions and strong, indirect light, growing in soil-based compost. Water only sparingly until shoots appear in spring, then keep moist and well fed until flowering. After flowering, allow to dry off completely, and store in a cool dry place until growth restarts. Propagate from bulb offsets.

E. pole-evansii *Giant Pineapple Flower*
Grows to 2 metres in the garden or greenhouse, but much smaller in the house. Leaves are undulating and the 30 cm flower has yellow-white flowers followed by ornamental berries.

E. zambesiaca *Pineapple Lily*
Underside of leaves are speckled with purple. Flowers are green and maroon, and remain on the plant for several weeks. Several other species are available.

EUONYMUS
E. japonica *Japanese Spindle Tree*
Basically an outdoor shrub, **Euonymus** can be grown indoors in good light and cool temperatures of 7°-18°C (45°-65°F). It prefers quite cold conditions, and in warm rooms may shed its fleshy leaves. Needs moderate watering in spring and summer, together with feeding, and should be kept fairly dry in winter. Grow in soil-based compost and propagate from cuttings, which are very slow to root. Most types grow to 1 metre in height, with woody stems, although some dwarfed forms exist. Those Euonymus kept in the home are usually among the many variegated varieties, having bright yellow streaks or blotches. All can be planted out in the garden when they outgrow the home. It is important to cut out any plain green shoots appearing on variegated plants, as these can otherwise 'take over'.

EUPHORBIA
(Spurge)

A huge and baffling family of plants, ranging through the familiar Poinsettia, prickly succulent shrubs, to completely globular cactus-like plants. All produce milky latex which is released if the plant is cut or damaged. This may be poisonous or irritant to the skin. This group is so diverse that its most important members are best treated as being quite unrelated.

E. fulgens *Scarlet Plume*
An attractive rambling shrub growing up to 1 metre in height, and carrying long slender leaves on arching stems. Orange-red flowers can be produced in autumn, winter or spring. Requires good light, even including direct sunlight. Thrives in normal warm room temperatures, but must be kept at 16°C (60°F) or more. Water freely in summer, but keep relatively dry in autumn and winter. Feed at monthly intervals during the growth phase, and grow in soil-based compost. Propagate from tip cuttings.

E. milii (E. splendens) *Crown of Thorns, Christ Plant*
Prickly rambling shrub up to 1 metre in height. Its 1 cm thick stems are densely covered with very sharp spines, and leaves are sparse. Tiny scarlet or yellow flowers are produced on the actively growing shoots, and appearing in profusion through the whole growing season. Should be pruned to keep the plant bushy. Grow **E. milii** in the sunniest available place at temperatures of 10°-30°C (50°-86°F). Keep moist during active growth and water only occasionally in winter. Cold draughts cause leaf drop (which can also take place in perfectly healthy plants). Feed at monthly intervals throughout the summer, and grow in a mixture of soil-based compost and sharp sand. Propagate from tip cuttings, taking care to stop the flow of latex by wetting the cut ends of parent stems and cuttings with water. Dry cuttings for a day before planting in a warm propagator, and then water only very lightly.

E. pulcherrima *Poinsettia, Christmas Star*
Popular decorative plant at Christmas, which is derived from a very large wild form. The cultivated varieties are dwarfed, and most grow to only 60 cm in height, with 12-15 cm leaves which have deeply serrated edges. Tiny yellowish flowers are produced in winter, which are surrounded by a group of large and spectacularly coloured bracts, usually scarlet, although pink, white and yellow forms are now available. Commercial growers stunt the plants and force them into flower at Christmas by a combination of controlled lighting and chemical treatments. In the home this cannot be achieved, and the best that can be done is to ensure that the plant is exposed to *only* natural light through autumn and winter. They are probably best discarded after flowering. Grow in good indirect light, at temperatures of 16°-21°C (60°-70°F) and avoid all draughts. Allow to dry out before watering. Feed at monthly intervals until autumn, and prune to remove straggly shoots. Propagate from tip cuttings as for **E. milii**. Grow in soil-based compost in the smallest practicable size of pot. This restricts the unnecessary production of masses of foliage.

Succulent Euphorbias
There are very many succulent Euphorbias, most of which closely resemble true cacti. Many produce leaves, which drop off to leave a bare spiny form. They all thrive in full sun at temperatures of 5°-30°C (41°-86°F). Water freely during active growth, and in winter, give only sufficient water to prevent the compost drying out completely. Feed at fortnightly intervals during the growth phase. Grow in a mixture of sharp sand and soil-based compost and propagate from shoot cuttings, which root very easily. Wet cut ends with latex to coagulate the latex, and allow cuttings to dry for three days before potting. Commonly cultivated forms include:

E. horrida *African Milk-Barrel*
Cactus-like plant producing club-shaped stems with long spines. Branches freely, and grows to a height of 30 cm.

E. obesa *Gingham Golf-Ball*
Globular plant, resembling a spineless barrel cactus, coloured purple-grey. Tiny flowers are produced on top of the plant. Must be propagated from seed.

E. pseudocactus
Tall branched form like the giant desert cacti. Stems are squarish in section edged with 1 cm spines. Can eventually grow to nearly 2 metres.

E. resinifera
Square section stems with spiny edges branching profusely and forming a dense hummock up to 30 cm.

E. tirncalli *Milkbush, Finger Tree, Pencil Tree*
Spindly shrub which soon loses all its tiny leaves, leaving smooth, cylindrical branched stems, less than 1 cm in diameter.

EXACUM
E. affine *Persian Violet*
Small, flowering perennial which is usually

discarded after flowering. Has glossy leaves and produces pale-blue star-shaped flowers with bright-yellow stamens in summer and autumn. Needs bright light, and can tolerate some sunlight. Thrives at normal room temperature with high humidity maintained by standing pot on damp gravel. Feed every two weeks while plants are flowering. Best grown from seed in soil-based compost. Plant seed in spring. Pick off flowers as they fade to prolong the flowering period.

Exacum affine

× FATSHEDERA
(Ivy Tree, Botanical Wonder)

A botanical oddity derived from a hybrid between only distantly related plants: FATSIA, and HEDERA, the common ivy. This plant retains characteristics of both ancestors, having large five-lobed leaves, carried on long thin stems, which usually need to be supported. It grows to 1–1.5 metres, and is an extremely hardy indoor plant. Grows well in light shade, and at temperatures of 4°-16°C (40°-60°F). May need extra humidity in centrally heated homes, by standing pot in damp gravel. Water only moderately, continue watering lightly through the winter to prevent leaf fall. Feed at fortnightly intervals during active growth. Pot in soil-based compost, and propagate from tip cuttings taken in spring or summer and raised in a propagator. Prone to attack by aphids and scale insects. A variegated form is available, which requires stronger light to maintain leaf colour.

FATSIA
F. japonica (Aralia japonica, A. sieboldii)
Aralia, Japanese Fatsia, Castor Oil Plant

Robust plant growing indoors or in the garden. Has very large leaves up to 40 cm wide, and divided into several finger-like lobes. Indoors the leaves are pale green while in the garden they become tough and dark coloured. Indoors, leaves are delicate and especially prone to damage from leaf cleaning chemicals or draughts. Several variegated forms are available. Grow Fatsias in indirect light, at temperatures of 16°-21°C (60-70°F). They will tolerate lower temperatures, however, becoming tough and leathery. Stand pot in damp gravel if air is very dry. Water plentifully during active growth, less in winter, but still sufficient to prevent leaf drop. Feed frequently throughout the growing season. Grow in a rich, well-drained, soil-based compost, preferably with added leaf mould, and pinch out shoots to encourage bushy growth. Propagate from tip cuttings or seeds. If you decide to transfer the plant to the garden, harden it off gradually by moving to a cooler position within the house. Prone to attack from red spider mite in dry conditions.

FAUCARIA
Small succulents, growing in low clusters. The paired leaves are thick and triangular, with the edges armed with fierce teeth. They produce large, yellow, daisy-like flowers in autumn. Grow in full sun, and temperatures of 5°-30°C (41°-86°F) and water well in sum-mer. Allow to become almost dry in winter. Feed at monthly intervals or less during the growth period, using only half the recommended strength of fertiliser. Grow in a mixture of sand and soil-based compost and propagate by dividing the clumps. Allow unrooted sections to dry off for three days before potting.

F. felina   *Cat's Jaws*
As **F. tigrina** below, but with narrower leaves and fewer teeth.

F. tigrina   *Tiger Jaw*
Grey-green 4 cm leaves with white speckles. Teeth are interlocked before the paired leaves separate and develop.

F. tuberculosa
Larger plant with leaves covered with warty growths. Fewer teeth along the edges.

FEROCACTUS
Group of fiercely spined, barrel-shaped cacti, most of which are spherical. In the wild they can grow to enormous size but in the home they seldom exceed 15 cm in diameter, growing in a perfect spiny ball. Most are difficult to induce to flower. Grow in full sun, at temperatures of 5°-30°C (41°-86°F), and if possible, put plants outdoors during sunny summer weather. Keep cool, but not freezing, during the winter rest period, when they should be allowed to dry out almost completely. At other times water moderately. Grow in a porous mixture of soil-based compost and sharp sand, and feed monthly during active growth with high-potash (tomato type) fertiliser. These cacti seldom produce offsets, so must be propagated from seed. They seldom produce flowers in the home.

F. acanthodes
Spherical blue-green cactus, notable for its long, hooked, pink or red spines, which develop their colour only in good light.

F. latispinus   *Devil's Tongue Cactus*
Grey-green spherical stem with clusters of white and red spines. In each cluster one spine is flattened, hooked and enlarged (3 cm by 0.5 cm). This Ferocactus is unusual in that it may produce its purple flowers in the home, provided it receives adequate sun.

FICUS
(Fig)

There are several hundred species of Ficus comprising trees, shrubs and climbers. Some are enormous (the Banyan tree), while others are small creeping plants. Almost all are grown for their stately evergreen foliage. Ficus need protection from direct sun, although as with other plants, variegated forms need stronger light than those with plain foliage. Most thrive in warm room conditions, or the conservatory, at temperatures of 16°-21°C (60°-70°F). They should be watered only moderately (but see **F. pumila**), and kept relatively dry in summer, giving only sufficient water to prevent the compost from drying out. Grow in well-drained, soil-based compost except for the creeping forms which do better in peat-based composts. These latter forms are easily rooted from tip cuttings, but the larger, erect forms are more difficult. They are usually propagated by air layering, but even this technique requires specialist care. The erect-growing Ficus can be induced to branch by cutting out the growing tip. In some species large amounts of sap will exude from the cut end of the stem, and this should be staunched by dusting the cut with powdered charcoal.

F. benghalensis *Banyan*
Large tree best suited to greenhouse or conservatory. Produces leathery 30 cm leaves, densely covered with reddish hairs as are the stems. A rather coarse-looking plant.

F. benjamina *Weeping Fig, Benjamin Fig*
Graceful weeping tree, growing slowly to 2 metres. Its fragile stem may need tying to supports. Leaves are up to 7 cm long, slender and pointed. Very prone to drop its leaves in insufficient light, as is the variegated form which has cream and green leaves. Does not have a true winter rest, but growth diminishes at this time of year. Scale insects often infest the woody bark on the main stem.

F. buxifolia
Recently introduced species have small, spoon-shaped leaves. Stems are reddish.

F. deltoides (F. diversifolia) *Mistletoe Fig*
Small bushy form with triangular or rounded, fleshy leaves covered with brown pits. Produces abundant yellow berries.

F. elastica *Rubber Plant*
The original and best known Ficus. Now usually grown as one of the many cultivated varieties including 'Decora' and 'Robusta'. These are much tougher than the original plant, but retain the stiff erect form with large glossy leaves. In the new varieties new leaves emerge from a bright red protective sheath. Seldom branches unless the growing point is cut off, and grows steadily into a very large tree. Various variegated forms are available with grey, cream and even pink markings.

F. lyrata (F. pandurata) *Fiddleleaf Fig*
Very large species developing into a stately tree. Leaves up to 40 cm long with waved edges and undulating surface. Tends to branch naturally or can be forced to do so by cutting out the growing tip.

F. pumila *Creeping Fig, Climbing Fig*
Small plant with thin, heart-shaped 2 cm leaves. Will trail or creep, forming a dense mat or climb rough surfaces such as brickwork or moss poles, clinging by means of tiny ivy-like roots. A rather delicate variegated form is available. F. pumila must never be allowed to become dry, or leaf drop will result. It tolerates deeper shade and cooler conditions than the other species and will survive outdoors in the summer months.

F. radicans (F. sagitta) *Rooting Fig*
Trailing plant often sold in variegated form. Has 3 cm narrow pointed leaves and very tough, wiry stems.

FITTONIA
(Snakeskin Plant)
Small and rather delicate creeping plants best grown in bottle gardens where they can obtain the high humidities they require. Fittonias have broad, paired, oval leaves, delicately marked with coloured veins. They need to be grown in light shade in humid conditions which can be achieved by standing the pot in damp gravel. Temperatures of 18°-24°C (65°-75°F) are required. They are very prone to leaf drop if too dry, or rot when wet. Keep just moist at all times, and feed every two weeks during active growth. Grow in peat-based compost and propagate by layering or tip cuttings. Young plants should be started off in a propagator. Pinch out tips to keep plant bushy.

F. argyroneura *Silver Net, Silver Snakeskin*
Small plant with rounded leaves covered by a network of silvery veins.

F. vershaffeltii *Painted Netleaf, Mosaic Leaf*
Larger than **F. argyroneura**, and with rich carmine veins on coppery leaves.

FORTUNELLA
(Kumquat)
Small trees for the conservatory or cool greenhouse, growing a little over 1 metre tall. They resemble and are closely related to CITRUS but are smaller and more manageable. They have short woody trunks, and are much branched, carrying glossy, green, pointed leaves. In spring and summer they produce small, fragrant, white flowers followed by slow-developing, miniature oranges. Grow in the brightest possible light at minimum temperatures of 10°C (50°F), and stand pots on damp gravel to increase humidity. Keep damp but

not waterlogged during active growth, and in winter water only sufficiently to stop the compost drying out. Feed during active growth with normal fertiliser, changing to high-potash (tomato type) fertiliser when flower buds appear. Grow in an open compost consisting of leaf mould or coarse peat mixed with soil-based compost. Grows easily from seed, which should be planted in autumn. Susceptible to attack by red spider mites and scale insects.

FREESIA

Many colourful hybrid Freesias can be grown in the home, although temperatures are generally rather warm for these outdoor plants. They thrive best in the conservatory or cool greenhouse, at temperatures of about 10°-16°C (50°-60°F). These are bulbous plants with stiff erect leaves. The funnel-shaped flowers are produced in sprays, in many different colours, and are extremely fragrant. Plant bulbs in autumn in soil-based compost and keep in a cool place until growth commences, after which they can be brought into the house in good light. Keep them moist up to and just after flowering then let them dry off until the next season. Propagate from offsets produced on the bulbs.

FUCHSIA

Familiar plants which produce masses of spectacular flowers, but which are not easy to grow in the home for any length of time. They thrive best in the conservatory or cool greenhouse where they can receive the strong light they need. There are literally hundreds of different types of Fuchsia; some erect, and some pendulous or trailing. Flowers have arching sepals and long trailing stamens and style. Colours range through white, pink, mauve, red and purple, often with contrasting colours in the same flower. These plants react badly to changes in conditions and are best raised from cuttings rather than purchased as a large plant. Grow Fuchsias in full sun, at a maximum temperature of 16°C (60°F), and give them a winter rest in a cooler spot (but protect from frost). They will grow well on the patio, but need protection in winter. Water plentifully through the growing season, and feed every week. Allow to become nearly dry in winter. Grow in soil-based compost and propagate from tip cuttings which root very easily. Pinch out growing tips to maintain a bushy habit, and prune severely in autumn. Very susceptible to attacks by white fly and aphids.

Freesia hybrid

GARDENIA
G. jasminoides *Cape Jasmine*
There are various species of Gardenia in cultivation, but G. jasminoides is the only type really suited for indoor cultivation. In the house it seldom exceeds 45 cm in height, although in the cool greenhouse or conservatory it reaches 2 metres. They need bright, indirect light and temperatures of 18°-21°C (65°-70°F). Steady temperatures of 18°C (65°F) or slightly less are absolutely essential when buds are developing. Temperature changes or draughts will cause bud drop. High humidity is important and plants should be stood in damp gravel and sprayed with water daily. Gardenias will not tolerate any lime, so unless you live in a soft water area they must be watered with rain-water or water obtained thawed from the frost in a refrigerator or freezer. Grow in a peaty, lime-free compost, and keep moist but not waterlogged at all times. Feed with 'acid' fertiliser at fortnightly intervals throughout active growth, and treat with iron sequesterene if yellow patches appear on the leaves. Propagate from 7 cm tip cuttings grown on in a heated propagator. The 7 cm white flowers are produced from June to December. Several varieties exist with dense bushy habit.

GASTERIA
(Ox-tongue, Lawyer's Tongue, Dutch Wings)
Group of compact succulent plants resembling the ALOE. Most produce their thick fleshy leaves in two tightly packed rows but some are slightly twisted into rosettes. Gasterias make ideal house plants, being extremely tolerant of dry centrally heated environments, and of underwatering. Unlike most succulents they do not like direct sunlight, but prefer strong, indirect light. Gasterias flower freely, producing long flower stalks with 15-20 tubular red or orange flowers in spring or summer. Keep at temperatures of 5°-30°C (41°-86°F), and if possible, grow outdoors in light shade during the summer. Give them a cool winter rest with very little watering. During the growing season water moderately. Do not feed Gasterias as this will make them develop too rapidly into soft unhealthy growth. Grow in a mixture of coarse sand and soil-based compost. Propagate from offsets which are produced profusely from the plant base. Allow offsets to dry for three days before potting up.
G. liliputana
Dwarf species growing up to 5 cm in height. Leaves grow in a spiral rosette and are dark green blotched with white.
G. maculata
The most common cultivated species with strap-like leaves up to 18 cm in length and 4 cm wide. In young plants leaves grow in flattened rows but become an untidy spiral as the plant grows. Leaves are shiny green with white speckles or blotches.
G. verrucosa *Wart Gasteria*
Tapered leaves up to 15 cm long with concave upper surface. Coloured dark green with white warty speckles. Leaves are arranged in flattened rows.

GEOGNANTHUS
(Seersucker Plant)
G. undulatus (Dichorisandra musaica undulata)
Small foliage plant grown for its decorative leaves which have a curious puckered surface. Leaves are deep green with silvery longitudinal strips and are deep maroon underneath, and look as though they are quilted. Small clusters of violet flowers are produced in summer. Geognanthus needs bright, indirect light and a minimum temperature of 18°C (65°F). Maintain high humidity by standing plant in moist gravel. Keep moderately damp at all times, and feed at two-week intervals throughout the growing period. Grow in well-drained, soil-based compost and propagate from tip cuttings in late spring. Old plants are best discarded and replaced by newly grown specimens.

GLORIOSA
(Glory Lily, Climbing Lily)
G. rothschildiana
Tropical climbing lilies which will grow in a well-lit window, or in the greenhouse or conservatory. They climb rapidly up supports clinging with their hooked leaf tips, reaching a height of 2 metres in a single season. Flowers are brilliant scarlet and orange with the petals turned back to show a bright yellow centre. Gloriosas grow from a large finger-like tuber, which is started into growth in spring. Keep at temperatures of 13°-18°C (55°-65°F), and feed well and keep moist during active growth. Plants will die back completely in winter and the tubers should be overwintered in a cool dry place.

GRAPTOPETALUM
Small rosette-forming succulent resembling ECHEVERIA. Stems are profusely branched, forming dense clusters of attractively coloured rosettes. Small bell-shaped flowers are

produced on 15 cm stems in summer. Grow in direct sunlight at normal room temperatures, keeping cool in winter. Water only moderately during active growth and keep almost dry in winter. Do not allow water droplets to wet the foliage. Grow in a mixture of coarse sand and soil-based compost. Feeding is generally unnecessary. Propagate from offsets or mature rosettes treated as cuttings.

G. pachyphyllum
Dwarf species with 3 cm rosettes, coloured bluish-grey. Produces red flowers.

G. paraguayense *Ghost Plant, Mother-of-Pearl Plant*
Rosettes up to 10 cm diameter with wide leaves, white with tinges of pink and grey. Produces white flowers.

GREVILLEA
(Silk Oak)

G. robusta
Very large Australian tree which is suitable as a house plant while young. The foliage is fern-like, with slightly furry leaves having silky undersides. Grown indoors Grevillea reaches a height of about 2 metres with a spread of 60 cm, but can be pruned to keep it within reasonable limits. Grow in light shade, although they will tolerate some direct sunlight. They grow in a wide range of temperatures from 4°-21°C (40°-70°F), and grow very rapidly at the higher temperatures especially if the atmosphere is humid. Water moderately throughout the year and feed fortnightly during active growth. Pot in peat-based compost. Difficult to propagate except from seed in a heated propagator.

GUZMANIA
Large bromeliad plants forming the typical rosettes of strap-like leaves with a central cavity or 'urn'. The leaves are less spiky than those of other bromeliads. They are grown for both foliage and flowers, which are very long lasting. The flowers arise from the centre of the rosette and are surrounded by large and bright-coloured bracts. Guzmanias prefer strong, indirect light and temperatures of 13°-18°C (55°-65°F). They require high humidity, which is achieved by standing pots in moist gravel. The compost should be peat-based with added chopped moss, and should be kept relatively dry. Water is provided mainly by topping up the water in the central urn of the rosette, except while the plant is in flower. Feed every two weeks throughout the year spraying the mixture over the foliage and into the central urn. Propagate from offsets produced from the base of the plant.

G. lingulata *Orange Star*
45 cm leaves arranged in a stiff rosette. Flowers are produced on a 30 cm stem and are short-lived; they are cream in colour. They are surrounded by large crimson bracts, which persist for many weeks after flowering has finished. Numerous colour varieties are available.

G. monostachya (G. tricolor)
40 cm narrow green leaves. The white flowers are produced on a tall slim spike and are covered by green bracts, striped with purple and tipped in orange-red. A variety with white striped leaves is available.

G. zahnii
A delicate-looking plant with slim semi-transparent leaves, 45 cm in length. The centre of the rosette is rusty-red, and the leaves have fine, red, longitudinal stripes on both upper and lower surfaces. Flowers are white or cream covered by deep red bracts.

Many hybrid forms of Guzmania are available.

GYMNOCALYCIUM
(Chin Cactus)
Large group of spherical desert cacti, most of which are quite small and easy to cultivate. They have deeply ribbed stems with spikes produced from areoles, and there is a deep notch or 'chin' beneath each areole, sometimes with connecting ridges between the 'chins'. Like most cacti they grow best in full sun. Otherwise becoming elongated and refusing to flower. The flowers are large and brightly coloured with a vase shape, and may be white, red, pink or yellow. Grow at normal room temperatures. They can withstand any normal room heat, but need a winter rest at 5°C (41°F) if they are to flower reliably. Water only sufficiently to prevent shrivelling over the winter, and water plentifully in spring and summer. Feed in the growing phase with a high-potash (tomato type) fertilizer, given every two weeks. Grow in well-drained compost comprising coarse sand and soil-based compost. Propagated very easily from offsets, which must be dried for three days before potting up. Protect from direct sun until well rooted.

G. baldianum (G. venturianum)
Bluish-grey coloured stem up to 6 cm diameter. Has about eleven broad ribs, and white or brownish spines. Flowers are purplish-red, 5 cm in length, and freely produced even on young plants.

G. bruchii (G. lafaldense)

Small plant, forming a dense clump up to 10 cm diameter. Has dainty white spines. Produces profuse pink flowers.

G. denudatum *Spider Cactus*

Larger species common in cultivation. Grows up to 15 cm diameter, with broad fleshy ribs. The short spines grow in clusters looking rather like spiders. Produces white or pale pink flowers.

G. mihanovichii

Popular species growing up to 6 cm in diameter. Ribs are narrow and sharp-edged, connected by narrow bands, and clusters of small yellowish spines. Usually grown in remarkable colour varieties which possess no chlorophyll, and can therefore, only survive when grafted on a suitable host plant. They are available in pink, red, blackish and bright yellow varieties, usually grafted on a triangular-sectioned forest cactus called HYLOCEREUS. This will not tolerate cold very well and should be kept at a minimum of 10°C (50°F) in the winter and not allowed to dry out like desert cacti. These coloured varieties really need to be regrafted after 2-3 years which is a specialised matter outside the scope of this book. Flowers are produced in summer and are usually cream or pink. Many other species of **Gymnocalycium** are available.

GYNURA

Grown for their attractive, furry, purple leaves. In summer these plants produce flowers with a disgusting smell, which should be picked off before they open. Leaves are saw-toothed, and the plants grow extremely rapidly during the summer months, providing adequate light is available. They require some direct sun for the full leaf colour to develop, and thrive at normal room temperatures down to a minimum of 13°C (55°F). Maintain high humidity by standing pots on moist gravel. Water well and feed at monthly intervals throughout the year. Do not allow water droplets to fall on the foliage. Grow in soil-based compost and propagate from tip cuttings, which root very easily. Pinch out tips to encourage bushy growth.

G. aurantiaca *Purple Velvet Plant, Royal Velvet Plant*

Stems which grow erect while young, then sprawl untidily. Large leaves up to 15 cm in length, dark green with purple veins and edges. Densely furred. Small daisy-like flowers may be produced in early spring.

G. sarmentosa (G. scandens) *Purple Passion Vine*

Trailing plant which needs supports if grown erect. Leaves are smaller and more slender than **G. aurantiaca**, deep purple and heavily furred.

Guzmania X Claudine

HAEMANTHUS
(African Blood Lily)

Bulbous plants which produce masses of tiny fluffy flowers in a globular cluster, carried on a fleshy 30 cm stem. Most flower before the leaves appear. They require bright light, with some sunlight. Grow in normal room temperatures and even in winter keep bulbs above 13°C (55°F). Plant bulbs so that the upper half is exposed and water sparingly until foliage appears. Water moderately throughout growing period. Evergreen species require minimal watering throughout the winter, while deciduous species should be allowed to dry out completely when leaves begin to yellow. Feed with high-potash (tomato type) fertiliser every two weeks during active growth. Grow in a soil-based compost and propagate from daughter bulbs separated during repotting in spring. Some species must be propagated from seed.

H. albiflos *White Paint Brush*
Evergreen species with fleshy leaves 30 cm long and 10 cm broad. Flowers are produced on a fleshy 20 cm stem in early autumn. Flower head is 5 cm across, with greenish-white flowers.

H. coccineus *Blood Lily, Ox-tongue Lily*
Large fleshy leaves which remain on the plant over winter and die off in spring, and followed in summer by the fleshy red-spotted flower stalk, carrying scarlet flowers.

H. katherinae *Blood Flower, Catherine Wheel*
Leaves are sometimes retained throughout the year and are 30 cm long, 8 cm wide, with undulating edges. In summer a large, fleshy flower stalk is produced carrying a 12 cm cluster of scarlet flowers.

H. multiflorus *Salmon Blood Lily*
Deciduous type, with a very large flower cluster, coloured pinkish-red and produced in late spring.

HAMATOCACTUS

Cylindrical desert cacti which have soft stems, and often grow in a slight spiral. They are deeply ribbed and have long spines. Flowers are funnel-shaped and are followed by attractive, berry-like fruit. They grow in direct sun or light shade, at normal room temperatures. They require a winter rest at 10°C (50°F) and will not tolerate temperatures below 5°C (40°F). During resting water only sufficiently to prevent complete drying out, and water moderately during active growth, when the plant should be fed with high-potash (tomato type) fertiliser. Grow in a mixture of coarse sand and soil-based com-

post. These cacti seldom produce offsets and are normally grown from seed.

H. hamatacanthus (Ferocactus hamatacanthus) *Turk's Head*
Initially spherical then elongating up to 60 cm long. Dark green, with about 13 deep ribs carrying whitish areoles. Spines are long and some are hooked. In young plants spines are reddish, gradually fading to white. Flowering commences on 10 cm plants, and flowers are yellow up to 6 cm diameter, and produced throughout summer.

H. setispinus *Strawberry Cactus*
Spherical species up to 10 cm across. Dark green stem with about 14 wavy-edged ribs. Areoles are grey and woolly. It flowers profusely, with yellow and scarlet 6 cm flowers.

HAWORTHIA

Extensive group of small Aloe-like succulents of which many are grown in the home or greenhouse. All have fleshy leaves arranged in rosettes and usually marked with white or cream or dark green. Some are tough and leathery, while others have softer leaves. Flowers are produced on thin wiry stems and are insignificant. The genus contains some very odd plants adapted for extreme desert conditions, but most grow readily in the home, thriving in light shade. They will grow at temperatures of 5°-30°C (41°-86°F), but prefer a cool winter rest at about 13°C (55°F). Grow in well-drained, soil-based compost with added coarse sand and water moderately in the growing season. Water just sufficiently to prevent drying out in winter. Feeding is seldom necessary. Very easily propagated from offsets.

H. attenuata *Cushion Aloe*
Attractively marked with bands of white tubercles across the 6 cm leaves. Several cultivated varieties are available.

H. margaretifolia *Pearl Plant*
Tough, curved, triangular leaves growing in an almost spherical rosette, up to 12 cm across. Speckled with coarse white tubercles, and soon forming dense clusters of rosettes.

H. maughanii *Cushion Aloe*
An odd desert form. Cylindrical leaves are arranged in rosettes, with their tips cut off square so the whole rosette has a flat upper surface. In the wild the whole plant grows flush with the soil surface with only the flat leaf tips exposed. Light enters the leaves through transparent 'windows'. During the rest period the thick roots contract, pulling the plant deeper into the ground.

H. rheinwardtii *Wart Plant*

Unlike most Haworthias, this has a 15 cm stem along which the blue-green leaves are tightly clustered and erect. Covered with coarse white tubercles. Very variable in form and several varieties exist.

HEDERA
(Ivy)

Well-known group of tough climbing or trailing plants grown for their attractive ever-green foliage. Ivies grow easily in room conditions provided they are given good light (but not direct sun) and kept reasonably cool: 4°-16°C (40°-60°F). At higher temperatures they will need extra humidity provided by water spraying or standing the pot on a tray of moist gravel. They must never be allowed to dry out completely, but the compost should be at least partly dry before watering. Feed every two weeks during active growth. The plants normally require training up moss poles or canes and can be pinched out to encourage bushy growth. Grow in soil-based compost and propagate by layering, tip cuttings, or cuttings which are allowed to develop roots while standing in a glass of water, before potting. Liable to attack from red spider mites.

H. canariensis *Canary Island Ivy*
Very large and vigorous ivy, with coarse leaves coloured dark green, with grey, cream and white marbling. Other colour varieties are available including some with reddish shoots and stems.

H. helix *English Ivy*
Available in a seemingly endless range of varieties. Variegated forms, crinkled leaves, and dwarfed leaves are all commonly available and some varieties only faintly resemble the original species.

HEDYCHIUM
(Ginger Lily, Kahili Ginger)

A beautiful but tender plant probably best suited to the greenhouse. Produces 1 metre stems and 30 cm strap-like leaves. Flowers produced in summer resemble orchids and are bright yellow with long protruding red stamens. The plant grows from a large creeping rhizome, and consequently requires a large pot. Grow in good, indirect light, and put out on the patio in mild sunny weather. Cut down the stems after flowering. Grow in temperatures of 16°-21°C (60°-70°F) and keep moist and well fed in the active growth period. In winter give only sufficient water to prevent drying out. Grow in soil-based compost and propagate by division of the rhizome in spring.

HELIOCEREUS
(Sun Cactus)
H. speciosus
A rather ungainly jungle cactus resembling EPIPHYLLUM. Has long, trailing, cylindrical stems with three to five ribs and small spines. Usually grows erect when young, then trails with stems up to 1 metre long. Spectacular flowers in spring which are up to 15 cm across and brilliant scarlet, with a bluish sheen. A white form is also available. Grow in good, indirect light and at normal room temperature. Like other jungle cacti, must be kept very moist in spring and summer and not allowed to dry out too much in winter. Feed fortnightly during active growth with a high-potash (tomato type) fertiliser. Grow in a mixture of coarse sand, leaf mould, and soil-based compost. Propagate from stem cuttings taken in spring or summer, which should be dried out for three days before potting up. Can also be grown from 8 cm lengths of stem (but make sure they are planted the right way up).

HELIOTROPIUM
× **hybridum** *Cherry Pie*
Popular plant usually treated as a temporary inhabitant of the home, and hardy enough to be grown outdoors. Has dark, wrinkled, oval leaves and produces large flat clusters of small fragrant flowers, typically violet, although mauve, pink and white varieties are also available. Flower in summer and autumn and occasionally at other times of year. Grow in good light, preferably including some direct sun, at temperatures from 13°-18°C (55°-65°F). They should be kept moist throughout the year and fed at fortnightly intervals during active growth. Pot in soil or peat-based compost, and propagate from stem cuttings in spring or autumn.

HELXINE
H. soleirolii (Soleirolia soleirolii) *Mind-your-own-business, Baby's Tears*
Prostrate creeping plant much used in mixed plant arrangements and in bottle gardens. Produces dense masses of tiny lettuce-green leaves, although a golden form is also available. If undisturbed a neat dome of foliage is produced which will eventually trail from the pot. Grow in light shade at normal room temperatures and protect from frost. Grows in soil or peat-based compost and needs only occasional feeding in summer. Propagates

itself by layering, and any detached portions will usually already have roots.

HEPTAPLEURUM
(Parasol Plant)
H. arboricola
Large and robust shrub resembling SCHEF-FLERA, and suited to large rooms, conservatories or the cool greenhouse. It has a tree-like growth with erect woody stems, and produces large fan-shaped leaves divided into about ten leaflets, each of which is lance-shaped and glossy green. It can be pruned to keep the plant bushy and prevent over-growth. The plant may need supports. Heptapleurum requires strong, indirect light, and a minimum temperature of 16°C (60°F) if leaf drop is to be avoided. Water moderately throughout the year and never allow the compost to dry out completely. Feed every two weeks from spring to autumn, and grow in soil-based compost. Propagate by stem cuttings taken in spring, dipped in hormone rooting powder, and grown on in a propagator. A less rampant variegated form is available.

HIBISCUS
Large genus of flowering tropical shrubs, only two of which are normally cultivated in the home. They grow to a large size unless kept drastically pruned, and are usually treated with dwarfing chemicals before being sold – these rapidly wear off! Hibiscus produces woody stems, with large saw-toothed ever-green leaves. Flowers are large and showy but short-lived, being rapidly replaced by others throughout spring and summer, although there are usually some flowers being produced all through the year. Hibiscus require bright light, preferably including some direct sun. They thrive at normal room temperatures which should not fall below 10°C (50°F) during the winter rest period. Keep moist from spring to autumn, and in the winter water only sufficiently to stop the compost drying out. These are vigorous plants which must be fed fortnightly while in active growth; with high-potash (tomato type) ferti-liser. Grow in soil-based compost and propagate from tip cuttings taken in spring and grown in a propagator. Cut back to about 15 cm in spring, just before new growth begins.
H. rosa-sinensis *Rose of China, Blacking Plant, Rose of Smyrna, Rose Mallow*
Produces 12 cm trumpet-shaped flowers of crimson with a black centre. Many colour varieties are available in white, yellow, pink and orange, and there is also a variety 'Cooperi', which has leaves variegated in cream and dark red. The name 'Blacking Plant' comes from the former use of ground-up petals to produce a black 'shoe polish'.
H. schizopetalus *Japanese Hibiscus, Japanese Lantern*
Slender drooping branches carrying 6 cm pendant flowers, with turned-back orange petals and a long columnar stamen.

HIPPEASTRUM
(Amaryllis)
× **hybrids**
Widely misnamed 'Amaryllis', Hippeastrums are large bulbous plants noted for producing an enormous and exotic flower before many leaves appear. They are usually sold as dry bulbs, up to 12 cm in diameter. These are planted in rich soil-based compost at any time from Christmas to spring, with the top third of the bulb exposed. They should be grown in bright light, at temperatures of 13°-18°C (55°-65°F), and watered lightly until shoots appear. Increase watering as the tips of the long strap-like leaves appear, shortly followed by the long fleshy flowering stem. This is topped by a cluster of trumpet-shaped flowers up to 15 cm across and available in most colours except blue. Begin feeding as soon as flowering finishes, and allow the plant to die back and dry up completely in late autumn. Remove all dead foliage and store in a completely dry place at 10°C (50°F). *See* separate entry under AMARYLLIS.

HOSTA
× **hybrids** *Funkia, Plantain Lily*
Familiar garden plants which can be grown indoors during the summer, or kept in tubs on the patio. They have lance-shaped leaves growing up to 60 cm in height, and usually heavily variegated with cream and green stripes. Hostas die back to their rhizomatous roots in winter, and therefore are usually only kept as temporary plants. Grow in light shade, preferably at cool temperatures 4°-21°C (40°-70°F). They must be kept moist and well fed in summer, and be kept fairly dry in winter, and until the new growth appears in spring. Grow in soil or peat-based com-post and propagate by dividing clumps in autumn. Very prone to attack by aphids.

HOWEA (KENTIA)
(Sentry Palm)
There are only two species in this genus of

palm, both of which are popular indoor plants. In the home, both grow to about 2 metres, with large arching fronds carrying leaflets up to 60 cm in length. Extremely tolerant of dry air conditions, so a very popular plant. Grow in anything from full sun to fairly deep shade, and at normal room temperatures. Do not allow winter temperatures to drop below 10°C (50°F). The tips of leaflets may become scorched in very dry atmospheres, so it may be beneficial to stand the pots on damp gravel to increase the humidity. These palms benefit from standing outdoors in mild weather. Keep moist and feed at two-week intervals in the active growth period. In winter give only sufficient water to prevent the compost drying out. Grow in soil-based compost and propagate from seed in a heated propagator. Seedlings develop very slowly. Prone to attack by red spider mite in dry atmospheres. Do not use leaf cleaning agents.

H. belmoreana *Curly Sentry Palm*
Long arching fronds, eventually developing a short thick trunk.

H. forsteriana *Flat Palm, Paradise Palm, Thatch-leaf Palm*
Slightly smaller and more compact than **H. belmoreana**, having its fronds carried more erect.

HOYA

A group of climbing or trailing evergreens with attractive fleshy leaves with a waxy surface. Produce clusters of fragrant, waxy white flowers. The flowers are slow to appear, but on mature plants will be produced on special flowering spurs year after year during the summer months. Each flower cluster contains up to 30 star-shaped flowers. Grow in hanging baskets or train up supports. Most types need direct sun or very strong indirect light, and grow at temperatures of 13°-21°C (55°-70°F). Water well during active growth but allow the compost surface to become dry before each watering. During winter give only sufficient water to prevent the compost drying right out. Feed during active growth with high-potash (tomato type) fertiliser. Propagate from stem cuttings dipped in rooting hormone and grown on in a propagator. Be careful not to pull off the flowering spurs when removing dead blossom. This would prevent flowering in subsequent years.

H. australis *Porcelain Flower*
Fast-growing climber with slim waxy leaves, lightly spotted with silver. Flowers are white with red centres.

H. bella *Miniature Wax Plant*
Dwarf form, at first erect, then spreading out into a pendulous shape. Has small dull-green leaves, sometimes speckled with white. Waxy white flowers have purple centres.

H. carnosa *Honey Plant, Wax Plant*
Large and vigorous climber usually available in its variegated form. Leaves are very thick and waxy, and up to 7 cm long. Flowers appear only on fully mature plants. Flowers are pinkish-white with a red star-shaped mark in the centre.

HYACINTHUS
× hybrids *(Hyacinth)*

Hyacinths are purchased as specially treated bulbs intended for indoor cultivation, which after flowering should be discarded or planted in the garden. Non-treated hyacinth bulbs are not suitable for growing indoors. Treated bulbs should be planted in late autumn/early winter in peat-based compost or fibrous compost sold especially for hyacinths, with the top of the bulb exposed. They should be watered lightly, then kept in a cool dark place for 6-10 weeks, while the roots develop. They can be left outdoors if necessary, well covered with peat or straw. When the plants are brought into a warm room, growth will take place rapidly. Keep moist once growth starts in earnest, and grow in strong, indirect light. Feeding is not necessary.

HYDRANGEA
H. macrophylla

This is the only Hydrangea normally grown indoors and even this is best treated as a temporary house plant, to be put in the garden after flowering. They are usually purchased on the point of flowering, and grow from 30-60 cm in height indoors. The plant has woody stems and large glossy leaves up to 15 cm long. Flower heads are made up of large clusters of flat four-petalled flowers in white, pink, red, blue or purple. Red varieties will produce blue flowers in areas with soft water or when grown in acid composts, while blue varieties turn red in limy conditions. Keep in bright indirect light in temperatures not exceeding 16°C (60°F). Keep very moist but not waterlogged and feed every two weeks. Repotting is unnecessary as the plant is soon to be discarded or planted in the garden.

HYLOCEREUS
H. undatus (Cereus triangulans)

An epiphytic forest cactus producing long

stems, triangular in section. They are best known for their use as a stock onto which other cacti are grafted. If allowed to develop they produce an untidy sprawling plant, with large white nocturnal flowers, up to 30 cm in length. Grow in light shade at normal room temperature with a minimum temperature of 6°C (45°F). Water well in active growth and feed at two-week intervals. Grow in fibrous compost or a mixture of soil-based compost and sharp sand. Propagate from stem cuttings.

HYMENOCALLIS
(Spider Lilies)
Bulbous plants for the warm greenhouse, producing long, strap-shaped leaves. Flowers have a trumpet-shaped centre surrounded by long spidery petals, usually white in colour, and up to 18 cm across. Grow in strong, indirect light in soil-based compost with the top of the bulb exposed above the surface. Keep well watered and fed during active growth. Propagate by division of bulb offsets. Many species and hybrids are available.

HYPOCYRTA
H. glabra (Nematanthus spp.) *Goldfish Plant*
A rather undistinguished plant with glossy oval evergreen leaves about 2 cm long, growing in pairs on a woody stem. The leaves have a fine red edge. Curious pouched yellow flowers are produced from an angular yellow

bud, but are inconspicuous. Grows to about 45 cm in height, preferring light shade. Prefers warm temperatures of 16°-21°C (60°-70°F) but will tolerate lower winter temperatures if not overwatered. Keep fairly dry at all times and feed once every month during active growth. Grow in soil-based compost and propagate from stem cuttings.

HYPOESTES
H. phyllostachya (H. sanguinolenta) *Baby's Tears, Freckle-face, Polka-dot Plant, Measles Plant*
Originally a rather uninteresting plant but now revitalised with the introduction of spectacularly coloured varieties. Hypoestes is a straggly plant when mature, but has a compact shrubby form while young, and if well pinched out. Leaves are pointed, oval in shape, dark olive-green in colour, and speckled with bright pink. In some varieties the pink may cover most of the leaf. Mauve flowers may be produced but are insignificant. Grow in good, indirect light at temperatures of 10°-16°C (50°-60°F), watering well. These plants will not tolerate drying out. In winter they should be watered sparingly. Feed every two weeks during active growth. Grow in soil-based compost and do not allow the plant to become pot-bound; pot on frequently. Propagates easily from tip cuttings, either planted out or rooted in water. Can also be grown from seed.

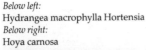

Below left:
Hydrangea macrophylla Hortensia
Below right:
Hoya carnosa

IMPATIENS
(Busy Lizzie, Patience Plant)
Small bushy plants with fleshy stems which are probably the most freely flowering indoor plants available. Flowers are produced in clusters or individually, and are pansy-like with a long spur protruding from the back. Colours are extremely variable but most are red, pink or white. Impatiens need bright light if they are to flower well but will be scorched by direct sunlight. They do well at normal room temperatures, but above 21°C (70°F) they will need extra humidity, achieved by frequent water spraying and by standing the pot in damp gravel. Water thoroughly during active growth and feed every two weeks. During the winter they should be kept relatively dry, but not so dry as to cause wilting. Grow in normal soil-based compost and do not allow the plant to become pot-bound. Propagates very easily from tip cuttings taken in spring which can be potted up or first rooted in a glass of water. Impatiens are very susceptible to aphids, white-fly and red spider mite.

I. repens
Creeping form which roots itself by layering. Red stems carry small waxy leaves and bright yellow 3 cm flowers.

I. wallerana (I. petersiana, I. sultanii, I. holstii) *Snap Weed*
The ancestor of the common hybrids now universally grown. Among the hybrids are plants with variegated leaves, bronze leaves and very large flowers up to 7 cm across. Most are of convenient dwarf size, growing up to about 40 cm, and easily kept bushy by regularly pinching out straggly growth.

IPOMEA
(Morning Glory)
× hybrids
These short-lived annual climbers produce large and brilliantly-coloured flowers in various shades of blue. They require sticks or a frame to which they cling with tendrils, growing very rapidly. They are usually raised from seeds sown in the spring in a heated propagator. Ipomeas grow in temperatures of 10°-18°C (50°-65°F) and are suitable for the home or the patio. They are grown in normal soil-based compost, and must be kept moist and fed every two weeks. Discard after flowering, or at first frost, and replace with seedlings the following spring.

IRESINE
I. herbstii *Beefsteak Plant, Bloodleaf, Chicken Gizzard*
An unusual but easily grown foliage plant with leaves coloured bright purplish-red, and bright red stems. It is a small shrubby plant which needs plenty of strong light, including some sunlight, if its full colour is to develop. Grows at normal room temperatures of 13°-18°C (55°-65°F) throughout the year and will not tolerate lower temperatures. Must be kept moist and well fed throughout the growing period. Pinch out growing tips to encourage bushy growth. Grow in soil-based compost, and propagate from tip cuttings which root very easily. Many people discard the original plant at the end of the year and grow on from cuttings.

IRIS
Many species and hybrids of Iris are cultivated, and several of the small forms are suitable for indoor growing, although they are best treated as temporary house plants. Irises grow either from creeping rhizomes or from bulbs and are usually hardy out of doors. All require good, indirect light and relatively cool room conditions of 7°-16°C (45°-65°F). They are best overwintered out of doors. Grow in normal soil-based compost.
I. pallida
Growing from a creeping rhizome this 30 cm Iris is easily propagated by division of clumps in spring. It must be kept well watered, but requires very well-drained compost.
I. reticulata
A typical Iris grown from a bulb. It can be treated like HYACINTHUS, by planting in a cool, dark place and only bringing indoors and watering *after* growth has started. This Iris will not tolerate very wet conditions.

IXORA
(Flame of the Woods, Jungle Geranium, Indian Jasmine)
I. coccinea
An interesting tropical shrub best suited to the greenhouse, although with care it can be grown in the home. It grows to a height of about 1 metre, and has glossy, heart-shaped 10 cm leaves. Ixora produces large flower clusters in summer. Flowers are tubular, with four spreading petals, and look rather like HYDRANGEA. There are several cultivated colour varieties, but that usually seen is a brilliant red. Ixora needs several hours of direct sun every day, and temperatures of 16°-21°C (60°-70°F). It will not tolerate low

temperatures. Humidity must be maintained with water sprays and by standing the pot in damp gravel. Ixora needs a relatively dry winter rest, but during active growth should be watered moderately, and fed fortnightly. Grow in a well-drained compost mixed from peat, leaf mould and coarse sand. Propagate from stem cuttings taken in spring, treated with rooting hormone and grown in a heated propagator.

Ixora coccinea

JACARANDA

J. mimosifolia (J. acutifolia, J. ovalifolia)

Tropical tree which can be grown in the home, conservatory, or put out on the patio during mild weather. Produces long, fern-like fronds up to 45 cm long, subdivided into dainty leaflets. It gradually loses its lower leaves producing a tree which is then usually replaced by younger specimens. Grow in direct sunlight, at cool room temperatures. A winter rest is essential at about 10°C (50°F). Water only moderately during active growth and feed every two weeks. In winter water only sufficiently to prevent the compost drying out. Grow in soil-based compost and propagate from seed. These must be soaked for 24 hours before planting to soften their tough coats.

JACOBINIA

Only two species of Jacobinia are commonly grown indoors. They are small bushy shrubs, with pointed, dark-green evergreen foliage. They grow vigorously and although they can be kept for many years if drastically pruned, are usually discarded when they become straggly and replaced by newly propagated young plants. Grow in bright light with some sun, at temperatures of 16°-21°C (60°-70°F). Keep moist and well fed during active growth, and do not allow compost to dry out completely during the winter rest. Grow in soil-based compost and propagate from tip cuttings taken in spring and rooted in a propagator. Pinch out growing tips to encourage bushy growth.

J. carnea   *Brazilian Plume, King's Crown, Pink Acanthus*

Grows up to 1 metre high and produces large, conical flower clusters in August and September. Flowers are tubular, 4 cm long, and coloured carmine or pink. This plant needs a prolonged winter rest at about 13°C (55°F).

J. pauciflora

Small plant looking very different from **J. carnea**. Grows to about 45 cm, with small, pointed leaves and individual drooping yellow-tipped scarlet flowers, which are produced from autumn right through the winter and into spring. Needs its annual rest after flowering, i.e. in late spring, when watering should be sparing until new growth begins.

JASMINUM

(Jasmine, Jessamine)

Large group of climbers or ramblers, most of which are cultivated out of doors. The three species described below can be grown in-doors, in the conservatory, or in a cool greenhouse. All grow vigorously, and need some support. They all require some direct sunlight if they are to flower. They prefer cool conditions but if humidity is high, will tolerate room temperatures up to 16°C (60°F). They are greedy plants, needing to be kept well fed during active growth, although they should not be overwatered, especially in winter. Grow in soil-based compost, and propagate from tip cuttings which root easily. Pinch out growing tips on young plants to encourage bushy growth.

J. mesnyi (J. primulinum)   *Yellow Jasmine*

Has long rambling stems, square in section, and needing supports. Produces 4 cm pale yellow flowers with darker centres in early summer. The flowers are not noticeably scented.

J. officinale   *White Jasmine*

The most common species. A rampant climber with small, finely divided leaves and square-sectioned stems. Produces tubular white flowers from summer to autumn, which are very strongly scented. Pale pink varieties are available.

J. polyanthum

Similar to **J. officinale**, but producing its flowers through the winter into late spring. Flowers are strongly scented, pink on the outside and white inside. Flowers successfully as a small specimen.

JUNIPERUS

There is a large group of species and hybrids of this well-known coniferous tree. Junipers have prickly blue-green foliage, with a characteristic resinous smell. They may have a normal tree-like habit, prostrate and creeping, or be stiffly erect. They will not tolerate indoor conditions, but are ideal for growing on the patio in large tubs. Take care to select a low- or slow-growing form, such as those recommended for the rockery. Grow in normal soil-based compost and never allow the compost to dry out.

Jasminum Mesneyi

KALANCHOE

A group of succulent plants grown either for their interesting foliage or for their flowers. Most are quite hardy and survive well in indoor conditions. Kalanchoes require bright light, preferably including some direct sunlight. They grow well in normal room temperatures of 10°-27°C (50°-81°F), and if possible should be rested during winter at around 10°C (50°F). They must be protected from frost. Water sparingly at all times, and during winter give only sufficient water to prevent drying out. Overwatering causes growth to become soft and floppy. Grow in a mixture of soil-based compost and sand, and feed at monthly intervals during the summer. Propagate as tip cuttings, or as outlined below.

K. blossfeldiana   *Christmas Kalanchoe, Flaming Katy*

Large fleshy leaves sometimes edged with red, and clusters of 30-50 small red flowers produced in winter, and carried on a 10 cm stalk. This species should be watered and fed while in flower. Many colour varieties are available. Propagate by pushing a detached leaf into the compost, stalk first. Keep relatively dry until well rooted. This plant is normally discarded after flowering.

K. marmorata (K. somaliensis)   *Pen Wiper*

Bushy plant up to 30 cm high producing large, waxy, bluish leaves with indented edges, and covered with brown blotches.

K. pumila

30 cm plant with small oval leaves, pinkish-green in colour, and completely covered with a white powdery coating. Stems droop gracefully, so the plant is ideal for hanging baskets. Clusters of small pink flowers are produced in late winter or spring.

K. tomentosa   *Pussy Ears, Panda Plant*

Produces large rosettes of fleshy oval leaves covered with dense silvery hairs. The hairs at the tip of the leaf are rusty-orange when young, and dark brown on older plants. Propagate from leaf cuttings or from severed rosettes.

KENTIA

See HOWEA

KOHLERIA

(Tree Gloxinia)

A group of evergreen flowering plants growing from heavily branched rhizomes. Stems are hairy, and carry pairs of saw-toothed leaves. Flowers are also hairy and foxglove-like. Kohlerias require bright light, with some direct sun (but need shade in mid-summer).

They require temperatures of up to 27°C (81°F), and the temperature should not be allowed to drop below 10°C (50°F) or the plant will die back. Maintain humidity by standing the pot in damp gravel. Water moderately during active growth and gradually reduce water after flowering. Plant can be kept active throughout the year by moderate watering, or can be allowed to die back by restricting water. Feed with 25% strength fertiliser at each watering. Grow in a mixture of peat-based compost and sharp sand, with a pinch of lime added. Propagate by separating rhizomes in spring, or from tip cuttings.

K. eriantha

Produces long stems which are restricted by growing in a small pot. May grow up to 1 metre in height. Small clusters of scarlet-orange flowers are produced in summer, each up to 4 cm long and carried on a long red stalk.

K. × 'Rongo'

Hybrid producing 30 cm white-haired stems and magenta flowers with white veining. May flower throughout the year.

Kalanchoe blossfeldiana

LACHENALIA
L. aloides *Cape Cowslip*
Bulbous plant suitable for the cool greenhouse or any sunny room where the temperature does not fall below 10°C (50°F). Lachenalia produces 30 cm strap-like leaves, mottled with purple. The flowers, which are produced on 30 cm purple blotched stems, are tubular and pendulous, coloured yellow with crimson and green tip. Flowers are produced in winter. Plant bulbs in groups with tips just below the surface of normal soil-based compost. Keep relatively dry until growth appears, then water and feed well until flowering. After flowering remove bulbs for storage in a cool dark place until summer.

LAELIA
(Amalia)
Epiphytic orchid which produces elongated pseudo-bulbs, each carrying one or two small fleshy leaves. A single short flower stem is produced from each pseudo-bulb carrying star-shaped flowers which persist for up to six weeks. Many are winter flowering. Grow in bright, indirect light and keep temperature 10°-16°C (50°-60°F) throughout the year. Maintain humidity by standing pots in damp gravel. Water moderately during active growth, and during winter water only sufficiently to prevent pseudo-bulbs from shrivelling. Feed during active growth with high-nitrogen foliar feed. Grow in a small pot and plant in the normal fibrous compost used for other orchids. Propagate by division of rhizome as active growth begins.
L. anceps
Purplish pseudo-bulbs produce 60 cm stem with about five 10 cm flowers coloured rich purple, with crimson and yellow lip. Flowers are produced in winter.
L. cinnabarina
Tall (up to 30 cm) reddish-green pseudo-bulbs. Clusters of up to twelve star-shaped orange-red flowers are produced on 20 cm stems in late winter or spring.
L. purpurata
45 cm pseudo-bulbs each carry a single large leaf up to 70 cm long. Flowers are produced in summer on a thick 30 cm stem, carrying up to six flowers. Each flower is 20 cm across, pink, mauve or white, with purple or crimson lip. Many other species are available.

LAELIOCATTLEYA
× hybrids
Laeliocattleya is a hybrid of LAELIA and CATTLEYA. This cross has produced a very wide range of colours and forms which are summer or winter flowering. They should be treated as LAELIA, and care should be taken not to allow the pseudo-bulbs to shrivel during the winter rest period.

LANTANA
L. camara *Yellow Sage*
The only one of this group of low-growing evergreens really suited to the home, or to the cool greenhouse or conservatory. Normally grows to 1 metre or more but, when the roots are confined by a pot, seldom exceeds 45 cm. It can be kept short and bushy by pruning hard. The leaves are rough and slightly saw-edged, and the stems are prickly. Flowers are produced in summer and autumn and consist of 5 cm heads containing many tubular, yellow or orange-red flowers. Sometimes both colours occur in the same flower head. White-flowered varieties are also available. Lantana requires good light, preferably including some direct sunlight. Normal room temperatures are adequate, with a brief winter rest at about 10°C (50°F). Water plentifully and feed well during active growth. During the winter rest period water only sufficiently to prevent the compost from drying out. Grow in soil-based compost and propagate from stem cuttings taken in mid-summer. Flowers more profuse on young plants taken from cuttings. Prone to attack by white-fly.

LAPAGERIA
L. rosea *Chilean Bell Flower, Copihue*
Evergreen climber best suited to the cool greenhouse or conservatory. Twines around wire supports and can reach a height of 4.5 m. Produces beautiful 7 cm bell-shaped, waxy crimson or white flowers from summer to autumn. Grow in strong, indirect light at temperatures of 10°-18°C (50°-65°F), and keep moist during active growth, feeding every two weeks. Keep drier in winter. Grow in lime-free, peat-based compost and propagate from seed sown in spring, or by layering in spring or autumn. Take care not to let the plant dry out.

LAURUS
L. nobilis *Bay Tree*
Familiar small evergreen tree which is ideally suited for cultivation in tubs on the patio. Grows best in full sun, sheltered from the wind, but may not survive very cold winters. Grow in soil-based compost and propagate from tip cuttings taken in late summer.

LILIUM
L. auratum *Golden-rayed Lily*
Lilies are not particularly easy to grow in the house, and thrive best in the cool greenhouse. **L. auratum** is one of the better types, especially if grown outdoors and brought in when ready to flower. It can grow to 1 metre or more in height with very large, typical lily flowers. The large scaly bulbs are planted in autumn in lime-free, peat-based compost. The pot is left outdoors completely covered in peat until growth starts, when the plant can be brought into a cool part of the house. Water freely, preferably with rain-water, and tie the developing plant to cane supports. Allow to dry off after flowering and repot outdoors after a short rest period. Propagate from offsets.

LITHOPS
(Living Stones, Mimicry Plant)
The popular name, Living Stones, accurately describes these very odd little plants, often mistakenly referred to as cacti. Lithops produce two fleshy, fused leaves growing from an underground stem. The tops of the leaves are flattened and about 3 cm across, looking as though they have been cut off, and in the wild grow with the flattened tips flush with the soil surface. The fleshy leaves are separated by a slit through which a large daisy-like flower is produced in late summer. These plants need some specialised care, but can be grown quite easily in the home if their needs are understood. Grow Lithops in direct sun at temperatures of 5°-30°C (41°-86°F). Water sparingly from May onwards and do not feed at all. Stop watering at the end of autumn and let the plant dry out completely. It will shrivel and appear to be completely dead, then in spring new leaves appear through the dried remains of the previous year's growth. Do not water at all until the old growth has shrivelled completely. Grow in a mixture of coarse sand and soil-based compost in deep pots to accommodate the long tap root. Propagate by dividing clumps, or from seeds, which grow surprisingly fast. Many species are available, most of which are difficult to distinguish, except by the specialist. Most are marbled or spotted in blue-green or brown. Liable to attack by mealy bug.

LIVISTONA
Group of large palms of which two species are grown as house plants, remaining relatively small while restricted by a pot. They produce large fan-shaped leaves divided into slim sections, which droop along part of their length. The long stems have saw-toothed edges, and a trunk is only produced on old specimens. Grow well in light shade at any normal house temperature and can withstand cold conditions (but not frost). Water only moderately and if temperatures exceed 16°C (60°F), continue watering through the winter. Otherwise give a winter rest period. Feed every two weeks during active growth. Pot in soil-based compost and propagate from seed. Young plants develop only slowly.

LOBIVIA
Group of typical barrel-shaped cacti, either spherical or elongated, and usually growing in clumps. They produce large, brightly coloured flowers which open during the day and close at night. To grow their spines and flowers Lobivias need direct sunlight. They benefit from being put outdoors in the summer. Grow at temperatures of 5°-50°C (41°-86°F), and give the plants a winter rest in a cool place. Water moderately in summer and very little in winter. Feed with high-potash (tomato type) fertiliser during active growth. Grow in a mixture of sharp sand and soil-based compost in wide shallow pots. Propagate from offsets, which often carry their own roots. Can also be grown easily from seed.

L. aurea
Roughly spherical, and eventually growing to about 10 cm in height, this cactus has about fifteen ribs, with spines up to 4 cm long. Flowers are brilliant lemon-yellow, and up to 8 cm across.

H. hertrichiana *Cob Cactus*
Spherical, 10 cm cactus, profusely offsetting from the base and having eleven ribs with yellowish spines. 7 cm flowers are brilliant scarlet. Many hybrids exist, crossed with CHAMAECEREUS or ECHINOPSIS.

LYCASTE
Among the easiest of the orchids for amateur cultivation, Lycaste grows from large egg-shaped psuedo-bulbs, each carrying several broad leathery leaves. Flower stems are produced from the base of the pseudo-bulbs, each carrying a single fragrant flower, waxy and very long lasting. Grow in light shade at temperatures of 10°-13°C (50°-55°F), and maintain humidity with water spraying or by standing pots in moist gravel. Water only moderately during active growth and allow to dry out between waterings. During the rest period water only enough to stop the pseudo-bulbs from shrivelling. Feed with a foliar

fertiliser once a month during active growth. Pot in well-drained orchid compost. Propagate by dividing rhizomes in spring, complete and pseudo-bulbs.

L. aromatica
Has large (7 cm) pseudo-bulbs, each producing several flower stems, with single 6 cm golden flowers produced in spring and summer.

L. cruenta
Pseudo-bulbs up to 10 cm high. Flowers are bell-shaped, coloured yellow and green, with a red interior. Flowers are produced in spring.

Many other species are available in different colours, with similar requirements.

Lithops glesinae

Lilium 'Firecracker'

MAMILLARIA

Very large group of barrel-shaped cacti, some spherical, and others columnar. Mamillarias are popular because they are easy to grow, not too large, and most are free-flowering. Many grow into dense clumps. Unlike superficially similar cacti, Mamillarias do not have ribs. Instead their areoles are carried on tubercles, arranged in a spiral around the stem. Flowers are produced in a ring around the top of the stem, and are often followed by coloured fruit. All Mamillarias are spiny, but these are relatively small and not too vicious. Mamillarias require direct sun if they are to thrive. Grow at temperatures of 5°-30°C (41°-86°F), and provide a winter rest at 10°C (50°F), when they should be watered only sufficiently to prevent complete drying out. At other times water only moderately and feed with high-potash (tomato type) fertiliser monthly during active growth. If possible, put them outdoors in mild weather. Do not allow water to collect on the concave upper surface, as this can stain the plant or cause rotting. Grow in a mixture of sharp sand and soil-based compost. Propagate from seed, or from offsets which should be dried for three days before potting up. Cream- or white-flowered Mamillarias seem to flower more freely, and at a smaller size than red- or mauve-flowered types.

M. bocasana *Snowball Cactus, Powder-Puff Cactus*
Blue-green stems are covered with dense, silky white hair, concealing long spines. Grows in dense clusters with each joint up to 5 cm in diameter. Produces yellow 1 cm flowers in spring. Very easy to grow.

M. elegans
Forms a stubby cylinder up to 10 cm high, when it begins to produce offsets around the base. Densely covered with small white spines, and larger brown-tipped spines. Flowers are purple-red, and produced in early spring, but only on mature plants.

M. erythrosperma
Small spherical stems up to 4 cm in diameter, spreading into large clumps. Each stem carries clusters of small white spines and large yellow spines, one of which in each group is hooked. Produces deep pink flowers in early summer.

M. hahniana *Old Lady Cactus*
Spherical stems up to 10 cm in diameter, and eventually producing offsets. Covered with dense curly 'wool', produced from the areoles and covering longer spines. Produces 2 cm crimson flowers in late spring on mature plants.

M. zeilmanniana *Rose Pincushion*
Small cylindrical species which slowly develops into a cluster. Covered with silver and brown spines. Particularly noteworthy as being one of the few red-flowered Mamillarias to flower freely at a small size. Produces its 1 cm purple-red flowers in summer. A white flowered variety is available. Many other species and hybrids of Mamillaria are available.

MANETTIA

M. bicolor *Firecracker Vine, Candy Corn Plant*
Evergreen climber which must be trained up supports or allowed to trail from a basket. Pointed leaves are rather nondescript, but the flowers are tubular, 2 cm long, hairy, and coloured orange with yellow tips. Manettias need bright, indirect light and temperatures of 16°-21°C (60°-70°F). They require a cool winter rest when their compost should be kept relatively dry. At other times water plentifully and feed every two weeks during active growth. Grow in soil-based compost, and prune in spring to prevent the plant from becoming straggly. Propagate from tip cuttings taken in spring or summer.

MARANTA

(Prayer Plant)
Group of evergreen plants with attractively marked and coloured leaves, which tend to fold shut at night. Oval or heart-shaped leaves are comparatively large and carried singly on long stems. Grow in light shade and do not expose plants to direct sunlight, which scorches them severely. They prefer a fairly constant 18°-24°C (65°-75°F), and require high humidities, which can be maintained by standing pots in moist gravel, and by frequent water spraying. Hard water leaves white lime marks on the leaves. Feed and keep well watered except during the winter rest, when they must be kept relatively dry. Grow in soil-based compost, and propagate by division of clumps or by cuttings taken in late spring. These plants are frequently confused with their relatives; CALATHEA, CTENANTHE and STROMANTHE.

M. leuconeura *Prayer Plant, Rabbit Tracks*
The only species commonly found in cultivation, and available in many colour varieties. Large oval leaves are carried at right angles to the stem, folding and rising erect at night. Leaves are light green with large purple blotches between the veins and are coloured

crimson below. Colour varieties may have cream, red or brown markings, which usually follow the line of the leaf veins.

MEDINILLA

M. magnifica *Cape Grape, Rose Grape, Love Plant*

A magnificent plant for the warm greenhouse but difficult to keep even in those conditions. Forms an evergreen shrub 1 metre or more in height, with woody stems carrying coarse 30 cm leaves. Produces spectacular flowers in large pendant clusters. Flowers are bright pinkish-red with purple anthers. Medinillas require strong, indirect light and temperatures of 18°-24°C (65°-75°F), and must be kept well watered and under conditions of high humidity throughout the year. Slightly less water is required in winter. Feed every two weeks as soon as flower buds appear, and continue feeding until autumn. Grow in a mixture of soil-based compost, leaf mould and coarse sand. Very difficult to propagate by cuttings, because of its very large leaves. Prune hard after flowering. Very liable to attack by red spider mites.

MICROCOELUM

See COCOS

MILTONIA

Small group of epiphytic orchids which all have characteristic flat, pansy-like flowers. Most have flattened egg-shaped pseudo-bulbs up to 10 cm in height. Each pseudo-bulb carries two or three narrow and delicate leaves. Flower stems are produced from the base of the pseudo-bulbs, and carry from one to twelve large flowers, which are usually velvety in texture. Grow Miltonias in light shade at a constant temperature around 18°C (65°F). They dislike any variations in temperature. Maintain high humidity by standing pot in moist gravel and daily water spraying. There is no rest period, so they should be watered moderately throughout the year. Feed monthly with high-nitrogen foliar feed. Pot in normal fibrous orchid compost and propagate by dividing the rhizome, complete with several pseudo-bulbs.

M. clowesii

Produces 60 cm flower stalks, carrying groups of 6.5 cm flowers. These have curious red-and yellow-barred petals, and a conspicuous pink blotched white lip.

M. spectabilis

Produces large individual flowers on 20 cm stems. 10 cm flowers are pale pink, with mauve-streaked lip.

M. warscewiczii

Groups of four or five flowers on 30 cm stems. Flowers reddish-brown with yellow tips to petals and sepals, with a purple and white lip, blotched with dark brown.

There are many colour varieties and hybrids of Miltonia.

MIMOSA

(Sensitive Plant, Touch-me-Not)

M. pudica

The only one of this genus of trees which is suitable for indoor cultivation. It has the typical feathery mimosa foliage and fluffy round flowers (although the florists' 'Mimosa' is actually an ACACIA). It is grown, however, for its odd habit of drooping its leaves when handled. As soon as the leaf is touched it begins to fold in on itself, and the effect can sometimes spread through large parts of the plant. After about an hour the plant recovers. The stems are spiny and hairy, and the fluffy flowers, produced in summer, are pink. Mimosa is a perennial, but becomes rather straggly, so is usually discarded after flowering and replaced with younger specimens. Grow in direct sunlight at normal room temperatures, maintaining high humidity by standing the pot in a tray of damp gravel. Water moderately, and do not allow the plant to dry out. Give a brief winter rest, and feed fortnightly during active growth with high-potash (tomato type) fertiliser. Grow in soil-based compost, and propagate from seed. Don't provoke the plant to droop too often, or it may become 'tired' and fail to recover for a long time.

MONSTERA

M. deliciosa *Swiss Cheese Plant, Mexican Breadfruit*

Familiar house plant with large heart-shaped leaves perforated, or split along their length. Fleshy stems sprawl or climb, aided by long aerial roots, which also absorb moisture from the air. Needs supports, such as moss poles. Few people realise the size this plant can reach, and mature specimens may have 7 metre stems carrying leaves 1 metre long. Mature leaves have more holes than the unbroken immature forms, which are often misleadingly sold as **M. pertusa** (an invalid name). Occasionally produces a 20 cm white lily-like flower followed by an edible fruit. A variegated form is available, which grows much less rampantly. Grow in good, indirect light, and avoid direct sunlight. Keep in temperatures of 16°-21°C (60°-70°F), and water sparingly throughout the year. If leaf tips wither, stand pot in damp gravel to increase humidity. Feed fortnightly during active growth (which in good conditions can be throughout the year). Grow in a mixture of soil-based compost and leaf mould. Propagate by air layering. Cuttings can be taken, but are large and awkward to handle. Clean leaves frequently with water – not with leaf cleaning agents.

MUSA
(Banana)
Banana plants are generally too large for indoor cultivation, although those described below are useful for greenhouse or conservatory cultivation. Bananas are large perennials with a stubby trunk-like base, from which rise very large leaves. Most are suitable for the warm greenhouse, requiring fairly high temperatures and high humidity. Grow in a mixture of leaf mould and soil-based compost and feed well during active growth. Propagate by division, suckers, or from seed (which germinates very slowly).

M. acuminata cavendishii *Canary Island Banana*
Dwarf form of the common banana, growing up to 2 metres in height. Flowers are yellow and green, with large red-brown bracts, followed by the characteristic fruit.

M. coccinea *Red Banana*
Small species growing up to 1 metre high. Yellow-green flowers are enclosed by bright red bracts, and are followed by orange fruit which is inedible. Hardier than most other members of the genus.

MYRTUS
(Myrtle)
Evergreen small trees or shrubs with strongly aromatic foliage. Leaves are small, dark green and pointed, and carried on densely branched stems. Flowers are 2 cm across, star-shaped, and almost obscured by a mass of fluffy yellow stamens. Myrtles need the strongest direct sun, but live well at room temperatures. They require a winter rest at about 6°C (45°F), otherwise leaf drop may occur. Water lightly during winter and more plentifully during active growth. Feed sparingly during active growth only. Grow in soil-based compost, mixed with peat. Myrtles prefer lime-free conditions. Propagate from tip or heel cuttings, which are very slow to root. Prune lightly to maintain bushy growth, and pinch out tips as required.

M. communis 'Microphylla' *Dwarf Myrtle*
The most commonly available myrtle, growing to no more than 50 cm.

M. communis 'Variegata'
Compact form with 4 cm leaves, edged with yellow.

Monstera deliciosa

NARCISSUS
(Narcissus, Daffodil)

Popular temporary plants for the home. Usually purchased as prepared bulbs 'forced' into flowering early, and discarded when flowering is finished, or planted out in the garden. There are several forms, including those producing clusters of small flowers, and large, single-flowered types which are popularly known as daffodils. Bulbs bought in autumn or winter are planted in bulb fibre so that the tip is just exposed. Pots must then be placed outdoors and covered with peat to a depth of at least 10 cm. When the growing tips emerge through the peat the pots can be brought indoors, where they will come into flower very rapidly. Keep as cool as possible to prolong flowering, ideally at no more than 16°C (60°F). Keep moist at all times. Always check with your supplier as to whether or not the bulbs you buy have been pre-treated by cooling. If so, they can be planted and grown indoors immediately. Otherwise they *must* be planted out as described above.

NEANTHE
See CHAMAEDOREA

NEMATANTHUS
See HYPOCYRTA

NEOREGELIA
Bromeliad plants which produce stiff, flattened rosettes of saw-edged leaves. Produce tiny flowers in the central urn at any time of year, and these are usually accompanied by dramatic colour changes in the foliage. Neoregelias need bright light, preferably with some direct sun. They require temperatures of 13°-18°C (55°-65°F), and cannot tolerate cooler temperatures. Humidity must be maintained by water spraying, and by standing pot in damp moss or gravel. Water moderately throughout the year and keep the hollow centre cup topped up with clean water. Feed every two weeks, adding the half-strength fertiliser to the water in the cup and compost. Keep compost moist but not excessively so. Grow in a mixture of peat, leaf mould and coarse sand. Propagate from offsets produced around the plant base which are frequently already rooted.

N. carolinae *Blushing Bromeliad, Cartwheel Plant*
Glossy green leaves forming a rosette up to 60 cm across. Tiny lavender flowers are produced in the central cup, when the centre of the plants turns brilliant red. Usually avail-

able as the variety 'Tricolor', which has green, white and pink striped leaves, and becomes more extensively coloured when flowering.

N. spectabilis *Fingernail Plant*
60 cm rosette of deep green leaves, striped grey on the underside. The leaf tips become bright red during flowering, the 'fingernails' of its popular name.

NEPHROLEPIS
Tropical ferns usually grown in hanging baskets, or in such a position that they can trail. They have long fronds, divided into small 'leaflets' which grow alternatively along the stem. They produce furry runners which creep across the compost and produce new plants where they root. Grow in good light but protect from direct sun which will scorch foliage. Grow at temperatures of 13°-18°C (55°-65°F) and protect from cooler temperatures. Maintain humidity by water spraying and by standing pot in moist gravel. Water plentifully throughout the year and feed every month. Grow in a mixture of peat and soil-based compost. Propagate from plantlets produced at tips of runners.

N. cordifolia *Erect Swordfern*
Stiff, arched fronds up to 60 cm in length.

N. exaltata *Boston Fern, Ladder Fern*
Similar to **N. cordifolia**, but with fronds 1 metre or more in length. There are many varieties, some of which have finely divided 'leaves' so that they have a feathery appearance. If ordinary leaves appear among this type of foliage they should be cut out to prevent the plant reverting to type.

NERINE
N. bowdenii
Bulbous plants which produce long strap-like leaves in autumn after flowering. Flowers are produced in large clusters, and are pink and lily-like, up to 12 cm across. Bulbs are planted in soil-based compost in summer and must remain completely dry until the flower shoot appears. Foliage appears after flowering, this eventually dies back and the bulbs must then be left unwatered until growth begins in the next autumn. Keep at temperatures of 10°-16°C (50°-60°F) and protect from frost. Propagate from offsets produced from the bulbs. Feed only during active growth.

NERIUM
(Oleander, Rose Bay)
N. oleander (N. indicum, N. odorum)
Large woody shrub which seldom grows to more than 2 metres in the house or conserva-

tory. Has large, pointed, willow-shaped leaves, carried on erect stems. Flowers are produced in small clusters, and are 3-4 cm across, usually pink, although many other colour varieties are available. Most are heavily perfumed. Flowers are produced in summer and autumn and occasionally at other times throughout the year. Grow in bright light, including some sunlight, and at temperatures of 13°-21°C (55°-70°F). Rest the plant at 10°C (50°F) or less during winter, when watering can be restricted. At other times keep compost moderately watered. Do not allow the plant to dry out completely. Feed at fortnightly intervals during active growth and cultivate in soil-based compost. Propagate from tip cuttings taken in summer. Prune well to remove straggly growth after flowering. Be careful not to get sap on the skin, as it is extremely poisonous. Liable to attack by scale insects and mealy bug.

NERTERA

N. granadensis (N. depressa) *Bead Plant, Coral Moss*

Tiny creeping plant looking very like HELXINE, and forming a dense circular pad of small, pale green leaves. The thin stems creep over the surface of the compost, rooting along their length, and eventually forming a pad about 15 cm in diameter, and 4 cm thick. Tiny flowers are produced followed by dense masses of 4 mm orange berries, quite out of proportion to the plant's size. Berries appear in late summer and persist for several months. Grow Nerteras in good light, including some sun, and keep them relatively cool, at about 10°-16°C (50°-60°F). They can be kept outdoors from spring until the berries are forming. In warmer temperatures they tend to produce rank, soft foliage. Maintain a high humidity with water spraying and water well throughout the year, but allow the surface of the compost to dry between waterings. Feed sparingly during the summer months only, and grow in a mixture of soil-based compost, peat, and sharp sand. Grow from seed, or by division of mature clumps.

NIDULARIUM

Typical Bromeliads, with a large rosette of strap-shaped leaves surrounding a central water storage vase or urn. Small flowers are produced in the vase, and at this time the leaves around the centre of the plant change colour. Nidulariums only flower when mature (after several years), and the flowering rosette then dies, to be replaced by offsets growing around it. Flowers can be produced at any time of year. Nidulariums should be grown in strong indirect light, at a minimum temperature of 13°C (55°F), and in humid conditions, maintained by standing pots in damp gravel. Compost should be kept moist throughout the year, and the central vase kept topped up with water. Feed with half-strength fertiliser at fortnightly intervals during active growth. Grow in normal fibrous bromeliad compost and propagate from offsets raised in a propagator.

N. fulgens (N. pictum) *Blushing Bromeliad*

Rosette up to 45 cm across with broad, pale green leaves speckled with darker green, with saw-edges. Centre of rosette becomes bright red when the tiny blue flowers are produced.

N. innocenti *Bird's Nest Bromeliad*

Similar to **N. fulgens** but with deep green leaves, which are held more erect, and have a metallic appearance. Leaves are purplish-red underneath. Centre blushes rust-red when the white flowers are produced.

NOTOCACTUS

(Ball Cactus)

Very popular desert cacti, spherical or cylindrical in shape. Grown for their spines, colouring and flowers. The stems are heavily ribbed, and the small areoles are set very close together. Some types produce offsets, while those which do not are more difficult to propagate. Flowers are produced at the top of the stem in summer. Typical cacti which must be grown in direct sun to promote flowering. Grow at temperatures of 5°-30°C (41°-86°F), and rest at 10°C (50°F) or less over the winter, when the compost should be allowed to dry almost completely. Water moderately during active growth, and feed with high-potash (tomato type) fertiliser. Grow in a mixture of soil-based compost and sharp sand. Propagate from offsets, which must be dried for three days before planting, or from seed. Liable to attack by mealy bug.

N. leninghausii *Golden Ball Cactus*

The most popular Notocactus, which is spherical at first, then becoming cylindrical. Covered in dense golden spines which are relatively soft to the touch. Produces large yellow flowers, but not until the plant is at least 15 cm tall.

N. ottonis

Small, clustering spherical Notocactus that grows very easily from seed. Produces large yellow flowers after two or three years. Rots if overwatered.

Many other species are available.

× ODONTIODA

Hybrid group of orchids, produced by crossing **Cochlioda** and ODONTOGLOSSUM. It resembles the latter, but is larger flowered. Various varieties are available. See ODONTOGLOSSUM for cultivation details.

ODONTOGLOSSUM

Group of epiphytic orchids which are relatively easy to grow. The creeping rhizome produces flattened, egg-shaped pseudo-bulbs, each carrying two or three strap-like leaves, which are deeply folded. Long arching flowering stems are produced from the base of the pseudo-bulbs, sometimes carrying 25 or more flowers, which may be produced continuously throughout the summer. Flowers are flattened in shape. Odontoglossums need strong, filtered light, and coolish temperatures of 10°-13°C (50°-60°F) throughout the year. They require high humidity, and their pots must stand in damp gravel, the plants being water-sprayed every day. Keep moderately damp, but allow compost surface to dry out between waterings, and feed periodically with foliar feed. Most types do not need a winter rest, although less watering may be necessary at this time. Pot in standard orchid compost, and propagate by dividing clumps, complete with pseudo-bulbs.

O. bictoniense

Popular orchid for the beginner, which grows rapidly, with flower spikes up to 100 cm in height, carrying greenish-yellow flowers with rust-brown blotches and a pink lip.

O. crispum

Large flowered type, producing flowers up to 12 cm across and as many as 30 flowers being carried on a single stem. Colours vary, but they are usually white with red and yellow speckles on the lip.

O. grande   *Tiger Orchid, Clown Orchid*

Popular orchid, with flowers up to 16 cm across, bright yellow with cinnamon bars. This Odontoglossum needs a distinct winter rest if it is to flower in the next summer.

O. pulchellum   *Lily-of-the-Valley Orchid*

Produces masses of small (1-2 cm) white flowers, waxy in texture, and very fragrant. Several flower stems may be produced from each pseudo-bulb. Quite hardy, and fast growing.

× ODONTONIA

Group of hybrid orchids resulting from a cross between MILTONIA and ODONTOGLOSSUM. Many types available.
See ODONTOGLOSSUM for cultivation details.

ONCIDIUM

(Dancing-lady Orchid, Butterfly Orchid)
Very large group of orchids with very varied shape and flowers. Most grow from large egg-shaped pseudo-bulbs, carrying a pair of large fleshy leaves. Flower stalks are produced from the base of the pseudo-bulb, and are often arching or pendulous. Flowers are relatively small and produced in large numbers. Unlike most orchids, Oncidiums need some direct sunlight and many benefit from extra artificial light during winter. Most grow well at cool temperatures of 10°-13°C (50°-60°F), and should stand on damp gravel to provide extra humidity. Regular water spraying is essential at higher temperatures. They need a month long rest after flowering, or during winter when humidity is reduced and less water given. At other times they should be watered moderately. When resting, water only sufficiently to stop pseudo-bulbs shrivelling. Give foliar feed at monthly intervals during active growth. Grow in standard orchid compost, and propagate by dividing the rhizome, complete with pseudo-bulbs, in spring.

O. ornithorhyncum

Long flowering stems are produced in winter, carrying up to fifty 2 cm lilac-pink blooms with bright yellow lip. Several spikes may be produced from each pseudo-bulb.

O. papilio   *Butterfly Orchid*

Delicate and beautiful orchid, which needs heated greenhouse conditions and resents over-damp conditions. Flowers are deep red, cross-barred with yellow, and are up to 10 cm across. They are balanced on their stalks in such a way that they move like a butterfly in the slightest draught. Flowers throughout the year.

Many other species are available.

OPLISMENUS

O. hirtellus 'Variegatus' (Panicium variegatum)   *Basket Grass, Ribbon Grass*

Rampantly growing variegated grass with broad leaves rather like TRADESCANTIA. Ideally suited to hanging baskets with its 45 cm trailing stems. Leaves are pointed, and striped in mid-green, cream, and pink. Best discarded after 1-2 years and replaced with new plants raised from cuttings. Grow in bright light, including some sunlight, and at temperatures of 13°C (55°F) or above. Water well during active growth and feed monthly. Rest in winter with only sufficient water to prevent compost drying out. Grow in standard soil-based compost, and propagate from cuttings taken in spring or summer, which are ridiculously easy to root.

OPUNTIA
(Prickly Pear)
Familiar group of cacti, characteristically having fiercely spined, flattened stems. However, there are many other forms, including cacti with long cylindrical stems, and some dwarf types which are almost barrel-shaped. All have one very nasty feature, which is the presence of groups of tiny spines called glochids, which are barbed and always seem to puncture the skin, however much care is taken during handling. They cause intense itching. Opuntias are undemanding cacti, living at temperatures of 10°-30°C (50°-86°F), and some surviving at temperatures close to freezing. They require as much sun as possible and benefit from being put outdoors in the summer. They need moderate watering in spring and summer when they should be fed at fortnightly intervals with high-potash (tomato type) fertiliser. Grow in a mixture of soil-based compost and coarse sand. Propagate by detaching a stem segment, drying it for three days, then rooting it as a cutting. Can also be easily raised from seed. Wrap plants in newspaper when handling or repotting.

O. basilaris *Beaver-Tail Cactus, Rose Tuna*
Typical prickly pear, with 10 cm oval segments covered with areoles containing reddish glochids, but few or no spines. Branches profusely to form a dense clump, up to 40 cm high. Unlike most Opuntias it occasionally flowers in the home with 5 cm red blossoms.

O. cylindrica
Columnar type, which can grow unbranched up to 1 metre in height. If the top is cut off it produces branches looking like a miniature verson of the giant desert cacti. The stem is covered with diamond shaped bumps, each carrying an areole.

O. microdasys *Bunny Ears*
The most commonly cultivated Opuntia, profusely branching with flattened stems about 7.5 cm long, and forming large clumps with age. Areoles are tightly packed over its surface, and the glochids are even more unpleasant than is usual with this genus. Handle with care; preferably *don't* handle!

O. robusta
The giant of the family which grows up to 6 metres tall in the wild. Segments are up to 30 cm in length and are extremely tough. The plant is usually dwarfed by being grown in a pot. Can stand garden conditions for at least

nine months of the year, but cannot cope with hard frost.

O. salmina
Small form with soft, cylindrical stems, heavily branching, and often tinged with pink. Grows up to 30 cm high. Flowers readily, producing 3 cm flowers in summer.

Many other species are available, together with a variegated hybrid.

OSMANTHUS
(False Holly)
O. heterophyllus 'Variegatus'
Slow-growing evergreen shrub with prickly, holly-like leaves of very variable shape. Grows very slowly to a height of 1 metre. Variegated forms are usually grown, and may have cream, pink or purple markings. There is also a true dwarf form growing up to 40 cm in height. Grow in direct sunlight in a cool, well ventilated position, such as a conservatory, at room temperatures preferably *below* 13°C (55°F). Water moderately during active growth and feed every two weeks. Needs very little water in winter. Grow in soil-based compost and propagate from tip cuttings taken in spring, and treated with hormone rooting powder.

Oncidium X 'Sultanmyre'

PACHYPHYTUM

Small succulents, which resemble the rosette-forming plants like ECHEVERIA, although the fleshy leaves are actually arranged in pairs. Flower in spring and summer, producing pendant flowers on a long spike. Grow in direct sunlight, at normal room temperatures. Need a winter rest at about 13°C (55°F), when water should be severely restricted. During active growth, water moderately but do not feed, or the plants will become too fleshy and soft. Grow in a mixture of sand and soil-based compost. Propagate easily from stem cuttings, which are dried for three days before potting up.

P. amethystinum (Graptopetalum amethystinum)

Grows up to 10 cm high, with erect stems which later droop over. Leaves are plump and about 3 cm long, coloured blue-green, with a mauve tinge.

P. oviferum *Moonstones*

Grows up to 15 cm high with clusters of 3 cm egg-shaped leaves, which are pinkish-grey and covered with an attractive silvery bloom. Produces white or red flowers at intervals throughout the year.

PACHYPODIUM

(Club Foot)

P. lamerei

Desert succulents resembling cacti, to which they are only distantly related. They resemble columnar cacti, but although spined, they lack the characteristic areoles. The plant is topped by a large tuft of elongated leaves. Not very easy to grow, but require full sun, and temperatures of 12°-30°C (54°-86°F), and will not tolerate cooler temperatures. Grow in a mixture of sand and soil-based compost, and water only sparingly, keeping them relatively dry in winter.

PACHYSTACHYS

P. lutea *Lollipop Plant*

Small shrub with large, lance-shaped leaves, growing to about 45 cm in height. Flowers are produced in summer, consisting of groups of golden yellow bracts, through which the tubular white flowers appear. Flowers continuously for several months and bracts remain attractive even after flowering has finished. Grow in strong, indirect light, at temperatures of 16°-21°C (60°-70°F), and water only moderately throughout the year. Feed every two weeks and grow in soil-based compost. Propagate from tip cuttings taken in spring and treated with rooting hormone

before potting up.

PALISOTA

P. elizabetha

Odd plant in which the enormous leaves grow straight from the compost without a separate stem. Leaves are undulating with a wide, pale-coloured central vein, and look rather like seaweed. Grows easily in light shade at temperatures of 16°-21°C (60°-70°F), and should be kept moist and well fed throughout the year. Grow in soil-based compost and propagate by division in the spring.

PANDANUS

(Screw Pine)

Tough plant resembling DRACAENA, with shiny, strap-like leathery leaves and a short woody stem. Leaves grow in a rosette, and are sharply pointed and toothed along their edges. Aerial roots produced from older plants buttress the trunk and help support it. Grow in some direct sunlight, at temperatures of 16°-21°C (60°-70°F), and maintain the humidity by standing the pot in damp gravel. Dry air will scorch leaf tips. Water moderately during active growth, and keep relatively dry in winter. Feed at two-week intervals during active growth. Grow in soil-based compost, and propagate from suckers produced around the base of the plant.

P. baptiste *Blue Screw Pine*

Viciously pointed and barbed leaves, with brilliant yellow stripes. Leaves are capable of causing an unpleasant cut. Can grow to a very large size.

P. veitchii *Variegated Screw Pine*

Grows up to 1 metre with attractive arched foliage, striped with white or cream. Just as heavily armed as **P. baptiste**, but smaller and more manageable.

PAPHIOPEDILUM

(Cypripedium) *Slipper Orchids, Lady's Slipper*

Group of ground-living orchids, deriving their popular name from the slipper-shaped lip in the flower. Leaves are broadly strap-shaped, leathery, and frequently blotched with green or purple. Leaves and flowers grow directly from a rhizome. Flowers are tough and waxy, and the upper sepal is usually a contrasting colour to the rest of the flower. Paphiopedilums usually flower in spring. They are moderately easy to grow, requiring good, indirect light, and do better if they receive some additional artificial light in winter. Most grow at temperatures of 13°-18°C

(55°-65°F), and will need frequent water spraying at higher temperatures. They should stand in trays of damp gravel at all times. Water moderately, allowing the compost surface to dry out between waterings, and restrict water from 4-6 weeks after flowering. Overwatering will cause the plant to rot. Feed with foliar feed every month, except for the rest period after flowering. Grow in normal orchid compost, and propagate by separating the rhizome.

P. callosum
Vigorous orchid with large leaves mottled in two tones of green. Flowers are produced on 45 cm stems and are about 8 cm across. Flowers are basically white, with green and purple stripes, and a purple lip.

P. hirsutissimum
Another species with mottled green leaves. Flower stem is covered with black hairs, and the flower has a complicated colour pattern, from deep purple to violet, pink and green, with wavy edges to the petals. Comparatively easy to grow and to flower.

P. insigne
Another popular orchid often recommended for beginners. It flowers in the winter with green, yellow and bronze blossoms. There are also pure yellow varieties.

P. spiceranum
Has short (15 cm) leaves, with purple undersurfaces. Flowers are carried on a short stem and are about 5 cm across. Flowers are generally bronze, with the upper sepal white with a central crimson or purple stripe. Not really suitable for the beginner.

P. venustum
Unusual form with blotched blue-grey and green leaves. Flowers are carried on a 30 cm stem, and are purple with green and white stripes on the sepals, which also carry distinctive, hairy black warts. Easy to grow and to flower.

PARODIA

Group of barrel-shaped desert cacti, spherical or becoming more elongated with age. Tubercles and areoles are arranged in spirals. Flowers are produced at the top of the stem in spring. They are generally very spiny and may not branch. Like all desert cacti, they thrive in full sun, and require temperatures of 5°-30°C (41°-86°F). They require a winter rest at around 10°C (50°F) when water should be severely restricted. At other times water only moderately. Grow in normal cactus compost: sharp sand and soil-based compost in equal parts. Roots may rot in winter if overwatered,

in which case damaged tissue should be cut away, and the plant treated as a cutting. For experts or experimenters, it is worth grafting such a damaged Parodia onto a more vigorous stock. Propagate by separating and planting offsets, or grow from seed.

P. aureispina   *Golden Tom Thumb*
Small barrel-shaped cactus with a bright green stem covered with yellow and white spines. The central spine in each areole is hooked. Flowers are 3 cm across and yellow in colour.

P. chrysacanthion
Popular spherical type growing slowly to about 12 cm diameter. Slender spines are pale yellow. Yellow flower produced in late spring.

P. sanguiniflora
Plump cylindrical species with hooked brown spines. Tubercles may merge into ribs. Mature plants tend to branch prolifically. Produces 5 cm blood-red flowers.

PASSIFLORA
(Passion Flower)
P. caerulea
Vigorous climbing plant which clings to its supports with spiral tendrils. Grown for its curious flowers, which are saucer-shaped, with a complex arrangement of stamens and style. Flowers are basically white, with purple filaments surrounding yellow and brown stigmas. Flowers are up to 7 cm diameter, and may be followed by peach-coloured, edible fruit. Passiflora should be grown in the brightest available light at normal room temperatures. It needs a winter rest at about 10°C (50°F), when watering should be minimal. During active growth it should be watered plentifully and fed with tomato type fertiliser. Grow in soil-based compost, and propagate from stem cuttings treated with hormone rooting powder. Prune drastically in spring before vigorous growth begins.

PEDILANTHUS
(Devil's Backbone, Jacob's Ladder, Ribbon Cactus)
P. tithymaloides smallii
Small succulent plant, noteworthy for its peculiar plump zigzag stems, growing up to 60 cm in length, and spreading or trailing. Leaves are pointed, up to 6 cm long, and deeply folded. There is also a variegated form with cream-edged leaves. Grow in bright light, including some direct sunlight. Pedilanthus prefers warm conditions of 18°-27°C (65°-80°F). Water sparingly and keep barely moist in winter to avoid rotting. Feed every

month while in active growth. Grow in soil-based compost with added sand, and propagate from cuttings. These exude milky acrid latex, which should be rinsed off both cut surfaces. Dry the cuttings for one or two days before potting up.

PELARGONIUM
(Geranium)
Confusingly, all the plants popularly known as 'geranium' are Pelargoniums. Even more confusingly, there is a true Geranium, which is quite different. All the types of Pelargonium grown indoors are hybrids, of which there are huge numbers of different types. There are four basic groups, discussed in more detail below. All Pelargoniums need direct sunlight if they are to thrive. They all do well at normal room temperatures, and should be given a winter rest at about 10°C (50°F); except for **P. domesticum** hybrids, which have to be rested after flowering in summer. During the rest period they should be watered only sufficiently to prevent compost from drying right out. Feed at fortnightly intervals with high-potash (tomato type) fertiliser during active growth. Grow in well-drained, soil-based compost, and propagate from tip cuttings taken in spring, and treated with hormone rooting powder. Pinch out growing tips to encourage bushy growth.

P. domesticum hybrids
Usually grow to 60 cm in height with plain green, oval leaves, having scalloped edges. Flowers are produced profusely in small clusters. Rest after flowering.

P. hortorum hybrids *Zonal Geranium*
Grow to 1 metre or more, with large leaves having a reddish ring or 'zone' on the leaf. Leaves may be marked with red, orange, or cream. Flowers are smaller than those of **P. domesticum** hybrids.

P. peltatum hybrids *Trailing Geraniums*
Prostrate or trailing types, with stems up to 1 metre in length. Stems are brittle and carry ivy-shaped leaves. Flower profusely in spring and summer.

Scented-leaved types
Most scented-leaved forms are garden plants, but there are a few hybrids and species small enough for indoor cultivation. Most will need extensive pinching-out to keep them compact and bushy.

PELLAEA
P. rotundifolia *Button Fern*
Most unfernlike, although Pellaea is a true fern. It has typical wiry fern stems, up to 30 cm in length, and spreading almost horizontally. They carry pairs of small circular leaflets or pinnae which are about 1 cm across. The stems or fronds are produced from a creeping rhizome. Pelleas grow well in moderate shade, at temperatures of 16°-21°C (60°-70°F). At higher temperatures they need frequent water sprays. Water plentifully throughout the year, but do not allow the plant to become waterlogged, especially at lower temperatures. Grow in peat-based compost or in a mixture of leaf mould and soil-based compost. Propagate by division of the rhizome. Guard against complete drying out, which will kill the plant.

PELLIONIA
Family of creeping plants, usually grown in arrangements with other more spectacular plants, as ground cover. Can also be grown in hanging baskets. Pellionias require strong, indirect light and temperatures of 13°-21°C (55°-70°F), and will be damaged by lower temperatures. Water plentifully during active growth, and in winter water only sufficiently to prevent the compost drying right out. Feed every two weeks during active growth. Grow in soil-based compost, with added peat or leaf mould. Propagates very easily from tip cuttings, or by layering.

P. daveaunea
Long pinkish stem carrying 5 cm leaves with saw-toothed edges, varicoloured in light green with blackish edges.

P. pulchra (P. repens) *Rainbow Vine, Satin Pellionia*
Purple stems, and deep green leaves with blackish veins and purple underside.

PENTAS
P. lanceolata (P. carnea) *Egyptian Star Cluster*
45 cm woody shrub with furry stems carrying lance-shaped furry leaves about 8 cm long. Flowers are produced in clusters in autumn or winter, and are tubular, opening to a star shape at the tip, coloured white, pink or mauve. Grow in bright light, preferably with some direct sun. Requires temperatures of 13°-21°C (55°-70°F), and will not tolerate lower temperatures. Water moderately, except for 4-6 weeks after flowering, when water should be restricted. Feed every two weeks during active growth. Grow in soil-based compost, and propagate from tip cuttings taken in spring or summer.

PEPEROMIA
Genus of small, mainly succulent foliage

plants, which usually have attractively coloured or shaped leaves. Their flowers are produced on spikes, but are insignificant. They grow best in light shade, but variegated types benefit from some sun. Peperomias grow well and easily at temperatures of 13°-18°C (55°-65°F), and will tolerate even lower temperatures if kept relatively dry. Maintain high humidity by standing pots in moist gravel. Water sparingly at all times, allowing compost to become dry to the touch before watering. Feed during active growth only, but use fertiliser at half-strength. Grow in peat-based compost. Propagate from tip cuttings taken in summer, or from leaf cuttings. Leaf stalks can be simply inserted into the compost, or leaves can be cut across and planted vertically. Pinch out young plants to encourage bushy growth.

P. argyreia (P. sandersii) *Water Melon Peperomia*

Large, heart-shaped succulent leaves up to 10 cm in length. Reddish stalk is attached off-centre, and silver and green banding follows the leaf veins, so each leaf resembles a perspective drawing of a water melon. Grows up to 30 cm high but requires care if it is to survive for long.

P. caperata *Emerald Ripple*

Has neat 3 cm leaves, dark green and deeply corrugated, carried on reddish stalks. Grows to about 12 cm, and dwarf varieties are also available.

P. magnoliifolia 'Variegata' (P. tithymaloides)

Desert Privet

Robust variegated plant with red stems, and very succulent oval leaves up to 10 cm long, and heavily variegated in green and cream. Grows erect at first, then trails.

P. scandens 'Variegata'

Climber or trailer, with stems up to 1 metre in length, with 4 cm heart-shaped leaves carried on pink stalks. Leaves are variegated in green, cream and yellow.

Numerous other species and varieties are also available.

PERESKIA

(Barbados Gooseberry)

P. aculeata

Only of interest because it is a cactus, although it looks nothing like one. Pereskia is a large, sprawling shrubby plant up to 1.5 metres high, with large leaves which drop in autumn. Its relationship to cacti is given away by the inconspicuous areoles and spines formed in leaf axils. Produces rose-like flowers, up to 4 cm across in late autumn on mature plants. Grow in full sun at temperatures of 10°-30°C (50°-86°F), and water well in spring and summer. Restrict water in winter. Feed at monthly intervals with high-potash (tomato type) fertiliser, during active growth only. Grow in soil-based compost, and propagate from stem cuttings or seed. Provide supports for stems.

PERSEA

P. americana (P. gratisiima) *Avocado Pear, Alligator Pear*

Usually grown as a curiosity from the large avocado stone or seed. Eventually forms a large tree with large, coarse leaves and a straight unbranched stem. Pinching out will encourage branching. Will not produce fruit in the home, the average conservatory or greenhouse. Requires a minimum temperature of 10°C (50°F) in winter, and any normal room temperature in summer. Spray with water to prevent leaf scorch, and water and feed well during active growth. Keep relatively dry in winter. Grow in soil-based compost. Propagate from avocado stones, which should be dried for at least a week, then planted to half their depth, pointed end down.

PETUNIA

hybrids

Familiar garden plant, ideally suited for growing in tubs on the patio. Must be grown in direct sun, and kept well watered and fed.

PHALAENOPSIS

Group of epiphytic orchids, many of which produce fleshy aerial roots. Leaves are broadly strap-shaped and limp. Clusters of flowers are produced on long flower stalks at any time of year. Phalaenopsis requires bright, indirect light, with extra artificial light during winter. Grow at temperatures of 18°-21°C (65°-70°F), and maintain high humidity by standing pots in moist gravel and mist-spraying with water daily. Do not allow water droplets to rest on the leaves. Water only moderately, and allow compost surface to dry out between waterings. No resting period is required. Give a foliar feed every month. Grow in standard orchid compost, in pots or hanging baskets. Propagate from plantlets produced on flowering stems after flowering has finished.

P. schilleriana

Spring flowering species, with beautiful leaves marbled in grey and silver, and coloured purple underneath. Flowers are produced in large clusters, and are 5 cm across,

and coloured brilliant mauve with a yellow throat. **Relatively** hardy and easy to flower.
P. stuartiana
Very similar to **P. schilleriana**, but with white flowers, speckled with purple. The lip is orange-yellow with red spots. Many other species and varieties are available.

PHILODENDRON

Popular foliage plants, which were among the first to become popular for indoor cultivation. All have large leathery leaves, and most are climbers or trailers. Climbing species cling to tree bark or moss poles with short aerial roots. Leaf shapes are very varied, and juvenile and adult leaves may be entirely different. All should be grown in good indirect light at temperatures of 16°-21°C (60°-70°F). They will not tolerate temperatures below 13°C (55°F), and are also damaged by cold draughts. Water moderately during active growth, and feed at fortnightly intervals. Give Philodendrons a short rest in December-January, watering only sufficiently to prevent compost from drying out. Grow in a mixture of soil-based compost and peat or leaf mould. Propagate climbing types by cuttings, or more easily, by layering. Non-climbing types should be propagated from seed.
P. bipennifolium *Fiddleleaf or Horse-Head Philodendron*
Large climber reaching 2 metres in height. Leaves are an elongated heart-shape, narrow in the middle, and up to 40 cm in length in mature specimens. Needs supports.
P. bipinnatifidum
Non-climbing species that produces a rosette of leaves up to 45 cm long, carried on 40 cm stalks. Leaves are deeply cut and palm-like. A short 'trunk' is produced in mature plants.
P. × 'Burgundy'
Interesting hybrid with 30 cm lance-shaped leaves, coloured reddish-green on the upper surface, and deep red below, with bright red shoots and stems. Grows slowly, and needs supports.
P. melanochrysum *Black-gold Philodendron*
Large but slow-growing climber with heart-shaped or oval leaves up to 60 cm long. Leaves are almost black with lighter leaf veins, and a velvety texture. Needs support as it climbs.
P. scandens *Heartleaf Philodendron*
The 'original' Philodendron grown as a house plant. Much smaller than most other plants of this group. Thin climbing stems carry 10 cm heart-shaped leaves. Can be grown as a climber, needing support on moss poles, or

can be allowed to trail. Pinch out tips to prevent the plant from becoming long and stringy. Many other species are available, but be cautious, some grow very large indeed!

PHOENIX

Slow-growing palms which are very suitable for indoor cultivation. All produce feathery fronds, divided into small leaflets or pinnae. Fronds are erect at first, then arch gracefully with increasing size. They are produced from a bulbous base which gradually elongates into a trunk. Grow in good indirect light at temperatures of 16°-21°C (60°-70°F). Water sparingly in spring, increasing water as growth commences, and feeding every two weeks. Reduce watering in autumn and winter, and cease feeding. Grow in soil-based compost and propagate from seed (except for **P. roebelenii**, which produces suckers which can be treated like cuttings). Seedlings grow extremely slowly.
P. canariensis *Canary Date Palm*
The hardiest species of Phoenix, producing a short bulging stem. A trunk is only produced after many years. Fronds are very stiff and pinnae are sharply pointed. Grows up to 2 metres when grown indoors.
P. dactylifera *Date Palm*
This is the commercial date palm, which has more bluish foliage than other species of Phoenix and more arching fronds. Grows fast, and produces a large tree – too quickly. Not as attractive as the other species.
P. roebelenii *Miniature Date Palm, Feather Palm*
Small species, seldom growing taller than 1 metre, with slim arching fronds, dusted with white scales. Produces a stem or trunk faster than the other species and often branches.

PHYLLITIS

P. scolopendrium *Hart's Tongue Fern*
A common house plant, but one which usually suffers in the overheated, dry conditions in most homes. Lettuce-green fronds are strap-like, and often have gracefully undulating edges. They are carried erect and arching in a loose rosette from a hairy creeping rhizome. The undersides carry a herring-bone pattern of brown spore cases. Some forms are available with frilled edges. Grow in medium light, and avoid direct sunlight. Tolerates temperatures down to 10°C (50°F), and requires high humidity, especially at high temperatures. Stand the pot in a tray of moist gravel. Keep moderately damp throughout the year, as the plant grows more

or less continuously. Feed monthly with half-strength fertiliser. Grow in peat-based compost, or in a mixture of leaf mould and soil-based compost. Propagate by separating part of the rhizome. Not an easy plant, since the fronds quickly become scorched and then look untidy.

PILEA

Small foliage plants which may be either creeping or erect. The erect forms are less successful, becoming straggly or bare-stemmed as the lower leaves drop. Foliage is noteworthy for the metallic markings developed in some species. Grow Pileas in moderate shade, at temperatures of 16°-21°C (60°-70°F). They require high humidity which means standing pots in damp gravel, and frequent water spraying. However, they should only be watered sparingly, letting the compost surface dry out between waterings. Feed every two weeks through spring and summer. Grow in a mixture of peat and soil-based compost. Propagate from tip cuttings, which root very easily, and discard leggy, old plants. Pinch out to encourage bushy growth.

P. cadieri *Aluminium Plant, Water-melon Pilea*
Erect form with raised silvery patches between the leaf veins. Leaves are about 6 cm long, but there is a much smaller dwarf form.

P. involucrata *Friendship Plant, Panamiga*
Small, fleshy leaves which are deeply quilted, and densely packed on the stems. Leaves are bronze-green, with purple undersides. An erect growing species.

P. nummariifolia *Creeping Charlie*
Small-leaved creeping species, with 2 cm leaves, having a quilted surface, and carried on thin red stems.

P. spruceana
Similar to **P. involucrata**, but a creeping form. Several colour varieties are available.

PINGUICULA
(Butterwort)
Genus of bog-living insectivorous plants. They all produce a flat rosette of pale green leaves with rolled edges. The upper surface secretes a sticky fluid which attracts flies, then traps and digests them. Grow in good indirect light at normal room temperature. Plant in a mixture of peat, sand and sphagnum moss, and stand the pot in a shallow dish of water. Will not tolerate hard water, so give only rain-water or water thawed from frost in a refrigerator or freezer. Produces

attractive 2 cm flowers on a thin stem in summer. Several species are available, and some have special growing requirements.

PIPER
P. crocatum *Climbing Pepper*
Attractive climbing or trailing vine. Thin stems carry heart-shaped 10 cm leaves with puckered surfaces. Waxy leaves are deep green with raised silvery-pink patches. The undersides are maroon. Grow in good indirect light at temperatures of 18°-24°C (65°-75°F). They will not tolerate temperatures much lower than 16°C (60°F), and resent sudden temperature changes. Stand pot in a tray of moist gravel and mist spray frequently. Water moderately throughout the year, and feed at fortnightly intervals during active growth. There is no true winter rest period. Grow in soil-based compost and propagate from stem cuttings raised in a propagator.

PISONIA
(Birdcatcher Tree)
P. umbellifera (Heimerliodendron brunonianum)
Small tree which seldom exceeds a height of 1 metre when grown in a tub or pot. Stem branches heavily, and carries leaves up to 30 cm by 8 cm, marked in dark and light green and yellow. The leaf rib exudes a sticky gum, hence the popular name. Grow in strong indirect light, and temperatures of 16°-21°C (60°-70°F). Pisonias will not tolerate temperatures below 10°C (50°F), and may be damaged by sudden temperature changes. Water moderately during active growth, and feed at fortnightly intervals. During winter water only sufficiently to stop the compost drying out. Grow in soil-based compost and propagate from tip cuttings taken in spring. Treat with hormone rooting powder and raise in a propagator.

PITTOSPORUM
Large shrubs or small trees for cool conditions. Suitable for the patio in mild weather. Pittosporums have tough leathery leaves with a glossy surface, and produce scented tubular flowers in summer. Grow in strong light, including some sunlight, and at temperatures of 10°-18°C (50°-65°F). Water well during active growth, but give a winter rest at about 10°C (50°F) and water only sufficiently to prevent the compost from drying out. Feed every two weeks during active growth. Prune in spring to remove straggly growth. Grow in soil-based compost and propagate from tip

cuttings in spring, or from seed.

P. tenuifolium *Kohuhu, Parchment Bark*
Often used by florists for its small lettuce-green leaves with undulating margins. Stems are black. Very attractive and very hardy. Variegated forms are available.

P. tobira *Japanese Pittosporum*
Heavy woody stems with large elliptical leathery leaves arranged in rosettes. Flowers are produced in summer, in small clusters.

PLATYCERIUM
(Staghorn Ferns)
Strange epiphytic ferns looking rather like a large bunch of seaweed. Large flat fronds are antler-shaped, fleshy, and covered in white down. They are carried on another form of frond, which spreads over and clasps a tree branch or the plant pot, absorbing water and trapping nutrients. Each year a new supporting frond is produced on top of that grown in the preceding year. Grows well in light shade, at temperatures of 16°-21°C (60°-70°F), and must be mist sprayed with water every day. Water thoroughly but allow compost to dry out between waterings. It is sometimes beneficial to submerge the whole pot in water for a few minutes. Water much less in winter, especially at lower temperatures. The fronds droop when over-dry, but will recover when watered. Feed once or twice each year. Grow either clinging onto bark, or potted in a mixture of peat and sphagnum moss. Propagate by division, which is difficult and may damage the plant. Prone to attack by scale insects. Platyceriums benefit by being put outdoors in summer rain.

P. bifurcatum *Antelope Ears*
Most common species with softly arching fronds, spreading or trailing. Fronds may eventually reach a length of 1 metre, with tips divided into finger-like segments.

P. grande *Regal Elk-Horn Fern*
Larger species with fronds up to 1.5 metres long, and growing erect, with drooping tips. Less furry than **P. bifurcatum**.

PLECTRANTHUS
Small plants in the 'cheap and cheerful' class. They may be erect and shrubby or creeping, and the latter are the more popular for growing in hanging baskets. They have soft, square-sectioned stems, and rounded leaves with toothed edges. Leaves are aromatic when touched. Flowers are produced in summer but are insignificant. Grow in some direct sunlight at warm temperatures of 16°-21°C (60°-70°F). In warm weather maintain humidity by standing pots in a tray of moist gravel. Give a winter rest at around 13°C (55°F), when watering should be minimal. Water well during active growth, but do not allow plants to become waterlogged. Feed at two week intervals during active growth. Grow in soil-based compost, and propagate from tip cuttings which root very easily. Pinch out growing tips to encourage bushy growth. Discard old plants, which become straggly.

P. australis *Swedish Ivy*
An erect or sprawling form with dark green leaves. Grows easily, and will live in quite deep shade.

P. coleoides 'Marginatus'
Variegated plant with white-edged leaves. At first erect, then trailing.

P. oertendahlii *Candle Plant*
The most popular species. A trailer with 60 cm stems carrying round, bronze-green leaves with silvery veins and purple edges and undersides.

PLEIONE
Group of orchids which are very suitable for house cultivation, thriving at low temperatures. They grow from a plump pseudo-bulb, which dies off each year. Pleiones produce sparse foliage, which is greatly overshadowed by the showy flowers. Grow at low room temperatures and in winter keep at 4.5°C (40°F), when water is withheld completely. Commence watering in spring, sparingly at first, then increasing as growth commences. Grow in a mixture of peat and sphagnum moss in light shade. Propagate from offsets in spring.

P. bulbococodioides (P. formosa)
Variable coloured flowers produced in spring or summer, typically with pink petals and a fringed and blotched white lip. Flowers are up to 10 cm across. Pure white varieties are available.

P. forrestii
Flowers are produced in mid-summer, and are yellow or orange, with rust-coloured blotches on the lip.

PLEOMELE
P. reflexa 'Variegata' **(Dracaena reflexa)**
Song of India
Universally known as Pleomele, although probably technically a DRACAENA. Beautiful decorative shrub or small tree growing very slowly and having tough woody stems. Leaves are carried in rosettes and are lance-shaped, up to 15 cm long and striped in green

and creamy yellow. Grows up to 2 metres high but may take twenty years to do so. Very expensive because of its slow growth. Grow in good indirect light at temperatures of 16°-21°C (60°-70°F), and maintain humidity by standing pot in tray of damp gravel. Do not overwater, and feed at two-week intervals from spring to autumn. Grow in soil-based compost with added leaf mould or peat. Propagate from tip cuttings taken in spring, treated with hormone rooting powder and raised in a propagator.

PLUMBAGO

P. auriculata (P. capensis) *Cape Leadwort*

Untidy climber with long thin stems carrying down-curved oval leaves. Flowers are produced in spring in small clusters, and are tubular, flaring into five blue petals. A white variety is also available. Plumbagos should be pruned heavily after flowering to produce fresh growth which will carry the next season's flowers. Grow in full sun at normal room temperatures. Rest in winter at around 10°C (50°F), when only sufficient water should be given to prevent the compost from drying out. Water plentifully, during active growth, and feed with high-potash (tomato type) fertiliser. Grow in soil-based compost and propagate from tip cuttings in spring. Do not take these from old, woody stems. Pinch out regularly to encourage bushy growth.

PLUMERIA

(Frangipani, Temple Tree)
P. rubra

Large tree for the conservatory or greenhouse, which grows to 3 metres or more. Produces large fleshy leaves, and large waxy pink flowers 5 cm across in summer. White, yellow and mauve forms are also available. Grow in minimum temperatures of 18°C (65°F), even in winter. Grow in good indirect light and keep well watered, with slightly less water in winter. Feed every two weeks during spring and summer, and spray with water every day in hot weather. Grow in soil-based compost and propagate from tip cuttings in early summer.

PODOCARPUS

P. macrophyllus *Buddhist Pine, Japanese Yew, Southern Yew*

Very unusually for a house plant, this is a conifer. It is a small tree with heavily branched stems carrying large, flattened, leaf-like needles up to 8 cm long. The needles are clustered in dense rosettes, and are extremely tough and leathery. Grow in light shade, or with some direct sunlight. Grow at temperatures of 10°-16°C (50°-60°F). At ordinary room temperature it grows continuously, but below 13°C (55°F) growth ceases, and the plant can be rested. Water only moderately during active growth, feeding every two weeks. If the plant is rested give only enough water to prevent drying out. Do not overwater. Grow in soil-based compost, in a relatively small pot. Propagate from tip cuttings treated with rooting hormone powder and raised in a propagator. Pinch out growing tip to encourage bushy growth.

POLYPODIUM

P. aureum (Phlebodium aureum) *Haresfoot Fern*

Fern producing fronds on wiry stems rising from a creeping rhizome, which is covered with furry scales. Fronds are up to 60 cm in length carried erect or arching. They are subdivided into smaller pinnae or leaflets, which are elongated and undulating. The underside of the pinna is dotted with brown spore cases. There are colour varieties with pale blue-green foliage. Grow in medium shade and do not expose to direct sunlight. Grow at normal room temperatures. Polypodium grows throughout the year, so a winter rest is not required. However, if temperatures drop below 13°C (55°F), restrict watering. At other times water plentifully, especially at temperatures of 21°C (70°F) or more, when mist spraying will be required, and the pot should stand on a tray of moist gravel. Feed each week, with half-strength liquid fertiliser. Grow in a mixture of leaf mould and soil-based compost. Propagate in spring by separation of part of the rhizome. The severed section should be pegged to the soil surface.

POLYSCIAS

Group of shrubs or trees which can grow tall but, with roots restricted by a pot, seldom outgrow their environment. They are very slow growing. Cultivate in strong, indirect light at temperatures of 16°-21°C (60°-70°F). They will not tolerate lower temperatures. Maintain humidity by standing the pot on a tray of damp gravel. Water moderately throughout the year, allowing the surface of the compost to dry out between waterings. Feed every two weeks from spring to autumn. The plant will continue to grow slowly through the winter. Grow in soil-based compost and propagate from tip cuttings taken in spring. Remove lower leaves, treat with hormone rooting powder and raise in a propagator. Very susceptible to attack by red spider mite.

P. balfouriana *Balfour aralia, Dinner Plant Aralia*

Has grey speckled stems carrying leaves which consist of three rounded leaflets. The leaflets have scalloped margins and a puckered surface, and are heavily variegated with creamy yellow, either on their margins or around the leaf veins.

P. guilfoylei 'Victoriae' *Geranium leaf aralia*

The type species is a large tree, but the variety 'Victoriae' grows to no more than 1 metre. It is slimmer and more erect than **P. balfouriana**, with large leaves divided into up to seven leaflets, coloured grey-green with a narrow white margin.

PRIMULA

The popular garden primulas can be grown indoors as temporary house plants, but even the tender forms, which will not survive outdoors in winter, need cool airy conditions when kept indoors. Most varieties flower in early spring. They all produce tubular flowers opening to a flattened shape carried in large clusters on erect stems. Leaves usually grow in an attractive rosette. Grow primulas in bright light, preferably with some sunlight, at temperatures of 10°-16°C (50°-60°F). At higher temperatures increase humidity by standing the pot in moist gravel. Water plentifully, but do not allow to become waterlogged. Feed every two weeks during the flowering season. Grow in soil-based compost. If the plant is to be kept after flowering, keep it cool and only lightly watered until growth starts in late winter. Prone to attack by red spider mite.

P. × kewensis

Yellow-flowered primula, having leaves with a waxy white coating, and toothed edges. Fragrant flowers produced from December to April.

P. malacoides *Baby or Fairy Primrose*

Small species with 1 cm mauve flowers (other colour varieties are available). Leaves are pale green and hairy, with toothed edges. Winter flowering.

P. obconica *German Primrose*

Vigorously flowering species with large hairy leaves which can cause an allergic rash in some people. 2 cm flowers are carried on a 30 cm stem, and are red, mauve or white, with a green central 'eye'.

P. sinensis *Chinese Primrose*

Has deeply ribbed and toothed hairy leaves. Produces a 30 cm flower stalk with 3 cm purple, red, pink or white flowers, with a bright yellow 'eye'. Petals are often frilled. Spring flowering.

PSEUDERANTHEMUM

(Purple False Eranthemum)

P. atropurpureum (P. kewensis, Eranthemum atropurpureum)

Small straggly shrub up to 1 metre high when grown indoors. Erect stems carry 12 cm leaves coloured purplish-green, with patches of cream, white and pink. 15 cm flower spikes in pink and white are produced in summer on mature plants. Grow in good, indirect light at temperatures in excess of 16°C (60°F), and maintain humidity by standing pots in damp gravel. Water moderately throughout the year, and feed fortnightly during active growth. Propagate from cuttings treated with rooting hormone, and raised in a propagator.

PTERIS

(Table Fern)

Large group of ferns which are popular house plants. Fronds are produced on wiry stems from creeping underground rhizomes. Fronds are tall and erect, often arching at the tips. Grow in bright, indirect light, and never expose to full sun. Grows well at normal room temperatures, but above 18°C (65°F) will need to be stood in moist gravel and mist sprayed daily. Will not tolerate temperatures below 13°C (55°F). Water plentifully at all times, since the plant grows actively throughout the year. Watering can be reduced slightly at lower temperatures. Feed every month with half-strength fertiliser. Grow in a mixture of leaf mould and soil-based compost, or in peat-based compost. Propagate by dividing rhizome in spring. May produce young ferns spontaneously as the microscopic spores germinate.

P. cretica *Cretan Brake*

Fronds are 30 cm in length having one large central pinna, and several smaller pinnae. Fronds are carried on a 15 cm black stalk. A variegated form is available with cream longitudinal stripes on the pinnae.

P. ensiformis *Sword Brake*

Has two types of frond. The larger fronds are up to 40 cm long, carrying large, paired pinnae. Smaller fronds are about 15 cm long. Fronds are carried on 15 cm stalks. A silvery variegated form is also available.

P. tremula *Australian Brake, Trembling Bracken*

Produces large fronds up to 60 cm by 30 cm. Fronds are yellow-green and pinnae are finely divided to give a fluffy appearance. The dark spore cases on the underside of the pinnae give the pinnae a black-edged appearance.

PUNICA

P. granatum 'Nana' *Dwarf Pomegranate*
Small shrubby bush growing very slowly to a maximum of 1 metre. Produces small leathery leaves, coloured glossy green. Flowers are produced in late spring to summer, and are orange-red and pendant, rather like a FUCHSIA flower. Flowers are followed by small yellowish pomegranates, which are barely edible. Leaves tend to drop after fruiting. Needs pruning to maintain a tidy shape. Grows in good light, including some direct sun, at temperature of 10°-18°C (50°-65°F), and prefers temperatures of around 13°C (55°F) for its winter rest. Water freely during active growth and in winter give only sufficient water to prevent drying out. Feed during active growth, at fortnightly intervals. Grow in soil-based compost and restrict roots by using smallish pots to encourage flowering. Propagate from cuttings taken in spring and treated with rooting hormone. Does not propagate very easily.

Primula beesiana

REBUTIA
(Crown Cacti)

A genus of small globular desert cacti that branch to form clumps. They are noteworthy for their profuse flowers, produced in late spring and summer, which often completely conceal the stems, and are produced even on very young plants. Flowers are produced low down, often in a complete ring about the stem, and remain for about a week, closing at night. Unlike most cacti, flowers open only a few times at a time, extending the flowering season. Rebutias should be given some protection from full sun in mid-summer. They need full sun at all other times. Grow them at temperatures of 5°-30°C (41°-86°F), and give them a winter rest at 10°C (50°F) or a little cooler, when only sufficient water should be given to prevent the compost from drying out. At other times, water moderately, and feed with high-potash (tomato type) fertiliser every four weeks during active growth. Grow in shallow pots, in a mixture of coarse sand and soil-based compost. Propagate from offsets, which should be dried out for three days before planting, or from seed. Liable to attack by mealy bug.

R. albiflora
A rare, white-flowered form which may flower while still only 1 cm across. It forms many dense clusters of small, white-spined stems.

R. calliantha
Larger species growing up to 12 cm tall and covered with short white spines. Produces circles of purple buds which open to spectacular 4 cm scarlet or orange flowers.

R. miniscula   *Red Crown*
Fast-growing form which will fill its pot with white-spined branches in a few years. Produces pinkish-red flowers.

R. senilis   *Fire Crown*
Spherical stems grow up to 7.5 cm across. Silvery white, hair-like spines are up to 3 cm long. Produces red, pink or yellow flowers. Many other species are available, and Rebutias also hybridize freely, seldom reproducing the expected characteristics when grown from seed.

RECHSTEINERIA
See SINNINGIA

RHAPIS
(Lady Palms)

Slow-growing palms with leaves divided into several blunt-ended leaflets. They are relatively short and take many years to develop any noticeable 'trunk', as lower leaves die off.

They require strong, indirect light, except in winter when they benefit from some direct sunlight. Grow in normal room temperatures, down to about 7°C (45°F), when growth ceases. Otherwise they grow throughout the year, and at higher temperatures do not need a winter rest. Water moderately during active growth, feeding once a month. If plants rest during colder conditions, restrict the watering accordingly. Grow them in comparatively small pots in soil-based compost and propagate from suckers produced from the base of the plant.

RHIPSALIDOPSIS
(Easter Cactus)

Popular jungle cacti, with flattened stems, branching repeatedly. They are first erect, then arch and droop, so they are suitable for growing in hanging baskets. Stems have notched edges, and small areoles with sparse brownish bristles. Flower profusely in spring. Grow in indirect light at normal room temperatures. Do not let temperatures drop below 10°C (50°F) and avoid temperature changes when buds are formed, as these may otherwise drop. No winter rest is needed, so Rhipsalidopsis can be watered throughout the year. Water well except at low temperatures, when they can be kept drier. In very warm conditions mist spraying with water is beneficial. Feed with high-potash (tomato type) fertiliser as soon as buds appear and stop feeding when flowering finishes. Grow in soil-based compost with added coarse sand. Propagates ridiculously easily from detached stem segments, which root within days.

R. gaertneri (Schlumbergia gaertneri)
4 cm flattened stems with a pinkish tinge when grown in good light. Flowers are scarlet, and up to 4 cm across, produced very freely in early summer.

R. rosea
Stem sections are up to 2 cm long and triangular or square when seen in cross-sections. Pink 2 cm flowers are flattened and star-shaped. There are many hybrids between **R. gaertneri** and **R. rosea**, producing flowers in pink, mauve and red.

RHIPSALIS
(Mistletoe Cactus)

Jungle cacti which look most uncactus-like, with unusual trailing stems in various forms. Some are rounded, some are thread-like, and still others produce flattened frond-like stems. Their flowers are small and fragrant and are followed by white berries, which stay on the plant for several weeks. Most flower in spring and sometimes again later in the year. Grow in light shade and if possible, put them outdoors in summer. Grow in normal room temperatures of 13°-24°C (55°-75°F), and maintain humidity by standing in moist gravel if temperatures are high. Mist spraying is also beneficial. Water plentifully in spring and summer, and only moderately in winter. Rhipsalis dislike hard water, so use rainwater or water thawed from frost in the refrigerator or freezer. Feed every month with high-potash (tomato type) fertiliser, and at two week intervals when buds are forming. Grow in peat-based compost with added coarse sand. Propagates easily from cuttings or detached stem segments. Detach the whole branch when making a cutting.

R. cassutha (R. baccifera)
Cylindrical stems up to 12 cm long, produced in a dense trailing cluster. Produces small cream flowers in summer.

R. crispata
Large flattened stems up to 60 cm in length and 10 cm broad. At first erect, then trailing. 1 cm cream flowers are produced in summer from notches on the edges of the stems.

R. pilocarpa
Cylindrical stems up to 40 cm long and 5 mm thick, in a dense trailing cluster, covered with small bristly spines. Stems have grooves running along them. 2 cm flowers are produced in late winter.

R. houlletiana
Produces a mixture of slim cylindrical branches and large flattened frond-like branches. These have notched edges and carry 1 cm cream flowers in spring and summer.

RHODODENDRON
(Azalea)
Rhododendrons grown indoors are invariably referred to as 'Azalea', although this botanical name is no longer valid. All are evergreen shrubs with large showy flowers, and are hybrids, in white, pink, mauve or red, usually with double flowers or frilled petals. They are normally kept as temporary plants, to be discarded after flowering, but can be kept with care for several years. Rhododendrons require bright indirect light, and cool room temperatures of 10°-16°C (50°-60°F). At temperatures above 21°C (70°F) they wilt rapidly. They must be kept permanently moist, and preferably given soft water, or water thawed from frost in the refrigerator or freezer. Otherwise, treat occasionally with

iron sequestrene to prevent leaf yellowing. Feed with special fertiliser for lime-hating plants, every two weeks from spring to autumn. Put in the garden after flowering and bring indoors only if frost threatens. Bring indoors again when buds have developed. Propagate from tip cuttings raised in a propagator.

R. obtusum × hybrids
Has glossy, deep green leaves and hairy stems. Flowers are up to 3 cm across.

R. simsii (Azalea indica) *Indian Azalea*
Leaves have hairs around their margins. Flowers are carried in clusters and are up to 5 cm across and usually bi-coloured.

RHOEO
R. spathacea (R. discolor) *Moses-in-the-Cradle, Boat Lily*
Looking rather like DRACAENA, Rhoeo produces a 40 cm wide rosette of stiff leaves with purple undersides, carried on a short fleshy 'trunk'. This develops as lower leaves are shed. Usually available as the variegated form in which the leaves are striped in yellow, and may have a pinkish tinge. May also produce side-shoots, which trail when the plant is grown in a basket. Grow in good indirect light at normal room temperatures with a minimum of 16°C (60°F), and maintain humidity by standing the pot on a tray of moist gravel. Keep moist at all times but drier in winter. Feed every two weeks during active growth. Avoid draughts and sudden changes of temperature. Grow in peat or soil-based compost, and propagate from offsets produced from the base of the plant, or from side-shoots treated as cuttings. Can also be grown from seed.

RHOICISSUS
Popular climbing vines, which cling to supports with spiral tendrils. They are extremely tough and vigorous, and may survive outdoors in mild areas. Can also be allowed to trail from hanging baskets. They grow rapidly in light shade, and may tolerate quite poor light. Grows well at normal room temperatures at 13°-18°C (55°-65°F), and does best with a winter rest at about 10°C (50°F), when only light watering should be given. At all other times keep plentifully watered and well fed. Grow in soil-based compost and propagate from tip cuttings in spring and summer. These root very easily. Pinch out growing tips to promote bushy growth.

R. capensis *Cape Grape*
Large heart-shaped leave up to 16 cm across,

and with toothed edges. Leaves are pale green and covered with reddish-brown hair underneath.

R. rhomboidea *Grape Ivy*
A familiar house plant growing to very large size if not pruned ruthlessly. Leaves are divided into three sections, each toothed, and bronze-green in colour. Stems are wiry and covered in brown hairs.

More decorative varieties are available in which the 'teeth' on the leaf edges are cut very deeply.

RHYNCHOSTYLUS

R. retusa *Foxtail Orchids*
Epiphytic orchid noteworthy for its amazing blossoms, which are produced in a densely packed trailing 'plume', up to 50 cm long. The flowers are waxy and fragrant, up to 2 cm across, and are usually white with pink or magenta speckles, and a magenta lip. The foliage grows to a height of about 60 cm, with pale green, strap-like leaves. Flowers are produced in early spring and are relatively short-lived. May flower again later in the year. Grows well in normal room conditions, with minimum temperatures of around 13°C (55°F). As with many other orchids, water should be restricted in autumn (although no real rest is necessary) and at other times the plant should be kept well watered. Feed during active growth with high-potash (tomato type) fertilisers, and grow in normal fibrous orchid compost. Propagate by division in the spring.

RICINUS

(Castor Oil Plant)
R. communis
Shrubby plant which eventually develops into a small tree. In the home it seldom exceeds 1 metre in height. Leaves are up to 30 cm across, and deeply divided into 5-7 leaflets. Produces small, insignificant flowers followed by spiny seed pods. Grow in good indirect light at normal room temperatures. Provide a winter rest at about 13°C (55°F), when watering should be reduced. At other times water moderately. Grow in soil-based compost and propagate from seeds. The seedlings grow very rapidly, so the plant is often treated as an annual.

There is one variety with deep maroon foliage and stems and another with a pale mid-rib to the leaf.

RIVINA

R. humilis *Baby Pepper, Rouge Plant, Blood-berry*

Spreading or creeping plant with thick, heart-shaped leaves, slightly hairy. Shoots spread to about 60 cm. Throughout spring and summer clusters of white or pink flowers are produced, which are followed by glossy scarlet berries in autumn. Grow in good, indirect light at temperatures of 16°-21°C (60°-70°F), and water well in spring and summer feeding every month. Keep relatively dry in winter. Grow in soil-based compost and propagate from seed. Usually treated as an annual, although it can be kept as a perennial. Pinch out tips to prevent straggly growth.

ROCHEA

Small shrubby succulents growing to about 45 cm with a 20 cm spread. The small leaves are close together on the stems, arranged in two neat rows. Tubular flowers are produced in spring and summer in 6 cm clusters. Colours are white or red. Grow in direct sun and at normal room temperatures but give a winter rest at 10°-13°C (50°-55°F), when watering must be severely restricted. During active growth water only moderately. Feed at fortnightly intervals with high-potash (tomato type) fertiliser when buds appear and through to the end of flowering only. Grow in a mixture of soil-based compost and coarse sand. Propagate from stem cuttings taken in spring and dried for three days before planting. Grows only slowly from seed. Prune plants hard in winter.

R. coccinea
The most popular type, with red flowers. A white variety is available, and also a variety with white-and-red flowers. Flowers of **R. coccinea** have a hyacinth-like perfume.

R. versicolor
Has longer, slimmer leaves than **R. coccinea**. Flower colours are white, pink or cream, speckled outside with red.

RUELLIA

R. makoyana *Monkey Plant, Trailing Velvet Plant*
Spreading or trailing plant with twiggy 60 cm stems. Lance-shaped leaves are velvety olive-green with silvery veins and purple underneath. Flowers are produced a few at a time from autumn right through the winter. Flowers are rich purplish-pink, trumpet-shaped, and 5 cm across. Grow in good, indirect light at temperatures of 16°-21°C (60°-70°F), and in a high humidity maintained by frequent mist spraying and standing the pot on moist gravel. Do not allow temperatures to fall below 13°C (55°F). Water moderately and feed

every two weeks except for a two-month rest after flowering, when only sufficient water should be given to prevent the compost drying out completely. Grow in a mixture of leaf mould or peat and soil-based compost. Propagate from tip cuttings taken in spring and treated with rooting hormone. Raise cuttings in a propagator. Pinch out tips to encourage bushy growth. Susceptible to aphid attack.

Ruellia makoyana

SAINTPAULIA
(African Violet)
Probably the most popular indoor plant of all, flowering freely through most of the year. Has large, fleshy, dark-green, heart-shaped leaves, growing in a spreading rosette. Flowers are carried on a fleshy stem in clusters, they are violet-like with a central yellow eye. Saintpaulias require bright, indirect light, and may benefit from some filtered sunlight. They will be scorched by mid-day sun, however. Adequate lighting will ensure that the plant flowers continuously throughout the year. They require warm room conditions of 16°-21°C (60°-70°F) and must be kept moist. Water with tepid water, onto the compost surface. Do not wet the leaves. Reduce watering if temperature falls below 16°C (60°F). Feed at every watering with quarter-strength fertiliser. Special fertilisers are commercially available for these plants. Grow in well drained peat-based compost in a smallish pot. Propagate by rooting individual leaves. Insert the leaf stalk into the compost and raise in a propagator. Saintpaulias are very susceptible to attack by mealy bugs, root mealy bugs, aphids, and cyclamen mites.

Saintpaulia × hybrids
Available in a limitless range of flower shapes and every colour but yellow. Varieties with double flowers and with frilled petals are available.

S. confusa
Rosette-forming species with small round leaves and blue-violet flowers.

S. grandifolia
Creeping form with large, thin leaves up to 10 cm across. Small violet flowers are carried in clusters on a short stalk.

S. ionantha
The basic form which gave rise to most of the Saintpaulia hybrids. Leaves are hairy with pinkish undersides. Flower stalks about 12 cm high.

S. schumensis
Small rosette-forming species with pale mauve flowers carried on a 5 cm stem.

SANCHEZIA
S.nobilis (S. nobilis, S. glaucophylla)
Upright shrub growing to 1 metre in height with woody stems. Carries large lance-shaped leaves up to 30 cm long, coloured dark green with greenish-yellow markings over the midrib and major leaf veins. Flowers are produced in early summer and are yellow and tubular up to 4 cm long and grouped in stiff erect clusters, with bright red bracts. Sanchezias should be grown in bright, indirect light at normal room temperatures and not below 13°C (55°F). Maintain high humidity during active growth by standing the pot on a tray of moist gravel. Water moderately during active growth and feed every two weeks. During the winter rest water only sufficiently to prevent compost from drying out. Grow in soil-based compost and propagate from cuttings taken after flowering and treated with hormone rooting powder. Raise in a propagator. These plants are often treated as annuals to be discarded after flowering.

SANSEVIERIA
(Mother-in-Law's Tongue, Devil's Tongue, Bowstring Hemp)
Popular, hardy, but slow growing plant. The stiff erect leaves are unmistakable, although there are also small rosette-forming types. Leaves are usually sword-shaped and grow directly from a thick creeping rhizome. Sansevierias spread slowly by branching from their rhizome, and can eventually burst their pot if too restricted. Flowers are occasionally produced on a spike but are insignificant. Sansevierias need good light and are best grown in full sunlight. They require warm conditions of 16°-21°C (60°-70°F), and are damaged at temperatures below 13°C (55°F). Water moderately during active growth, letting the surface of the compost dry out before further water is given. Feed once a month during active growth with half-strength fertiliser. Do not overwater during winter. These plants are unlikely to be damaged by too-dry conditions, but are easily destroyed by rot in cool, damp conditions. Grow in a well drained mixture of coarse sand and soil-based compost. Propagate by division of rhizomes, complete with roots and leaves. They can also be propagated by planting 5 cm sections of leaf, as cuttings, but the resulting plants will lose any variegated markings the parent plant may have had.

S. cylindrica
A scarce form with cylindrical 90 cm leaves with cylindrical sections, about 3 cm thick. Leaves have longitudinal ribs.

S. liberica
Typical erect fleshy leaves, striped with broad bands of almost pure white.

S. trifasciata
Stiffly erect leaves up to 90 cm in height and about 7 cm broad. They are marbled in green and grey and have undulating edges. The variegated form with yellow edges is much more popular.

S. trifasciata 'Hahnii' forms a tiny rosette not taller than 10 cm, and with yellow-edged leaves. Silver flecked varieties are also available.

SARRACENIA
(Pitcher Plant)
An odd-looking, insectivorous plant. Produces tall tubular leaves or 'pitchers', with a 'lid' at the top. Flies are lured into the pitcher, past inward pointing hairs which trap them, falling into a pool of digestive fluid. Attractive flowers are produced, but pitcher plants are grown mostly for the odd-looking and brightly coloured leaves. Leaves are up to 80 cm long, and often veined or blotched in red or purple. Small forms are also available, but those commercially available are usually mixed hybrids to be grown from seed. Sow seed on a mixture of chopped sphagnum moss and peat, and water with soft water thawed from the frost in the refrigerator or freezer. After germination seeds should be grown in a mixture of 6 parts moss peat, 2 parts perlite, and one part sand in cool, humid conditions. The pot should stand in a dish containing 2 cm of soft water. Do not feed with fertilisers because these will damage the plant.

SAXIFRAGA
S. stolonifera (S. sarmentosa) *Mother-of-Thousands, Beefsteak Geranium, Creeping Sailor*
One of the easiest plants to cultivate. Produces rosettes of rounded leaves, dark green with silvery veins and coloured pink underneath. Leaves are up to 8 cm across and are hairy. Long creeping stems are produced, carrying small plantlets which root where they touch the compost. Flower spikes are produced in late summer carrying white star-shaped flowers. Ideal for growing in hanging baskets. Variegated forms are available with leaves edged with white, and tinged with pink. Grow in light shade, although brief exposure to sun will be beneficial, especially for the variegated types. Grow in cool room temperatures of 10°-16°C (50°-60°F). At higher temperatures provide extra humidity by standing pots on moist gravel. Do not allow temperatures to fall below 7°C (45°F). Water plentifully during active growth and reduce watering gradually after flowering, giving very little water over the winter period. Feed every month during active growth. Grow in well drained, soil-based compost and propagate by planting the small plantlets. Prone to attack by aphids.

SCHEFFLERA
(Brassaia)
Genus of evergreen shrubs and trees which all have tough foliage. The leaves are large and divided into several lance-shaped segments. They tend to grow tall and straight, and are best pinched out to encourage bushiness *before* they reach the ceiling. Grow in good indirect light, in normal room temperatures. In winter, provide minimum temperatures of 13°-16°C (55°-60°F). At cooler temperatures leaves will drop. Water moderately during active growth and feed every two weeks. During the winter rest give only sufficient water to stop compost from drying out completely. Grow in soil-based compost, and propagate by air layering or by growing from seed. Cuttings can be taken but are difficult to root. Liable to attack by mealy bug.
S. actinophylla *Queensland Umbrella Tree, Starleaf*
Grows to 3 metres or more. Leaves are deep glossy green and divided into 5-7 leaflets, which may be 30 cm in length.
S. digitata *Seven Fingers*
Leaflets are up to 18 cm long, and are relatively broader than **S. actinophylla**.
S. venusta
A form with narrow undulating leaflets, which is shorter and more compact than the other species. May have up to ten leaflets in each leaf.

SCHIZOCENTRON
(Spanish Shawl)
S. elegans (Heterocentron elegans)
Trailing or creeping plant usually grown in hanging baskets. Has pointed oval leaves carried on hairy pink stems, which root to the compost along their length. Produces rose-purple, four-petalled flowers in summer which are up to 2 cm across. They have prominent purple stamens. Grow in good, indirect light at temperatures of 16°-21°C (60°-70°F), and maintain humidity by standing pot on moist gravel. Water moderately throughout the year and guard against drying out when grown in a hanging basket. Feed every month. Grow in a mixture of peat and soil-based compost. Propagate from cuttings or by division of the plant.

SCHLUMBERGIA
(Zygocactus) *Christmas Cactus*
The most popular cactus grown indoors usually purchased in bud, and often not flowering again, because its undemanding requirements have not been understood.

These are epiphytic cacti, requiring shade and plenty of moisture. They produce small, flat, jointed stem segments, which at first arch, then trail gracefully. The areoles and tiny bristles are situated in notches at the edge of the segments. Flowers are spectacular and are usually produced around Christmas time. Flowers may be up to 6 cm long, and the flowering period is usually prolonged. Grow in good, indirect light, and avoid artificial lighting as the plants come into bud. In the home, the plants' 'calendar' becomes confused as artificial lighting changes the apparent length of the day, and flowering is often delayed until spring. Grow in normal room temperatures of 13°-24°C (55°-75°F), and put outdoors in the shade in mild summer weather. Water plentifully except for a brief rest after flowering, preferably using soft rainwater, or water obtained by thawing frost from the refrigerator or freezer. Feed every two weeks with high-potash (tomato type) fertiliser, except during the brief rest period. Grow in a mixture of coarse and peat-based compost. Propagate from cuttings in spring and summer. Each cutting should consist of two or three segments.

Schlumbergia × hybrids
Very many available, most with magenta flowers. Segments have rounded notches and tips.

S. truncata *Crab Cactus*
Edges of the segments are deeply notched and edged with spikes as are the tips of the segments. Flowers are white, pink or red. Occasionally supplied as a 'standard', grafted on a tall columnar cactus, but it does not survive long.

SCILLA
(Wood-hyacinths)
Small bulbous plants grown variously from their foliage (which is often speckled), or their flowers. There are two forms: hardy Scillas, and tender plants. Hardy Scillas can only be flowered indoors for one season, after which they are usually planted outside. Tender species last for years, but need a winter rest, although their foliage persists through the year. Hardy Scillas dry off completely. Bulbs are small with a papery skin. Hardy Scillas are kept cool and in the dark for two to three months after planting in the autumn. They are gradually exposed to indirect light as the shoots appear. Tender Scillas require some direct sun. All grow at normal room temperatures and tender Scillas should be rested at 10°-16°C (50°-60°F), when little water is given.

At other times all Scillas should be kept moderately watered and fed monthly. Grow in soil-based compost. Propagate tender Scillas from bulbs produced as clumps. Hardy Scillas cannot be propagated indoors.

S. adamii
Tender species with narrow fleshy leaves up to 20 cm in length, striped with fine brown-red lines. Flowers are produced in clusters in spring. They are small, starry, and coloured in rich purple.

S. ovallifolia
Tender Scilla, with sparse foliage. Leaves are undulating and spotted with dark green. Small green flowers are produced in spring.

S. tubergeniana
Hardy form which produces 2 cm blue flowers in spring.

S. violacea (Ledebouria socialis) *Silver Squill*
Tender species with 10 cm fleshy pointed leaves, coloured grey-green and mottled with deep olive. Underside of leaves is purple. Clusters of small greenish-white flowers are produced in spring.

SCINDAPSUS
Genus of climbing plants with attractive variegated foliage, closely related to PHILODENDRON, which they resemble. Can grow very large, but easily kept to a reasonable size by pinching out and pruning. They climb moss poles or bark, clinging with small roots. Leaves are a lop-sided heart shape, and are leathery and shiny, up to 20 cm in length in the home. Can be grown upright, on supports, or allowed to trail. Grow in strong, indirect light at temperatures of 16°-24°C (60°-75°F), and give a winter rest at about 16°C (60°F) or a little cooler. They may need mist spraying in warm conditions or can be stood over a tray of moist gravel. Water moderately during active growth and feed every two weeks. During the winter rest water only sufficiently to prevent the compost drying out. Grow in soil-based compost and propagate from tip cuttings which root easily.

S. aureus (Epipremnum aureum) *Devil's Ivy, Pothos Vine*
Has angular stem, and irregular bright yellow streaks on the leaves. The variety 'Golden Queen' is almost completely yellow. 'Marble Queen' is creamy white with green speckles.

S. pictus *Silver Vine*
Similar to **S. aureus**, but with silvery blotches on the deep green leaves.

SCIRPUS
S. cernuus
Graceful grass-like plant related to bullrushes.

The slender leaves grow upright at first, then arch over and trail for as long as 60 cm in a graceful spray. Tiny flowers are carried at the end of the leaves. Scirpus grows from a creeping underground rhizome. Grow in light shade at normal room temperature. They grow continuously in temperatures down to 13°C (55°F), and should be kept very wet, or even stood in water. At temperatures of 7°-13°C (45°-55°F) they should be rested and kept relatively dry. Feed every four weeks during active growth, and pot in soil-based compost. Propagate by division of clumps in spring.

SEDUM
(Stonecrop)
Very large family of succulent plants, of very varied form. All have fleshy stems, and fleshy stalkless leaves. Flowers may be decorative, but these plants are grown more for their decorative foliage. Most are very easy to grow, provided they can be kept in full sun. They live in normal room temperatures and require a winter rest at about 10°C (50°F), when watering is severely restricted. At other times water moderately. Feeding is not necessary, except once or twice during the summer when high-potash (tomato type) fertiliser can be given. Grow in a mixture of coarse sand and soil-based compost, and propagate from stem cuttings with the lower leaves removed, dried for three days before planting. In species with plump leaves these can be rooted by planting them upright in dryish compost.

S. adolphi *Golden Sedum*
15 cm form with a rosette of thick, blunt-pointed leaves, coloured yellowish-green with a red edge. White flowers are produced in clusters in spring.

S. lineare 'Variegatum'
Arching stems which become prostrate, carrying groups of three slim leaves edged with white. Flowering stems are upright, carrying clusters of yellow flowers.

S. morganium *Donkey's Tail*
Long trailing stems up to 1 metre in length, completely obscured by fleshy leaves with a powdery bloom. Pink flowers are produced on the ends of the stems in large plants. Leaves are easily broken off in handling.

S. rubrotinctum *Christmas Cheer, Jelly Beans*
Small plant growing up to 20 cm high with swollen, club-shaped leaves, glossy green with a red blush. The red colour increases if the plant is kept dry in a very sunny position. May become prostrate, and root itself to the compost.

S. sieboldii 'Medio-Variegatum' *October Plant*
Small trailing plant with circular, saw-toothed leaves about 1.5 cm across. Leaves are arranged in clusters of three. The leaf centre is striped in cream, and the edge is red. Clusters of pink flowers are produced in autumn.

Many other species are available.

SELAGINELLA
Interesting plants intermediate between mosses and ferns. They form dense hummocks of pale green foliage, and can creep or trail. Younger plants have a semi-upright form of growth. Tiny scale-like leaves are flattened on either side of the slender stems. Like ferns, Selaginellas reproduce with spores, and these are produced on the tips of the stems. Grow Selaginellas in moderate shade and at normal room temperatures. They can only live in very humid atmospheres, so are ideal for culture in bottle gardens. Otherwise, mist spray them every day with tepid water and stand pots on moist gravel. Water plentifully throughout the year, and feed every two weeks with quarter-strength fertiliser. Grow in a mixture of coarse sand and peat-based compost. Propagate with cuttings taken in spring.

S. emmeliana (S. pallescens) *Sweat Plant, Moss Fern*
Erect species growing up to 30 cm high. Tiny leaves have white edges. There is also a golden variety.

S. kraussiana *Club Moss*
Fast-growing, creeping species often used as ground cover in mixed plant displays. There are golden and variegated varieties.

S. martensii
Semi-erect form with arched stems supported by trailing roots. Leaves are much larger than the other species. Variegated forms are available.

SELENICEREUS
(Queen-of-the-Night)
Very large forest cactus for the heated greenhouse or conservatory. Produces long straggly stems up to 5 metres in length and 2.5 cm thick, which can be trained across the roof of the greenhouse. Stems are heavily spined. Produces astonishing 30 cm, white, fragrant flowers, which open at night. Grow in good, indirect light, at temperatures of 7°-30°C (45°-86°F), and keep moist and well fed throughout the year. Feed at fortnightly intervals with high-potash (tomato type) fertiliser. Grow in soil-based compost with added bone-meal, and propagate from stem cuttings

in spring.

SENECIO

Enormous genus of plants, of which those grown as house plants are succulents. They are very diverse, having in common only their nonedescript daisy-like flowers. Some have succulent stems; others succulent leaves. All require good light, and the general rule is that the more succulent the plant, the stronger the light required. They grow in normal room temperatures at 5°-30°C (41°-86°F), and appreciate a winter rest at 10°C (50°F) or less, with minimal watering. The most succulent forms should be watered only sparingly at all times. Feed this type during active growth with high-potash (tomato type) fertiliser every month. Senecios with more orthodox leaves can be fed with ordinary liquid fertiliser. Highly succulent types should be grown in a mixture of coarse sand and soil-based compost. Leafy forms grow in soil or peat-based compost. Propagate from cuttings. Prone to aphid attack.

S. articulata (Kleinia articulata) *Hotdog Plant, Candle Plant*
Fleshy cactus-like stems about 12 cm long, branching profusely into jointed segments. Stems have a silvery bloom. Grows in winter to produce flattened blue-green leaves which fall off in spring, leaving a scar on the stem. These plants rest during summer and autumn.

S. macroglossa 'Variegatus' *Waxvine, Cape Ivy*
Long trailing or climbing stems with ivy-shaped fleshy leaves, variegated with cream patches, and with pink stems. Stems grow to about 1 metre in length. Keep moist and well fed.

S. mikanoides *German Ivy, Water Ivy*
Similar to **S. macroglossa**, but with larger, deep green leaves, having six or seven lobes, and deeply indented veins. Produces long trailing stems. Keep moist and well fed.

S. rowleyanus *String of Beads*
Peculiar creeping or trailing plant, producing thin string-like stems, on which are 'strung' completely spherical glossy green leaves about 6 mm in diameter, exactly like a 'String of Beads'. Stems trail to about 60 cm, or creep to produce a dense mat. Grow in direct sun. May produce fragrant white flowers in autumn.

SETCREASIA

S. purpura *Purple Heart*
Trailing plant with 10 cm lance-shaped leaves. Both leaves and stems are coloured rich purple, and are slightly hairy. Colour fades to purplish-green in poor light. Small pink flowers are produced on the stem tips in spring and summer. Stems grow erect to about 20 cm, then trail for 60 cm or more. For best leaf colour, grow where the plant receives some direct sun. Grows in normal room conditions, at 10°-16°C (50°-60°F), and continues to grow throughout the year. No rest is required and Setcreasias should be watered moderately and fed every two weeks while growing actively. Allow compost to dry out between waterings. Grow in soil-based compost and pinch out frequently to encourage bushy growth.

Propagate from cuttings, which root very easily.

SIDERASIS
S. fuscata
Temperamental plant for the heated greenhouse or bottle garden. It produces a beautiful rosette of white-striped, olive-green leaves, with rich maroon underside, and is covered with fine reddish hairs. Flowers are produced on a short stalk in summer, these are 2 cm across and purplish-pink. Grow in good, indirect light at a steady 21°-23°C (70°-75°F), and avoid any temperature fluctuations. Maintain high humidity by standing pots in a tray of moist gravel. Water moderately throughout the year, allowing the surface of the compost to dry out between waterings. Feed every month. Grow in a mixture of coarse sand, peat and soil-based compost. Propagate by dividing clumps and separating the rosettes.

SINNINGIA
(Gloxinias)
Most Sinningias are miscalled 'Gloxinia', which is an entirely different plant. They are tuberous rooted plants, with velvety leaves and large, showy, trumpet-shaped flowers. Grow in strong, indirect light at temperatures of 13°-18°C (55°-65°F). During the winter rest keep the tubers at 10°C (50°F). At temperatures above 23°C (75°F), mist spray and stand on a tray of damp gravel to maintain humidity. Water plentifully except in cold conditions, when the compost surface should be allowed to dry before watering. Reduce watering as the leaves fade and die off, and keep tubers completely dry until spring. Feed with high-potash (tomato type) fertiliser every two weeks after flowering, and until foliage dies back. Grow in a mixture of soil-based compost, peat and coarse sand, with added lime. Propagate from stem or leaf

cuttings, or from seed.

S. cardinalis *Cardinal Flower, Helmet Flower*
10 cm hairy leaves with scalloped edges, marked in dark green along leaf veins. Deep red flowers are produced on 25 cm stems. Flowering takes place over the whole of autumn. Flowers are elongated and tubular.

S. leucotricha *Brazilian Eidelweiss*
Leaves and stems are densely covered with white hairs. 15 cm leaves are oval, with down-turned edges. Tubular pink flowers are produced in summer and autumn.

S. pusilla
Tiny, free-flowering dwarf form growing to only 4 cm high, and flowering continuously through the year. Hybrids are available with many shades of pink, white and purple.

S. regina *Cinderella Slippers*
Large white-veined leaves, with purple undersides and toothed edges. Flowers are produced in autumn and are tubular and up to 8 cm long, coloured purple.

S. speciosa *Florist's Gloxinia*
The most familiar type, available in a wide range of hybrids of various colours. Produces large, coarse, saw-toothed leaves, which are densely furred. Flowers are produced in summer on 10 cm stalks and are extremely large and variable in form and colour. Frilled and multi-coloured varieties are available.

SMITHIANTHA
(Naegelia) *Temple Bells*
Temporary plants with large hairy leaves produced from a rhizome. Leaves are heart-shaped, with coarsely toothed edges. Flowers are produced in winter on a large spike. They are tubular, with a five-lobed mouth and are about 4 cm in length. Flowering may continue for a month or more. Grow in light shade at a temperature of 16°-21°C (60°-70°F). Water moderately; too much, or too little water will damage the foliage. Feed every week with quarter-strength fertiliser. Grow in peat-based compost, mixed with coarse sand and chopped sphagnum moss. Propagate by dividing rhizomes while they are dormant. Can also be grown easily from seed. Let the plant die back after flowering, and withhold watering. Store rhizomes in a cool dark place until ready for planting in late summer.

S. cinnabarina
Grows up to 60 cm high with 15 cm leaves covered with reddish hairs. Flowers are orange-red with a yellow throat, speckled with red.

S. zebrina
Grows up to 75 cm high. Leaves are deep green with purplish veins. Flowers are red with yellow bands and yellow petals and throat.

SOLANUM
(Jerusalem Cherry, Capsicum)
Small bushy shrubs growing to about 50 cm, having nonedescript dark green leaves and small flowers. They are grown solely for their large bright-coloured berries, which persist for several months. They produce berries in winter, and are best put out in the garden during summer, ready for flowering in late autumn. Grow in a sunny position and under cool conditions of 10°-16°C (50°-60°F). Maintain high humidity by standing plants on moist gravel and frequent mist spraying. Water spray plants kept outdoors during the summer. Water plentifully and give a short rest before putting out of doors, giving minimal water. Feed every two weeks except during the rest period. Grow in soil-based compost and propagate from seed raised in a propagator. Pinch out growing tips on young plants to encourage bushy growth. Prone to attack by white-fly.

S. capistratum *False Jerusalem Cherry, Winter Cherry*
Leaves are hairy, oval and undulating, carried on densely branched stems. Flowers are 1 cm across, white with yellow stamens. Oval berries are initially green, changing to tomato-orange. Variegated leaf forms are available.

S. pseudocapsicum *Jerusalem Cherry, Christmas Cherry*
Similar to **S. capistratum**, but more vigorous and hardier. Berries are more spherical, larger and longer lasting, and are usually produced in December.

SONERILA
S. margaritacea
Creeping plant with 25 cm red stems carrying 10 cm lance-shaped leaves, which are deep green with silvery-white speckles, and purple-red underneath. Produces small clusters of three-petalled pink flowers in summer and autumn. Grow in strong, indirect light, at normal temperatures with a minimum temperature of 18°C (65°F); maintain a high humidity with frequent water sprays, and stand the pot on moist gravel. The plant should be watered moderately throughout the year, feeding at two week intervals. There is no winter rest period, as Sonerila grows continuously. Grow in a mixture of peat-based compost and leaf mould. Propagate in spring or summer, using tip cuttings treated

with rooting hormone and raised in a propagator.

SOPHRONITIS
S. coccinea (S. grandiflora)
This is a very pretty dwarf epiphytic orchid which is relatively easy to grow in the home. It resembles a tiny CATTLEYA growing no taller than 7.5 cm, from a small clump of bulbs. Single flowers are produced, about 6.5 cm across, and are usually coloured scarlet with a speckled yellow lip. Other colours are available. Grow in medium shade at temperatures of 10°-13°C (50°-55°F), and at high humidities. They must be watered plentifully in summer, and less in winter, although they do not have a true winter rest. Grow in a mixture of standard orchid compost and chopped sphagnum moss, and feed during active growth with high-potash (tomato type) fertiliser. Can be grown in normal shallow pots or in a hollow on a piece of cork bark. Propagate by division in spring. Unfortunately, this tiny orchid is short-lived and seldom survives for long even under ideal conditions.

SPARMANNIA
S. africana *African Hemp, Indoor Linden, Indoor Lime*
Tall indoor shrub, growing up to 2 metres or more in height. Branches naturally to produce an attractive miniature tree, with 20 cm heart-shaped, hairy leaves. Edges of the leaves are coarsely toothed. The stems gradually become woody in older plants. Small clusters of 3 cm white flowers are produced in winter. These have conspicuous purple-tipped yellow stamens. Double-flowered varieties are available. Grow in good, indirect light at temperatures of 16°-21°C (60°-70°F), and in warm weather stand pot in damp gravel to maintain humidity. Water moderately during active growth, allowing compost surface to dry between waterings, and feed every two weeks. Rest in winter giving only sufficient water to prevent compost from drying out. Grow in soil-based compost and propagate in spring from tip cuttings. These may be planted or first rooted in water. Prune to maintain good shape. Liable to attack by mealy bugs.

SPATHIPHYLLUM
(Peace Lily)
S. wallisii
Grows from an underground rhizome, producing lance-shaped leaves up to 15 cm long, carried on 15 cm stalks. Produces a yellowish spike of tiny flowers, surrounded by a graceful white spathe. The blossom is carried on a long stalk and persists for several weeks. Flowers are produced a few at a time, throughout spring and summer, and sometimes into the winter. **S. wallisii 'Mauna Loa'** is a hybrid with large leaves and a very large spathe. Grow Spathiphyllum in light shade at temperatures of 18°-21°C (65°-70°F), and never let temperatures drop below 13°C (60°F). At these warm temperatures there will be no rest period. Water moderately and feed at fortnightly intervals from spring to late autumn. Stand pot on moist gravel to maintain humidity. Grow in peat-based compost, and propagate by dividing rhizomes in spring. Prone to attack by red spider mites.

SPREKELIA
S. formossisima *Aztec Lily, Jacobean Lily*
Bulbous plant producing 10 cm scarlet orchid-like flowers in midsummer, carried on a 50 cm stem. Bulbs are planted in soil-based compost with the tip exposed. Grow in full sun, at temperatures of 10°-16°C (50°-60°F), and water and feed well until foliage dies back in late summer. Then withhold all water until growth starts in the spring. Commence watering sparingly and increase as plant develops. Propagate by dividing offsets after two or three years.

STANHOPEA
Group of epiphytic orchids noted particularly for their eccentric growth style. Flower stalks grow *downwards*, through the compost, and emerge through the bottom of the hanging basket in which they must be grown. Their foliage is strap-like and up to 35 cm long, emerging from an egg-shaped pseudo-bulb. Flowers are very complex in shape. Relatively easy to grow in light shade requiring cool conditions of 10°-13°C (50°-55°F). They must be kept well watered during active growth and fed with high-potash (tomato type) fertiliser. Flowers are produced in summer and water should be gradually reduced into the winter, when a rest is given. Grow in normal orchid compost in an open sphagnum-lined wire basket so the flowering shoot can emerge. Propagate by division. Various species are available, and are difficult to distinguish.

STAPELIA
(Carrion Flower, Starfish Flower)
Group of succulents resembling erect cacti. They have branched square-sectioned stems

with notched edges, which are actually vestigial leaves. They are grown for their remarkable flowers which are interesting rather than pretty. These have a distinct disadvantage of smelling like decaying flesh. Flowers are star-shaped and fleshy, produced from spring to autumn. Grow in direct sunlight and temperatures of 16°-30°C (60°-86°F). At lower temperatures they develop fungus diseases. Water very carefully. They will shrivel if too dry, and bloat and rot if too wet. It is safest to stand the pot in tepid water for a few minutes, only watering again when the top surface of the compost is dry. Feed with high-potash (tomato type) fertiliser during active growth. Grow in a mixture of coarse sand and soil-based compost and use only sand for the top 2 cm of the mixture. Grows easily from seed or from offsets, which are usually already rooted. Do not overwater young plants.

S. hirsuta

Produces 30 cm stems about 2 cm thick. Flowers are 10 cm across, coloured cream and purple, and covered in dense hairs. The flower is less offensively smelly than the other Stapelias.

S. nobilis (S. gigantea) *Giant Toad Plant, Zulu Giant*

Produces enormous flowers, up to 30 cm across, coloured yellow with reddish-purple lines. Stems are only about 15 cm tall. Flowers spasmodically and smells moderately badly.

S. variegata *Starfish Plant, Star Flower, Toad Plant*

The most common type with 15 cm stems about 1 cm thick, mottled with purplish-green. The flowers are 6 cm across, coloured pale yellow with purple-brown spots, and have a disgusting smell.

STENOCARPUS

S. sinuatus *Wheel of Fire, Firewheel Tree*

A very large tree, restricted to about 2 metres when grown in a pot. Has pale green leaves with reddish undersides, up to 45 cm long, and deeply lobed. Mature plants in good condition may produce 6 cm yellow and scarlet wheel-shaped clusters of flowers, in summer and autumn. Grow in strong light with some direct sun. Grows well at normal room temperatures, down to a minimum of 10°C (50°F). Water plentifully during active growth and feed every two weeks. Water sparingly in winter. Grow in soil-based compost and propagate from seed, raising seedlings in a propagator.

STENOTAPHRUM

S. secundatum 'Variegatum' *Buffalo Grass, St Augustine's Grass*

Vigorous and attractive variegated grass for the hanging basket. Stems are flattened and blunt-ended, up to 30 cm in length. They are attractively striped in cream and green. Grow in bright light, including sun if possible, at temperatures of 10°-16°C (50°-60°F). They will not tolerate lower temperatures. At higher temperatures, stand them above trays of moist gravel to prevent scorching. Water plentifully during active growth and feed every month. During winter water only sufficiently to prevent the compost drying out. Grow in soil-based compost. Propagation is simplicity itself. Just pull off a tuft and plant it. Prune hard to remove dry and browning leaves.

STEPHANOTIS

(Floradora, Wax Flower, Madagascar Jasmine)

Popular but temperamental flowering plant needing special care in the average home. It is a climber which has deep green, leathery leaves, up to 10 cm long. White flowers are tubular, 3 cm long, with a waxy texture. Their perfume is extremely strong and fragrant. Can grow to 3 metres or more under good conditions. Grow in good, indirect light, at temperatures of 18°-21°C (65°-70°F) and avoid temperature fluctuations. Under no circumstances let the temperature fall below 13°C (55°F). Water plentifully during active growth. Restrict water during the winter rest, but never allow compost to dry out. Spray with water daily in hot weather. Feed every two weeks during active growth. Grow in soil-based compost and propagate from cuttings, treated with rooting hormone and raised in a propagator. Do not move the plant when in bud or in flower, or buds will drop. Prone to attack by scale insects.

STRELITZIA

S. reginae *Bird of Paradise Flower, Crane Lily*

Large and spectacular flowering plant growing to 1-1.5 metres high. The 45 cm leaves are leathery and oval, carried on long stalks. Flowers are produced in spring and summer on 1 metre stems. They have a remarkable bird-like shape, consisting of a green horizontal bract, 18 cm long, from which appears a crest of orange and purple flowers. These are very long lasting. Surprisingly, this exotic plant is undemanding. Grow in full sun at normal room temperatures of 13°-24°C (55°-

75°F). It requires a long winter rest, kept cool and very dry. At other times Strelitzia is watered moderately, and fed every two weeks. Grow in a soil-based compost and propagate by division of large plants. They resent disturbance, and will probably stop flowering for a year after division. Can be grown from seed – if you are prepared to wait for up to 10 years for flowers! May be attacked by scale insects.

STREPTOCARPUS
(Cape Primrose, Cape Cowslip)
Group of flowering plants which occur in various forms. Some are very odd in that they form only one large leaf, and often die immediately after flowering. Others are more orthodox, producing neat clusters of tubular flowers with a flared mouth. Grow in good, indirect light at temperatures of 16°-21°C (60°-70°F). At higher temperatures provide extra humidity by standing pots in damp gravel. Water moderately and do not allow the plant to become waterlogged. Rest in the winter giving only enough water to prevent the compost from drying out. Feed every two weeks during active growth with high-potash fertiliser. Grow in a mixture of soil-based compost, leaf mould or coarse peat and coarse sand. Propagate from leaf cuttings taken in spring. Cut leaf across and plant it upright in compost, raising the cutting in a propagator. Liable to mildew and to attack by mealy bugs.
S. polyanthus
A single-leafed type which may produce a few smaller leaves. Main leaf is 30 cm long, hairy, with scalloped edges. Produces many stems with clusters of 3 cm yellow flowers with blue edges.
S. rexii
Grows in a small rosette of wrinkled, dark green leaves. Flowers are produced on 15 cm stems and are mauve, with purple lines.
S. saxorum   *False African Violet*
Spreading shrubby plant with hairy grey-green leaves with turned-down edges. Flowers are carried in small clusters on long stalks and have a white tube with violet or dark red lobes. Numerous hybrids are available.

STREPTOSOLEN
S. jamesonii (Browallia jamesonii)   *Firebush, Marmalade Bush*
A beautiful shrub for the conservatory or cool greenhouse. It grows to 2 metres, spreading widely with long arched branches. Small leaves are wrinkled and hairy. In the summer it produces clusters of orange-red trumpet-shaped flowers, about 2 cm across. Must be grown against supports. Grow in good light including some sun. Tolerates a wide range of temperatures down to 4°C (40°F) in winter. It can be put out on the patio in summer. Water moderately and feed every month during active growth. In winter keep fairly dry and prune out straggly growth. Grow in soil-based compost and propagate from tip cuttings. Liable to attack from white-fly.

STROBILANTHES
S. dyeranus (Perilepta dyerana) *Persian Shield*
Small shrub carrying 15 cm oval leaves with finely toothed edges. Leaves are dark green with a metallic purple irridescent sheen on the upper surface and are purple underneath. Pale blue, tubular flowers are produced in late summer. Strobilanthes is more attractive while young, and is usually discarded when it reaches 60 cm in height. Grow in good, indirect light, at normal room temperatures, down to a minimum of 13°C (55°F). Water moderately during active growth and feed every two weeks. In winter give only sufficient water to prevent the compost drying out. Grow in a mixture of soil-based compost and peat or leaf mould. Propagate from stem cuttings taken in spring. Treat cuttings with rooting hormone and raise in a propagator.

STROMANTHE
Genus of plants closely resembling CALATHEA and MARANTA. A creeping rhizome produces attractive, bluntly oval leaves with a small point at the tip. The leaves are patterned with a herring-bone pattern. Grow in medium shade at warm temperatures of 18°-24°C (65°-75°F). Maintain a high humidity by standing pot on moist gravel and by frequent mist spraying. Water moderately throughout the year and never allow the plant to dry out. Feed with half-strength fertiliser every month, except in winter. Grow in peat-based compost and propagate by division of the rhizome, complete with several leaves.
S. amabilis   *Peacock Plant*
Small compact plant with 18 cm leaves striped in green and grey-green. The undersides of the leaves are grey-green.
S. sanguinea
Has large glossy leaves up to 50 cm long and 15 cm broad. Upper surface is marked in light and dark green, with a deeply indented central vein. Leaf undersides are purple.

SYNGONIUM

Genus of climbing plants rather similar to PHILODENDRON. The leaves vary in shape as the plant matures and generally are most attractive in young plants. Syngoniums can be trained up supports, or allowed to trail. Leaves are glossy and tough, and in the juvenile form are deeply lobed. Adult leaves are divided into several separate leaflets. Grow Syngoniums in good, indirect light and protect from direct sun. They grow in normal room temperatures down to a minimum of 16°C (60°F) or a little less. In hot weather maintain humidity by standing the plant in a tray of damp gravel. Water moderately and feed every two weeks during active growth. In winter give only sufficient water to prevent the compost drying out. Grow in a mixture of soil-based compost and peat. Propagate from tip cuttings taken in spring. Treat with rooting hormone and raise in a propagator.

S. auritum *Five Fingers, Goosefoot Plant*
Fleshy, dark green leaves have three lobes in immature plants, while in mature plants they are divided into five distinct leaflets and are up to 35 cm long.

S. podophyllum *Arrowhead Vine*
The most common Syngonium, which produces when young 15 cm leaves shaped like arrow heads on stiffly erect leaves. In mature leaves, there are up to seven distinct leaflets. Several varieties are available, and the best are creamy-white with green edges and green speckles.

Syngonium auritum

TETRASTIGMA

T. voinieranum (Cissus voinieranum)
Chestnut Vine, Lizard Plant, Javan Grape
This large and rather coarse vine is known as Lizard Plant because of the ease with which it drops whole sections of stem and leaves. It grows very rapidly, and clings to supports with spiral tendrils. Leaves consist of several 15 cm leaflets with saw-toothed edges, and with hairy undersides. Suitable for the conservatory or cool greenhouse. Grow in strong, indirect light, at normal warm room temperatures of 16°-21°C (60°-70°F). Water moderately and feed every two weeks during active growth. In winter give only sufficient water to prevent the compost drying out. Grow in soil-based compost, and propagate from stem cuttings taken in spring or summer. Pinch out young plants to encourage bushy growth.

THUNBERGIA

(Black-eyed Susan, Clock Vine)
T. alata
Attractive flowering climber which, although a perennial, is usually discarded after flowering. Triangular, 7.5 cm leaves are carried on the long twining stems which climb any available supports. Five-petalled flat flowers are produced through the summer, coloured bright yellow or orange, with a conspicuous dark brown 'eye'. Thunbergia must be exposed to direct sun if it is to flower. Grows in normal room temperatures of 13°-18°C (55°-65°F), and will tolerate cooler conditions for brief periods. Water plentifully while in flower and feed every two weeks. If the plant is to be kept over the winter, reduce watering to a minimum. Grow in soil-based compost and propagate from seed sown in early spring.

TILLANDSIA

A large group of very diverse bromeliad plants. Some are tiny, inconspicuous plants and others are large and spectacularly coloured. They grow in rosettes, and their roots are small and used largely to support the plant, absorbing water and nourishment through their leaves. Grow in strong, indirect light at temperatures of 16°-21°C (60°-70°F) when they will grow continuously. At lower temperatures they may need a winter rest. Provide extra humidity by standing plants over moist gravel and mist spraying frequently. Do not overwater, as the feeble roots may rot. Feed with half-strength fertiliser every month, using a high-potash (tomato type) fertiliser. Grow in normal bromeliad compost and propagate from offsets. Several small species Tillandsia are marketed as 'Air Plants'. They are exclusively epiphytic and are supplied with detailed culture instructions.

T. cyanea *Pink Quill, Silver Bird*
Produces a rosette of arching 30 cm leaves, coloured grey-green with a reddish line on the underside. A strange blossom is produced in spring or summer, consisting of an elongated flattened oval of bracts 15 cm long and 7.5 cm broad, and coloured bright pink. From between the bracts, rich purple flowers emerge, maturing one at a time over a period of several weeks. The bracts persist for two months or more, then the rosette dies off, and is replaced by growth from the offsets which cluster around the base of the plant.

T. lindenii (T. lindeniana) *Blue-Flowered Torch*
Similar to **T. cyanea**, but a little larger and producing blue and white flowers from the pink bracts.

T. usneoides *Spanish Moss, Grey Beard*
Often seen in films of Louisiana swamps, festooning the trees with a trailing mossy growth. Produces long trailing stems covered in tiny silvery leaves. Usually grown from a hanging basket or fastened to a piece of cork. Needs spraying with water daily, and occasional foliar feeding with quarter-strength high-potash (tomato type) fertiliser.

TOLMIEA

T. menziesii *Piggy-Back Plant, Mother-of-Thousands*
Foliage plant carrying 7.5 cm leaves which are hairy, heart-shaped, and saw-edged. Leaves are carried on long stalks, producing a pale green hummock about 30 cm high. Tiny plantlets are produced at the leaf base and can be removed and used for propagation. A very undemanding plant, growing easily in shade or bright light, at normal cool room temperatures of 7°-18°C (45°-65°F). It should be watered moderately and fed every two weeks during active growth, and during winter watered only sufficiently to prevent the compost drying out. Grow in soil-based compost. Liable to attack by red spider mites. A variegated form is available.

TRACHYCARPUS

T. fortunei *Windmill Palm*
A large palm which remains small indoors due to its very slow growth. Produces large, fan-shaped fronds carried on long tooth-edged stems. As leaves emerge from the plant's base they are folded like a fan, and

covered with dense hair. The leaves unfold to produce many slender segments. The 'trunk' develops slowly and is covered in dense, hair-like fibre. The trunk develops as fronds die, and are cut off. Grow in full sun at normal room temperatures, down to a minimum of 7°C (45°F) in winter. Stand outdoors in mild weather. Water moderately and feed every two weeks during active growth. Reduce watering a little in winter, unless the plant is kept in cold conditions, in which case only sufficient water should be given to stop the compost drying out. Grow in soil-based compost and propagate from seed – a very slow process.

TRADESCANTIA
(Inch Plant, Wandering Jew, Spiderwort)
Popular and familiar trailing plants, with soft fleshy stems up to 40 cm in length. Leaves are pointed and soft, usually with variegated lengthwise stripes. They are grown and propagated very easily, so are usually treated as temporary plants to be discarded when they become untidy. Grow in good light, preferably including some direct sunlight, if the variegated leaf colouring is to be preserved. Grow in temperatures of 10°-16°C (50°-60°F), and do not expose to lower temperatures. Water plentifully during active growth and feed every two weeks. In winter allow the top layer of compost to dry out before watering. Grow in soil-based compost, preferably with added coarse sand to improve drainage. Propagated very easily from tip cuttings taken in spring or summer. Pinch out growing tips to encourage bushy growth.

T. albiflora
Usually only seen in the variegated forms, striped in yellow or in white and mauve. Leaves are 5 cm in length.

T. blossfeldiana
Has 8 cm dark green leaves with purplish undersides. Variegated forms mix plain cream and part-coloured leaves on the same plant. Shoots may have a pink tinge.

T. fluminensis
Very similar to **T. albiflora** but leaves have purple undersides, and stems may be purple.

T. sillamoutana
The 5 cm leaves are densely covered with white hair, which also covers the stiff wiry stems. Unlike the other species the flowers are conspicuous and are reddish-purple.

TRICHOCEREUS
Tall, erect desert cacti, branching only from the base. They can grow large, but grow very slowly in the home, and take years to reach a height of 25 cm. Stems have many angular ribs, and the areoles are large, spiny and conspicuous. Grow in full sun and place outdoors in good summer weather. Can be kept at temperatures between 5°-30°C (41°-86°F) and during winter must be rested at 10°C (50°F) or less. Water moderately during active growth and feed every two weeks with high-potash (tomato type) fertiliser. During the winter rest give only sufficient water to prevent complete drying out. Propagate from seed, or from offsets produced at the base of the plant. Dry out for three days before potting up.

T. chilensis
This species has 10-17 ribs carrying large areoles with brown spines. Stems are about 7 cm in diameter. Large specimens produce 15 cm white flowers, which open at night.

T. spachianus
Grows to about 1 metre with stems having 10-15 ribs. Areoles are soft and white with short, yellowish spines. Flowers are up to 18 cm long, coloured greenish-white, but produced only on very old plants. Often used as a vigorous stock for grafting purposes.

TULIPA
(Tulip)
Popular outdoor plants, grown indoors only temporarily. There are very many species and hybrids with widely differing shapes and colours. Plant in bulb compost in autumn, water well, and keep the pot in a cool dark place (but protect from freezing). When growth emerges, gradually bring into full light then bring into a warm room for flowering. Keep in good light and at cool temperatures of 10°-16°C (50°-60°F). Water moderately but do not feed. After flowering, plant the bulbs in the garden where they may flower again after a couple of years. When buying tulips for indoor cultivation try to purchase dwarf rockery types, which are less leggy than the usual garden forms.

VALLOTA
(Scarborough Lily)
V. speciosa (V. purpurea)
Bulbous plants very similar to the related HIPPEASTRUM. Leaves are strap-shaped and up to 60 cm long. Flowers are produced in late summer, on the 60 cm stem. They are trumpet-shaped and up to 10 cm across, carried in clusters of up to ten flowers. Flowers are usually scarlet, and white or pink varieties are also available. Plant bulb in spring, with the tip exposed above the soil-based compost. Water sparingly until growth begins, and never allow the compost to become too wet. Grow in bright light, preferably including some sun, and feed fortnightly with high-potash (tomato type) fertiliser during the spring and summer. There is no true resting period, but watering should be reduced in winter. Grow at temperatures of 13°-18°C (55°-65°F). Propagate by division in late spring, separating offset bulbs.

VANDA
An unusual epiphytic orchid in which many strap-like leaves are produced along the single stem, arranged in a flat fan. Long fleshly aerial roots are often produced. Vanda should be grown in bright, indirect light, and supplementary artificial light may be needed in winter. Grow at normal room temperatures throughout the year, and maintain high humidity by standing pot in moist gravel and spraying daily. Water plentifully at all times, and feed every month with half-strength fertiliser. Grow in standard orchid compost and propagate from cuttings – but this is a risky process since the whole plant may die.
V. cristata
Grows to about 30 cm, producing sprays of 4 cm flowers coloured greeny-yellow, with blood-red speckles and stripes.
V. teres
Very tall plant growing to 2 metres in height with short, stiff cylindrical leaves. Flowers are produced in small sprays and are 7.5 cm across, coloured white, purple and pink, with a red and yellow lip and throat.

Several other species and many hybrids are available.

VELTHEIMIA
(Forest Lily)
Attractive winter-flowering bulbous plant. The large bulbs are planted in autumn in soil-based compost mixed with coarse sand, with the top third of the bulb exposed. Large, undulating strap-like leaves are produced, followed by a long flower spike with a large cluster of tubular flowers. The plant dies back in late spring and the bulb remains dormant until the following autumn. Grow in direct sun but keep well ventilated, in a temperature range of 16°-21°C (60°-70°F). Do not allow temperatures to exceed 21°C (70°F). Water sparingly after planting and only moderately in full growth. Stop watering completely during the summer rest. Feed each month with half strength high-potash (tomato type) fertiliser during the growth phase. Propagate by separation of offsets in autumn.
V. capensis (V. glanca, V. roodeae)
Blue-green strap-like leaves, 30 cm in length, and slightly undulating. Flower stem is 30 cm high, and flowers are pink, yellow tinged.
V. viridifolia (V. bracteata)
Leaves are bright green, up to 40 cm long, and less undulating than **V. capensis**. Flower stalk is purple-blotched and up to 60 cm high. Flowers are pink, tinged with green.

VRIESIA
Spectacular rosette-forming bromeliads with a characteristic central vase or urn containing water. Leaves are stiff, broad and strap-like, and are usually striped or blotched. Flowers are produced on a spike, enveloped in brightly coloured scale-like bracts, which persist on the plant for several weeks. Flowers are produced only on older plants. Grow in strong, indirect light at temperatures of 16°-21°C (60°-70°F), and maintain high humidity by standing pot in a tray of damp gravel. Keep compost only moderately watered, and relatively dry in winter. Keep the central vase topped up with water and apply half-strength fertiliser each month during active growth, watering it into the compost and into the central vase. Grow in standard bromeliad compost, and propagate from offsets or from seed. After flowering the main rosette gradually dies off and is replaced by offsets around the base.
V. fenestralis (Tillandsia fenestralis) *Netted Vriesia*
Produces a broad rosette up to 60 cm across, with leaves 5 cm across, marked with a conspicuous network of veins, and with purple blotches underneath. Flowers are yellow within greenish bracts.
V. hieroglyphica *King of Bromeliads*
Large rosette up to 75 cm across, which is bright green with purplish-brown irregular bands. A 60 cm stalk carries many small yellow flowers and is branched heavily, unlike other Vriesias.

V. splendens (V. speciosa)   *Flaming Sword*
A 60 cm rosette of tough leaves which are dark green with purplish cross bands. Flower stalk is 60 cm tall, with brilliant red bracts, from which the yellow flowers are produced.

Several other species are available, but most lack the attractive leaf markings of the species described above.

VUYLSTEKEARA

Hybrid orchids of obscure ancestry. In form and cultural needs they closely resemble ODONTOGLOSSUM. Vuylstekeara grows in normal room conditions at 10°-16°C (50°-60°F), and is suitable for the beginner, flowering relatively easily. Unlike most orchids it is capable of adapting to varying environments.

Veltheimia capensis

× **WILSONARA**

Spectacular hybrid orchid which produces a 'Christmas Tree'-shaped flower spike containing very large numbers of flowers. Its foliage grows from plump psuedo-bulbs, and the flower spike is produced from their bases. Grow in good, indirect light protecting from sun. Grow in temperatures of 10°-13°C (50°-55°F) and feed at monthly intervals. Keep moderately watered throughout the year. Grow in standard orchid compost and propagate by division in spring or autumn. Several varieties are available with flowers in many colours.

Wisteria

YUCCA

Y. aloifolia *Boundary Plant, Dagger Plant*

The only member of this large genus commonly grown indoors. Yuccas are imported as lengths of sawn-off woody stems, which are rooted to produce new green foliage. They have sword-like leaves arranged in a rosette and larger leaves may droop. The trunk grows to 2 metres or more, but develops quite slowly. Rosettes carry sharply tipped, deep green leaves up to 60 cm long. Variegated forms are sometimes available, striped longitudinally in yellow, white, or pink. Grow in bright light, including some sun, and put outdoors in mild weather. Yuccas thrive at temperatures of 10°-21°C (50°-70°F), and should be rested in winter, watering only when compost feels very dry. Water moderately during active growth and feed every two weeks. Grow in soil-based compost and propagate from offsets, which are produced only occasionally.

Vanda arachnoides

ZANTEDESCHIA

(Richardia)   *Arum, Calla Lily*

Attractive flowering plants growing from begonia-like rhizomes. Large leaves are produced which are usually arrow-shaped. Flowers consist of an erect, finger-like spadix around which is wrapped a large, showy spathe. The flower is carried on a long stem. These are marsh plants, and their special needs must be met for successful cultivation. Plant in soil-based compost and keep moist until growth appears. Feed every two weeks and water plentifully until flowering, after which watering is reduced until the leaves wither. The plants can then be rested with only occasional watering. When in active growth, Zantedeschias can be stood in a dish of water – one of the very few plants to withstand water-logging. In most cases the rest period is in summer. Propagate by removing offsets during the rest period, or from seed (which is a long, slow process).

Z. aethiopica *White Arum Lily*

The largest species, with leaves up to 45 cm long, carried on long stalks. The flower is carried on a fleshy 1 metre stem, and has a yellow spadix wrapped round with a creamy white 20 cm spathe.

Z. elliottiana   *Golden Calla*

This species has 30 cm leaves heavily dappled with translucent silvery-grey speckles. Flowers are produced on 60 cm stems, and are golden yellow tinged with green.

Z. rehmannii   *Pink Calla*

Slender 30 cm leaves with translucent silvery streaks. The flowers are pink, red or purplish. Many hybrid plants are available, in varying colours and forms.

ZEBRINA

(Wandering Jew)

Z. pendula (Cyanotis rittata)

Very similar to the related TRADESCANTIA, Zebrina is a variegated trailing plant. Its pointed oval leaves are 5 cm long and have a striped irridescent upper surface, with silvery bands, and are purple-red underneath. They are fast-growing plants with inconspicuous flowers. Grow in bright light, to preserve the attractive colouring, at temperatures of 13°-18°C (55°-65°F). Water moderately and feed every two weeks during active growth. In winter water only sufficiently to prevent the compost drying out. Grow in soil-based compost, and propagate with tip cuttings which root very easily. Pinch out growing tips to encourage bushy growth. Discard old plants when they become leggy or their leaves drop.

ZYGOCACTUS

See SCHLUMBERGIA

PLANT NAME	PLANT TYPE		LIGHT			COMPOST						HEIGHT			REMARKS
	FLOWERING	FOLIAGE	FULL SUN	INDIRECT	SHADE	PEAT-BASED	SOIL-BASED	CACTUS	BROMELIAD	ORCHID	OTHER	UP TO 30cm	30-60cm	OVER 60cm	
Abutilon Hybridum	●	●	●	●			●							●	
Abutilon Megapotamicum	●		●	●			●							●	
Abutilon Pictum	●	●	●	●			●							●	
Acacia Armata	●		●	●			●							●	
Acalypha Hispida	●			●		●	●							●	
Acalypha Wilkesiana		●												●	
Acer Palmatum		●	●			●	●							●	Patio only
Achimenes Erecta	●			●		●							●		
Achimenes Grandiflora	●					●							●		
Achimenes Longiflora	●					●							●		
Acokanthera Spectabilis	●			●		●							●		
Acorus Gramineus		●		●			●					●			
Adenium Obesum	●		●			●	●					●			
Adiantum Capillus-Veneris		●			●	●	●					●			
Adiantum Hispidulum		●			●	●	●					●			
Adiantum Raddianum		●			●	●	●						●		
Aechmea Chantinii	●	●		●					●				●		
Aechmea Fasciata	●	●		●					●				●		
Aechmea Fulgens	●	●		●					●				●		
Aeonium Arboreum		●	●					●						●	
Aeonium Haworthii	●	●						●					●		
Aeonium Tubuliforme		●						●				●			
Aeonium Undulatum		●						●						●	
Aerides Fieldingii	●			●						●			●		
Aeschynanthus Lobbianus	●	●		●		●									Trailing
Aeschynanthus Marmoratus		●		●		●									Trailing
Aeschynanthus Speciosus	●	●		●		●									Trailing
Agapanthus Africanus	●		●				●							●	
Agapanthus Praecox	●		●				●							●	
Agave Americana	●	●	●	●			●							●	
Agave Filifera	●	●	●	●			●							●	
Agave Passiflora		●	●				●					●			
Agave Victoria-Reginae		●	●				●						●		
Aglaonema Commutatum		●		●			●					●			
Aglaonema Crispum		●		●			●						●		
Aglaonema Pseudobracteum		●		●			●							●	
Allamanda Cathartica	●			●			●								Climber
Alocasia Indica		●		●		●	●							●	
Alocasia Macrorrhiza		●		●		●	●							●	
Alocasia Sanderiana		●		●		●	●							●	
Aloe Arborescens		●	●					●						●	
Aloe Aristata		●		●				●				●			
Aloe Jacunda		●	●					●				●			
Aloe Variegata		●						●				●			
Alteranthera Amoena		●		●		●						●			
Amaryllis Belladonna	●		●	●		●							●		
Amorphophallus Bulbifer	●				●	●								●	
Amorphophallus Rivieri	●	●			●	●								●	
Ananas Bractiatus	●	●		●		●								●	
Ananas Comosus	●	●		●		●							●		
Anchusa Capensis	●		●			●							●		Annual
Angraecum Eburneum	●			●						●			●		Warm greenhouse
Angraecum Sesquipedale	●			●						●				●	Warm greenhouse
Anigozanthus Manglesii	●	●		●			●							●	
Anthurium Andreanum	●	●			●	●								●	
Anthurium Crystallinum	●	●			●	●							●		
Anthurium Scherzeranum	●	●			●	●							●		
Antigon Leptopus	●		●				●								Greenhouse, climber
Aphelandra Chamissoniana	●	●			●	●	●						●		
Aphelandra Squarrosia	●	●			●	●	●						●		
Aporocactus Flagelliformis	●	●				●	●								Trailer
Aporocactus Mallisonii	●	●				●	●								Trailer
Araucaria Excelsa		●			●		●							●	
Araujia Sericofera	●			●			●								Climber
Ardisia Crispa/Crenata		●		●			●							●	Red berries
Aristolochia Altissima	●			●			●								Greenhouse, climber
Aristolochia Elegans	●			●			●								Greenhouse, climber
Arthropodium Cirrhatum	●			●			●						●		
Arundinaria		●		●		●	●						●	●	Various types
Asclepias Curassavica	●			●		●								●	
Asparagus Asparagoides		●		●			●							●	Climber
Asparagus Densiflorus Sprengeri		●		●			●								Trailer
Asparagus Densiflorus Myersii		●		●			●						●		
Asparagus Densiflorus Setaceus		●		●			●						●		
Aspidistra Eliator		●			●		●						●		
Asplenium Bulbiferum		●			●	●							●		
Asplenium Daucifolium		●			●	●							●		
Asplenium Nidus		●			●	●								●	

PLANT NAME	PLANT TYPE		LIGHT			COMPOST						HEIGHT			REMARKS
	FLOWERING	FOLIAGE	FULL SUN	INDIRECT	SHADE	PEAT-BASED	SOIL-BASED	CACTUS	BROMELIAD	ORCHID	OTHER	UP TO 30cm	30-60cm	OVER 60cm	
Astrophytum Asterias	●	●	●					●				●			
Astrophytum Myriostigma	●	●	●					●				●			
Astrophytum Ornatum	●	●	●					●				●			
Aucuba Japonica		●		●	●			●						●	Also on patio
Babiana Stricta	●			●			●						●		
Barleria Lupina	●	●		●		●	●							●	Warm greenhouse
Bauhinia Variegata	●		●				●							●	
Beaucarnia Recurvata		●		●	●		●							●	
Beaumontia Grandiflora	●			●			●								Rambler, warm greenhouse
Begonia Boweri	●	●		●			●					●			
Begonia 'Cleopatra'	●	●	●				●					●			
Begonia 'Lucerna'	●	●		●			●							●	
Begonia Maculata	●	●		●			●							●	
Begonia Masonica		●			●		●						●		
Begonia Rex Hybrids		●		●			●					●			
Begonia Semperflorens	●		●				●					●			
Begonia Hiemalis	●			●			●						●		
Begonia Tuberhybrida	●		●				●						●		
Beleropone Guttata	●				●		●							●	
Bertolonia Maculata	●	●		●			●						●		Trailer
Bertolonia Marmorata	●	●		●			●						●		Trailer
Bifrenaria Harrisonii	●			●						●			●		
Billbergia Nutans	●	●	●						●				●		
Billbergia × Windii	●	●	●						●				●		
Blechnum Brasiliense		●			●				●					●	
Blechnum Gibbum		●			●				●					●	
Bougainvillea × Buttiana	●		●				●								Climber
Bougainvillea Glabra	●		●				●								Climber
Bouvardia × Domestica	●				●		●							●	
Brassolaeliacattleya Hybrids	●			●						●				●	
Breynia		●		●		●								●	
Browallia Speciosa	●		●				●								Annual, trailer
Browallia Viscosa	●		●				●								Annual, trailer
Brunfelsia Pauciflora	●						●						●		
Bryophyllum Daigremontianum		●	●					●						●	
Bryophyllum Tubiflorum		●	●					●						●	
Bulbophyllum × Hybrids	●			●						●		●		●	
Buxus Sempervirens		●	●				●						●		Patio only
Caladium × Hortulanum		●		●		●							●		
Calanthe Vestita	●			●			●						●		
Calathea Bachemiana		●			●	●							●		
Calathea Insignis		●			●	●								●	
Calathea Makoyana		●			●	●								●	
Calathea Ornata		●			●	●							●		
Calathea Picturata		●			●	●						●			
Calathea Zebrina		●			●	●							●		
Calceolaria × Herbeohybrida	●			●			●					●			Annual
Callistemon Citrinus	●		●				●							●	
Camellia Japonica	●			●		●								●	Patio only
Campanula Isophylla	●			●			●								Trailer
Canna × Hybrida	●		●				●							●	Also for patio
Cantua Buxifolia	●			●			●								Climber
Capsicum Anuum			●				●						●		Red fruit
Carex Morrowii		●					●					●			
Carpobrotus Edulis	●	●	●				●								Trailer
Caryota Mitis		●		●			●							●	
Caryota Uris		●		●			●							●	
Catharanthus Roseus	●		●				●						●		
Cattleya Aurantiaca	●			●						●		●			
Cattleya Bowringiana	●			●						●			●		
Cattleya Intermedia	●			●						●			●		
Cattleya Labiata	●			●						●			●		
Cattleya Triannaei	●			●						●			●		
Celosia Argentia	●		●	●		●	●						●		
Cephalocereus Senilis		●	●					●						●	
Cereus Jamacaru	●	●	●					●						●	
Cereus Peruvianus	●	●	●					●						●	
Ceropegia Woodi		●	●					●							Trailer
Chamaecyparis Spp.		●	●				●							●	Patio only
Chamaecereus Silvestrii	●	●	●					●				●			
Chamaedora Elegans		●			●		●							●	
Chamaedora Erumpens		●			●		●							●	
Chamaerops Humilis		●	●				●							●	
Chlorophytum Comosum		●	●				●						●		
Chrysalidocarpus Lutescens		●	●				●							●	
Chrysanthemum Frutescens	●	●	●				●							●	
Chrysanthemum × Morifolium	●	●	●				●					●			
Cibotium Schiedei		●		●		●								●	

PLANT NAME	PLANT TYPE		LIGHT			COMPOST						HEIGHT			REMARKS
	FLOWERING	FOLIAGE	FULL SUN	INDIRECT	SHADE	PEAT-BASED	SOIL-BASED	CACTUS	BROMELIAD	ORCHID	OTHER	UP TO 30cm	30-60cm	OVER 60cm	
Cineraria × Hybrids	●			●			●					●			
Cissus Antartica		●		●	●		●							●	Climber/rambler
Cissus Discolor		●		●			●								Climber/rambler
Cissus Striatus		●		●			●								Climber/trailer
Citrus Limon	●		●				●							●	Fruit
Citrus Mitis	●		●				●							●	Fruit
Citrus Sinensis	●		●				●							●	Fruit
Cleistocactus Strausii	●	●	●					●						●	
Clematis Hybrids	●		●				●								Climber, patio only
Clerodendron Thomsoniae	●			●			●							●	Climber
Cleyera Japonica		●		●			●							●	
Clivia Miniata	●		●				●						●		
Cobea Scandens	●		●	●			●								Climber, also for patio
Cocos Wedelliana		●		●			●							●	
Codiaeum Variegatum		●		●			●							●	
Coelogyne Cristata	●			●						●			●		
Coelogyne Ochracea	●			●						●			●		
Coelogyne Pandurata	●			●						●				●	
Coffea Arabica	●	●		●			●							●	Red berries
Coleus Blumei		●	●	●			●						●		
Columnea × Banksii	●			●		●									Trailer
Columnea Gloriosa	●			●		●									Trailer
Columnea Linearis	●			●		●							●		
Columnea Microphylla	●			●		●									Trailer, very large
Conophytum Bilubum	●	●	●					●				●			
Conophytum Frutescens	●	●	●					●				●			
Cordyline Australis		●	●	●		●	●							●	
Cordyline Indivisa		●	●	●		●	●							●	
Cordyline Terminalis		●	●	●		●	●						●		
Cotyledon Orbiculatum	●	●	●					●					●		
Cotyledon Undulata	●	●	●					●				●			
Crassula Arborescens		●	●					●						●	
Crassula Argentea		●	●					●					●		
Crassula Deceptrix	●	●	●					●				●			
Crassula Falcata	●	●	●					●				●			
Crassula Lycopodioides		●	●					●				●			
Crassula Rupestris	●	●	●					●				●			Sprawling or trailer
Crinum × Powelli	●		●					●						●	
Crocus	●			●			●					●			Keep cool indoors
Crossandra Infundibuliformis	●			●			●						●		
Cryptanthus Acaulis		●		●	●				●			●			
Cryptanthus Bivittatus		●		●	●				●			●			
Cryptanthus Bromelioides		●		●	●				●			●			
Cryptanthus Fosterianus		●		●	●				●				●		
Cryptanthus Zonatus		●		●	●				●			●			
Ctenanthe Lubbersiana		●		●			●							●	
Ctenanthe Oppenheimiana		●		●			●							●	
Cuphea Hyssopifolia	●		●	●			●						●		
Cuphea Ignea	●		●	●			●						●		
Cyanotis Kewensis		●		●				●							Trailer
Cyanotis Somaliensis		●		●				●							Trailer
Cycas Revoluta		●	●	●				●						●	Very slow growing
Cyclamen Persicum	●			●			●					●			
Cymbidium Spp.	●			●						●			●		
Cyperus Altenifolius		●	●	●			●							●	Keep very wet
Cyperus Papyrus		●	●	●			●							●	Keep very wet
Cyrtomium Falcatum		●			●		●							●	Added peat in compost
Darlingtonia Californica	●	●	●	●							●			●	
Datura Cornigera	●			●			●							●	
Datura Sanguinea	●			●			●							●	
Datura Suaveolens	●			●			●							●	
Davallia Canariensis		●			●	●							●		
Davallia Trichomanoides		●			●	●							●		
Dendrobium Infundibulum	●			●						●			●		
Dendrobium Kingianum	●			●						●		●			
Dendrobium Nobile	●			●						●				●	
Dichorisandra Reginae		●		●			●							●	Upright or sprawling
Dieffenbachia Amoena		●		●			●							●	
Dieffenbachia Camilla		●		●			●						●		
Dieffenbachia Exotica		●		●			●						●		
Dieffenbachia Picta		●		●			●							●	
Dionea Muscipula		●	●								●	●			
Dioscorea Discolor		●	●				●								Climber
Dipladenia Splendens	●			●			●								Climber
Dizygotheca Elegantissima		●			●		●							●	
Dracaena Deremensis		●		●			●							●	
Dracaena Draco		●	●				●							●	
Dracaena Fragrans		●		●			●							●	

PLANT NAME	FLOWERING	FOLIAGE	FULL SUN	INDIRECT	SHADE	PEAT-BASED	SOIL-BASED	CACTUS	BROMELIAD	ORCHID	OTHER	UP TO 30cm	30-60cm	OVER 60cm	REMARKS
Dracaena Marginata		●		●			●							●	
Dracaena Sanderana		●		●			●								
Dracaena Succulosa		●		●			●					●			
Drosera Spp.	●	●	●								●	●			
Echevaria Agavoides	●	●	●					●				●			
Echevaria Derenbergii	●	●	●					●				●			
Echevaria Gibbiflora		●	●					●					●		
Echevaria Harmsii	●	●	●					●						●	
Echevaria Setosa	●	●	●					●				●			
Echinocactus Grusonii		●	●					●						●	Grows very slowly
Echinocactus Horizonthalonius	●	●	●					●				●			
Echinocereus Knippelianus	●	●	●					●				●			
Echinocereus Pectinatus	●	●	●					●				●			
Echinocereus Pentalophus Pr	●	●	●					●				●			Trailing or sprawling
Echinopsis Eyriesii	●	●	●					●				●			
Echinopsis Multiplex	●	●	●					●				●			
Elettaria Cardamomum		●			●		●							●	
Epidendrum Ibaguense	●			●						●				●	
Epidendrum Pentotis	●			●						●			●		
Epidendrum Vitellinum	●			●						●			●		
Epiphyllum Spp.	●	●		●		●								●	Added sand/leaf mould
Episcia Cupreata	●	●		●		●									Creeping form
Episcia Dianthiflora	●	●		●		●									Creeping form
Episcia Reptans	●	●		●		●									Creeping form
Erica Canaliculata	●			●		●								●	
Erica × Hyemanalis	●			●		●							●		
Eucalyptus Globulosus		●	●				●							●	Also for patio
Eucalyptus Gunii		●	●				●							●	Also for patio
Eucharis Grandiflora	●				●		●						●		
Eucomis Pole-Evansii	●			●			●							●	
Eucomis Zambesiaca	●			●			●						●		
Euonymus Japonica		●	●				●							●	Also for patio
Euphorbia Fulgens	●		●	●			●							●	Rambler
Euphorbia Milii	●		●					●						●	
Euphorbia Pulcherrima	●			●				●						●	
Euphorbia Horrida		●	●					●				●			
Euphorbia Obesa		●	●					●				●			
Euphorbia Pseudocactus		●	●					●						●	
Euphorbia Resinifera		●	●					●				●			
Euphorbia Tirucalli		●	●					●						●	
Exacum Affina	●		●	●			●					●			
× Fatshedera		●			●		●							●	
Fatsia Japonica		●		●			●							●	
Faucaria Felina	●	●	●					●				●			
Faucaria Tigrina	●	●	●					●				●			
Faucaria Tuberculosa	●	●	●					●				●			
Ferocactus Acanthodes		●	●					●				●			
Ferocactus Latispinus	●	●	●					●				●			
Ficus Benghalensis		●		●			●							●	
Ficus Benjamina		●		●			●							●	
Ficus Buxifolia		●		●			●							●	
Ficus Deltoides		●		●			●						●		
Ficus Elastica		●		●			●							●	
Ficus Lyrata		●		●			●								
Ficus Pumila		●		●		●						●			Creeping or trailing
Ficus Radicans		●		●		●						●			Creeping or trailing
Fittonia Argyroneura		●			●	●						●			Creeping
Fittonia Verschafeltii		●			●	●						●			Creeping
Fortunella Spp.	●		●				●							●	Orange fruit, added peat/leaf mould
Freesia	●			●			●					●			Keep cool
Fuchsia Spp.	●		●				●							●	Also for patio
Gardenia Jasminoides	●			●		●									Climber, soft water
Gasteria Liliputana		●		●				●				●			
Gasteria Maculata		●	●	●				●				●			
Gasteria Verrucosa		●	●	●				●				●			
Geognanthus Undulatus	●	●		●				●				●			
Gloriosa Rothschildiana	●			●		●									Climber
Graptopetalum Pachyphyllum	●	●	●					●				●			
Graptopetalum Paraguayensis	●	●	●					●				●			
Grevillea Robusta		●		●		●								●	
Guzmania Lingulata	●	●		●					●				●		
Guzmania Monostachya	●	●		●					●				●		
Guzmania Zahnii	●	●		●					●				●		
Gymnocalycium Baldianum	●	●	●					●				●			
Gymnocalycium Bruchii	●	●	●					●				●			
Gymnocalycium Denudatum	●	●	●					●				●			
Gymnocalycium Mihanovichii	●	●	●					●				●			
Gynura Aurantica		●	●				●						●		Sprawling form

PLANT NAME	FLOWERING	FOLIAGE	FULL SUN	INDIRECT	SHADE	PEAT-BASED	SOIL-BASED	CACTUS	BROMELIAD	ORCHID	OTHER	UP TO 30cm	30-60cm	OVER 60cm	REMARKS
Gynura Sarmentosa		●	●				●								Trailer
Haemanthus Albiflos	●		●				●						●		
Haemanthus Coccineus	●		●				●						●		
Haemanthus Katherinae	●		●				●						●		
Haemanthus Multiflorus	●		●				●						●		
Hamacactus Hamatacanthus	●	●	●					●					●		
Hamacactus Setispinus	●	●					●					●			
Haworthia Attenuata		●		●				●				●			
Haworthia Margatifolia		●		●				●				●			
Haworthia Maughanii		●	●					●				●			
Haworthia Rheinwardtii		●		●				●				●			
Hedera Canariensis		●		●			●								Also for patio, climber
Hedera Helix		●		●			●								Also for patio, climber
Hedychium Spp.	●			●			●							●	
Heliocereus Speciosus	●	●	●				●								Sprawling form, added leaf mould/sand
Heliotropium × Hybridum	●		●			●	●					●			
Helxine Soleirolii		●		●	●	●	●								Creeping form
Heptapleurum Arboricola		●		●			●							●	
Hibiscus Rosa-Sinensis	●		●				●							●	
Hibiscus Schizopetalus	●		●				●							●	
Hippeastrum Spp.	●		●				●							●	
Hosta × Hybrids		●		●	●	●	●							●	Also for patio
Howea Belmoreana		●	●	●	●		●							●	
Howea Forsterana		●		●	●		●							●	
Hoya Australis	●	●	●	●		●	●								Climber/trailer
Hoya Bella	●	●	●	●		●	●								Climber/trailer
Hoya Carnosa	●	●	●	●		●	●								
Hyacintha × Hybrids	●		●	●		●						●			
Hydrangea Macrophylla	●			●			●						●		
Hylocereus Undatus	●	●		●			●							●	Sprawling form, added peat/sand
Hymenocallis Spp.	●			●			●						●		
Hypocyrta Glabra	●	●		●	●		●						●		
Hypoestes Phyllostachya		●		●			●					●			
Impatiens Repens	●			●			●								Creeping form
Impatiens Walleriana	●			●			●						●		
Ipomea × Hybrids	●		●			●	●								Annual climber, indoors or patio
Iresine Herbstii		●	●				●						●		
Iris Pallida	●			●			●					●			
Iris Reticulata	●			●			●						●		
Ixora Coccinea	●	●		●							●			●	Peat/leaf mould/sand
Jacaranda Mimosifolia		●	●				●							●	
Jacobinia Carnea	●		●				●							●	
Jacobinia Pauciflora	●		●				●						●		
Jasminum Mesnyi	●		●				●								Vigorous climber
Jasminum Officinale	●		●				●								Vigorous climber
Jasminum Polyanthum	●		●				●								Vigorous climber
Juniperus Spp.		●	●	●		●	●					●	●	●	Patio only
Kalanchoe Blossfeldiana	●		●	●			●					●			Added sand
Kalanchoe Marmorata		●	●				●					●			Added sand
Kalanchoe Pumila		●	●				●					●			Added sand
Kalanchoe Tomentosa		●	●				●					●			Added sand
Kohleria Erianthus	●		●	●		●								●	Added sand and lime
Kohleria × 'Rongo'	●		●	●		●						●			
Lachenalia Aloides	●		●	●		●						●			
Laelia Anceps	●			●						●				●	
Laelia Cinnabarina	●			●						●				●	
Laelia Purpurata	●			●						●				●	
Laeliocattleya × Hybrids	●			●						●				●	
Lantana Camara	●		●	●			●						●		
Lapageria Rosea	●			●		●									Climber
Laurus Nobilis		●	●	●			●								Patio only
Lilium Auratum	●			●		●								●	
Lithops Spp.	●	●	●					●				●			
Livistona Spp.		●		●	●		●					●		●	
Lobivia Aurea	●	●	●					●				●			
Lobivia Hertrichiana	●	●	●					●				●			
Lycaste Aromatica	●			●						●			●		
Lycaste Cruenta	●			●						●			●		
Mamillaria Bocasana	●	●	●					●				●			
Mamillaria Elegans	●	●	●					●				●			
Mamillaria Erythrosperma	●	●	●					●				●			
Mamillaria Hahniana	●	●	●					●				●			
Mamillaria Zeilmanniana	●	●	●					●				●			
Manettia Bicolor	●		●				●								Climber
Maranta Leuconeura		●			●		●							●	
Medinilla Magnifica	●			●			●							●	Warm greenhouse, added leaf mould/sand
Miltonia Clowesii	●			●						●				●	
Miltonia Spectabilis	●	●		●						●			●		

PLANT NAME	FLOWERING	FOLIAGE	FULL SUN	INDIRECT	SHADE	PEAT-BASED	SOIL-BASED	CACTUS	BROMELIAD	ORCHID	OTHER	UP TO 30cm	30-60cm	OVER 60cm	REMARKS
Miltonia Warscewiczii	●			●						●			●		
Mimosa Pudica	●	●	●				●							●	
Monstera Deliciosa		●		●			●								Climber, added leaf mould
Musa Accuminata Cav.		●		●			●							●	Added leaf mould
Musa Coccinea		●		●			●							●	Added leaf mould
Myrtus Communis	●	●	●				●						●		Added peat
Narcissus Spp.	●			●		●						●	●		
Neoregelia Carolinae		●	●						●				●		
Neoregelia Spectabilis		●	●						●				●		
Nephrolepis Cordifolia		●			●		●						●		Added peat
Nephrolepis Exaltata		●			●		●							●	
Nerine Bowdenii	●			●			●						●		
Nerium Oleander	●		●				●							●	
Nertera Granadensis		●	●	●			●								Orange berries, added peat/sand
Nidularium Fulgens		●							●				●		
Nidularium Innocenti		●							●				●		
Notocactus Leninghausii	●	●	●					●					●		Very slow growing
Notocactus Ottonis	●	●	●					●				●			
Odontioda	●			●						●			●		
Odontoglossum Bictoniense	●			●						●				●	
Odontoglossum Crispum	●			●						●				●	
Odontoglossum Grande	●			●						●				●	
Odontoglossum Pulchellum	●			●						●			●		
× Odontonia	●			●						●			●		
Oncidium Ornithorhyncum	●			●						●				●	
Oncidium Papilio	●			●						●			●		Warm greenhouse
Oplismenus Hirtellus		●	●			●							●		
Opuntia Basilaris	●	●	●					●					●		
Opuntia Cylindrica		●	●					●						●	
Opuntia Microdasys		●	●					●				●			
Opuntia Robusta		●	●					●						●	
Opuntia Salmina	●	●	●					●				●			
Osmanthus Heterophylla		●	●				●							●	
Pachyphytum Amethystinum		●	●					●				●			
Pachyphytum Oviferum		●	●					●				●			
Pachypodium Lamerei		●	●					●				●			
Pachystachys Lutea	●			●			●						●		
Palisota Elizabetha		●			●		●						●		
Pandanus Baptiste		●	●				●							●	
Pandanus Veitchii		●	●				●							●	
Paphiopedalum Callosum	●			●						●			●		
Paphiopedalum Hirsutissimum	●			●						●			●		
Paphiopedalum Insigne	●			●						●			●		
Paphiopedalum Spiceranum	●			●						●		●			
Paphiopedalum Venustum	●			●						●			●		
Parodia Aureispina	●	●	●					●				●			
Parodia Chrysacanthion	●	●	●					●				●			
Parodia Sanguiniflora	●	●	●					●				●			
Passiflora Caerulea	●		●				●								Climber, also for patio
Pedilanthus Tithymaloides		●	●	●			●								Trailing, added sand
Pelargonium Domesticum	●		●				●						●		
Pelargonium Hortorum	●		●				●							●	
Pelargonium Peltatum	●		●				●							●	Trailer
Pelargonium (Scented Leaved Types)		●	●				●							●	
Pellea Rotundifolia		●			●	●						●			
Pellionia Daveaunea		●		●			●								Creeping form, added peat/leaf mould
Pellionia Pulchra		●		●			●								Creepers form, added peat/leaf mould
Pentas Lanceolata		●	●				●						●		
Peperomia Argyreia		●		●		●						●			
Peperomia Caperata		●		●		●						●			
Peperomia Magnoliifolia		●	●			●						●			
Peperomia Scandens		●		●		●									Climber/trailer
Pereskia Aculeata	●	●	●				●	●						●	
Persea Americana		●		●			●							●	
Petunia × Hybrids	●		●				●					●			Patio only
Phalaenopsis Schilleriana	●	●	●							●			●		
Phalaenopsis Stuartiana	●	●	●							●			●		
Philodendron Bipennifolium		●		●			●								Added peat. Climber
Philodendron Bipinnatafidum		●		●			●							●	Added peat.
Philodendron × Burgundy		●		●			●								Added peat. Climber
Philodendron Melanochrysum		●		●			●								Added peat. Climber
Philodendron Scandens		●		●			●								Added peat. Climber or trailer
Phoenix Canariensis		●		●			●							●	
Phoenix Dactylifera		●		●			●							●	
Phoenix Roebelanii		●		●			●							●	
Phyllitis Scolopendrium		●			●	●							●		
Pilea Cadieri		●			●	●	●						●		
Pilea Involucrata		●			●	●	●					●			

PLANT NAME	PLANT TYPE		LIGHT			COMPOST						HEIGHT			REMARKS
	FLOWERING	FOLIAGE	FULL SUN	INDIRECT	SHADE	PEAT-BASED	SOIL-BASED	CACTUS	BROMELIAD	ORCHID	OTHER	UP TO 30cm	30-60cm	OVER 60cm	
Pilea Nummulariifolia		●			●	●	●								Creeping form
Pilea Spruceana		●		●		●	●								Creeping form
Pinguicula	●	●		●							●	●			
Piper Crocatum		●		●			●								Climber or trailing
Pisonia Umbellifera		●		●			●							●	Greenhouse only
Pittosporum Tenuifolium		●	●				●							●	Keep cool. Also for patio
Pittosporum Tobira		●	●				●							●	Keep cool. Also for patio
Platycerium Bifurcatum		●		●	●	●				●			●	●	
Platycerium Grande		●		●	●					●				●	
Plectranthus Australis		●	●				●					●			
Plectranthus Coleoides		●	●				●					●			Also trailing
Plectranthus Oertendahlii		●	●				●								Trailer
Pleione Bulbococodioides	●			●						●			●		
Pleione Forrestii	●			●						●			●		
Pleomele Reflexa		●		●			●							●	Added peat. Very slow growing
Plumbago Auriculata	●		●				●								Climber
Plumeria Rubra	●			●			●							●	
Poducarpus Macrophyllus		●		●			●							●	
Polypodium Aureum		●			●		●						●		Added leaf mould
Polyscias Balfouriana		●		●			●							●	
Polyscias Guilfoylei		●		●			●							●	
Primula × Kewensis	●		●	●			●					●			Keep cool
Primula Malacoides	●		●	●			●					●			
Primula Obconica	●		●	●			●					●			
Primula Sinensis	●		●	●			●					●			
Pseuderanthemum Atropurpureum	●	●		●			●							●	
Pteris Cretica		●		●		●							●		
Pteris Ensiformis		●		●		●							●		
Pteris Tremula		●		●		●								●	
Punica Granatum	●	●	●	●			●							●	Yellow fruit
Rebutia Albiflora	●	●	●					●				●			
Rebutia Callianthus	●	●	●					●				●			
Rebutia Miniscula	●	●	●					●				●			
Rebutia Senilis	●	●	●					●				●			
Rhapis Spp.		●		●			●							●	
Rhipsalidopsis Gaertneri	●	●		●			●								Trailing. Added sand
Rhipsalidopsis Rosea	●	●		●			●								Trailing. Added sand
Rhipsalis Cassutta	●	●		●		●									Trailing. Added sand. White berries
Rhipsalis Crispata	●	●		●											Trailing. Added sand. White berries
Rhipsalis Pilocarpa	●	●		●											Trailing. Added sand. White berries
Rhipsalis Houlletiana	●	●		●											Trailing. Added sand. White berries
Rhododendron Obtusum		●		●		●								●	Keep cool
Rhododendron Simsii		●		●		●								●	Keep cool
Rhoeo Spathacea		●		●		●	●							●	
Rhoicissus Capensis		●		●	●		●								Trailing or climber
Rhoicissus Rhomboidea		●		●	●		●								Trailing or climber
Rhyncostylus Retusa	●			●						●			●		Trailing blossom
Ricinus Communis		●		●			●							●	
Rivina Humilis		●		●			●								Creeping. Red berries
Rochea Coccinea	●	●	●					●					●		
Rochea Versicolor	●	●	●					●					●		
Ruellia Makoyana	●	●		●			●								Trailer. Added peat
Saintpaulia × Hybrids	●			●		●						●			
Saintpaulia Confusa	●			●		●						●			
Saintpaulia Grandifolia	●			●		●						●			Creeping form
Saintpaulia Ionantha	●			●		●						●			
Saintpaulia Schumensis	●			●		●						●			
Sanchezia Nobilis	●	●		●			●							●	
Sansevieria Cylindrica		●	●				●							●	Added sand
Sansevieria Liberica		●	●				●							●	Added sand
Sansevieria Trifasciata		●	●				●							●	Added sand
Sansevieria Trifasciata 'Hahnii'		●	●				●					●			Added sand
Sarracenia Spp.	●	●		●							●	●	●	●	
Saxifraga Stolonifera		●		●			●					●			Also creeping/trailing
Schefflera Actinophylla		●		●			●							●	
Schefflera Digitata		●		●			●							●	
Schefflera Venusta		●		●			●							●	
Schizocentron Elegans	●	●		●			●								Added peat. Trailing or creeping
Schlumbergia × Hybrids	●	●		●		●							●		Added sand. Also trailing
Schlumbergia Truncata	●	●		●		●							●		Added sand. Also trailing
Scilla Adamii	●		●				●					●			
Scilla Ovallifolia	●			●			●					●			
Scilla Tubergeniana	●		●				●					●			
Scilla Violacea	●	●	●				●					●			
Scindapsus Aureus		●		●			●								Climber/Trailing
Scindapsus Pictus		●		●			●								Climber/Trailing
Scirpus Curnuus		●		●	●		●					●			Part trailing
Sedum Adolphi	●	●	●					●				●			

PLANT NAME	FLOWERING	FOLIAGE	FULL SUN	INDIRECT	SHADE	PEAT-BASED	SOIL-BASED	CACTUS	BROMELIAD	ORCHID	OTHER	UP TO 30cm	30-60cm	OVER 60cm	REMARKS
Sedum Lineare	●	●	●					●				●			Prostrate form
Sedum Morganium	●	●	●					●				●			Trailing
Sedum Rubrotinctum		●	●					●				●			
Sedum Sieboldii	●	●	●					●							Trailing
Selaginella Emmeliana		●			●	●						●			Added sand
Selaginella Kraussiana		●				●						●			Added sand
Selaginella Martensii		●			●	●							●		Added sand
Selenicereus Spp.	●	●		●			●							●	Rambling form. Added bone meal
Senecio Articulata		●	●					●				●			
Senecio Macroglossa		●		●		●	●								Trailing or climbing
Senecio Mikanoides		●		●		●	●								Trailing or climbing
Senecio Rowleyanus		●	●					●							Creeping or trailing
Setcreasia Purpura		●		●			●					●			Eventually trailing
Siderasis Fuscata	●	●		●			●						●		Warm greenhouse
Sinningia Cardinalis	●		●				●					●			Added peat/sand/lime
Sinningia Leucotricha	●		●				●					●			Added peat/sand/lime
Sinningia Pusilla	●		●				●					●			Added peat/sand/lime
Sinningia Regina	●		●				●					●			Added peat/sand/lime
Sinningia Speciosa	●		●				●					●			Added peat/sand/lime
Smithiana Cinnabarina	●				●	●						●			
Smithiana Zebrina	●				●	●								●	
Solanum Capistratum			●				●						●		Orange/red berries
Solanum Pseudocapsicum			●				●						●		Orange/red berries
Sonerilla Margaritacea	●	●		●		●						●			Creeping form. Added leaf mould
Sophronitis Coccinea	●			●						●		●			Added sphagnum moss
Sparmannia Africana	●	●		●			●							●	
Spathiphyllum Wallisii	●			●		●						●			
Sprekelia Formosissima	●			●			●						●		
Stanhopea Spp.	●			●						●			●		Grow in wire basket
Stapelia Hirsuta	●	●	●					●				●			
Stapelia Nobilis	●	●	●					●				●			
Stapelia Variegata	●	●	●					●				●			
Stenocarpus Sinuatus	●	●	●				●							●	
Stenotaphrum Secundatum		●		●			●					●			
Stephanotis Spp.	●			●			●								Climber, delicate
Strelitzia Reginae	●		●				●							●	
Streptocarpus Polyanthus	●			●			●					●			Added peat
Streptocarpus Rexii	●			●			●					●			Added peat
Streptocarpus Saxorum	●			●			●					●			Added peat
Streptosolen Jamesonii	●		●				●							●	Greenhouse/conservatory
Strobilanthes Dyeranus	●	●		●			●							●	Added peat
Stromanthe Amabilis		●		●	●	●						●			
Stromanthe Sanguinea		●		●	●	●								●	
Syngonium Auritum		●		●			●								Climber. Added peat
Syngonium Podophyllum		●		●			●								Climber. Added peat
Tetrastigma Voinieranum		●		●			●								Rampant climber
Thunbergia Alata	●		●				●								Climber
Tillandsia Cyanea	●	●		●					●			●			
Tillandsia Lindenii	●	●		●					●				●		
Tillandsia Usneoides		●		●							●				Trailing
Tillandsia 'Air Plants'	●	●		●							●	●			
Trachycarpus Fortunei		●	●				●							●	
Tradescantia Albiflora		●	●	●			●								Trailing
Tradescantia Blossfeldiana		●	●	●			●								Trailing
Tradescantia Fluminensis		●	●	●			●								Trailing
Tradescantia Sillamontana		●	●	●			●								Trailing
Trichocereus Chilensis	●	●	●					●						●	Very slow growing
Trichocereus Spachianus	●	●	●					●						●	Very slow growing
Tulipa	●		●			●							●		Also on patio
Vallota Speciosa	●		●				●						●		
Vanda Cristata	●			●						●		●			
Vanda Teres	●			●						●				●	
Veltheimia Capensis	●		●				●					●			
Veltheimia Viridifolia	●		●				●						●		
Vriesia Fenestralis	●	●		●					●				●		
Vriesia Hieroglyphica	●	●		●					●					●	
Vriesia Splendens	●	●		●					●					●	
Vuylstekeara × Hybrids	●			●						●		●			
× Wilsonara	●			●						●		●			
Yucca Aloifolia		●	●				●							●	Also on patio
Zantedeschia Aethiopica	●			●			●							●	
Zantedeschia Elliottana	●	●		●			●						●		
Zantedeschia Rehmannii	●	●		●			●						●		
Zebrina Pendula		●	●	●			●								Trailing

236

Some unrelated species share the same popular name and are indicated by an asterisk.

Aeroplane Propeller Plant	*Cotyledon falcata*
African Blood Lily	*Haemanthus*
African Hemp	*Sparmannia africana*
African Lily	*Agapanthus*
African Milk Barrel	*Euphorbia horrida*
African Violet	*Saintpaulia*
Air Plants	*Tillandsia*
Alligator Pear	*Persea americana*
Aluminium Plant	*Pilea cadieri*
Amalia	*Laelia*
Amaryllis	*Hippeastrum*
*Amazon Lily	*Eucharis grandiflora*
*Amazon Lily	*Eucomis*
Amazon Zebra Plant	*Aechmea chantinii*
Angel's Tears	*Billbergia nutane*
Angel Wings	*Caladium hortulanum*
Antelope Ears	*Platycerium bifurcatum*
Aralia	*Fatsia japonica*
Areca Palm	*Chrysalidocarpus lutescens*
Arrowhead Vine	*Syngonium podophyllum*
Arum	*Zantedeschia*
Australian Brake	*Pteris tremula*
Australian Maidenhair	*Adiantum hispidulum*
Autumn Cattleya	*Cattleya labiata*
Avocado Pear	*Persea americana*
Azalea	*Rhododendron*
Aztec Lily	*Sprekelia formosissima*
Baboon Flower	*Babiana stricta*
Baby Echeveria	*Echeveria derenbergii*
Baby Pepper	*Rivina humilis*
Baby Primrose	*Primula malacoides*
*Baby's Tears	*Helxine soleirolii*
*Baby's Tears	*Hypoestes phyllostachya*
Balfour Aralia	*Polyscias balfouriana*
Ball Cactus	*Notocactus*
Ball Fern	*Davallia trichomanoides*
Bamboo Palm	*Chamaedorea erumpeus*
Banana	*Musa*
Banyan	*Ficus benghalensis*
Barbados Gooseberry	*Pereskia*
Bar-room Plant	*Aspidistra*
Barrel Cactus	*Echinocactus grusonii*
Basket Grass	*Oplismenus hirtellus*
Bay Tree	*Laurus nobilis*
Bead Plant	*Nertera granadensis*
Beaver-Tail Cactus	*Opuntia basilaris*
Beefsteak Geranium	*Saxifraga stolonifera*
*Beefsteak Plant	*Iresine herbstii*
*Beefsteak Plant	*Acalypha wilkesiana*
Belgian Evergreen	*Dracaena sanderana*
Belladonna Lily	*Amaryllis belladonna*
Benjamin Fig	*Ficus benjamina*
Birdcatcher Tree	*Pisonia umbellifera*
Bird of Paradise Flower	*Strelitzia reginae*
Bird's Nest Bromeliad	*Nidularium innocenti*
Bird's Nest Fern	*Asplenium nidus*
Bishop's Hood	*Astrophytum myriostigma*
Black-eyed Susan	*Thunbergia*
Black-Gold Philodendron	
	Philodendron melanchrysum
Blacking Plant	*Hibiscus rosa-sinensis*
Black Orchid	*Coelogyne pandurata*
Black Tree Aeonium	
	Aeonium arboreum 'Schwarzkopf'
Bladder Flower	*Araujia sericofera*

Bleeding-Heart Vine	*Clerodendron thomsoniae*
Blood Flower	*Haemanthus katherinae*
Bloodberry	*Rivina humilis*
Bloodleaf	*Iresine herbstii*
Blood Lily	*Haemanthus coccineus*
Blue-Flowered Torch	*Tillandsia lindenii*
Blue Screw Pine	*Pandanus baptiste*
*Blushing Bromeliad	*Neoregelia carolinae*
*Blushing Bromeliad	*Nidularium fulgens*
Boat Lily	*Rhoeo discolor*
Boston Fern	*Nephrolepis exallata*
Botanical Wonder	*× Fatshedera*
Bottle-Brush	*Callistemon citrinus*
Bottle Palm	*Beaucarnea recurvata*
Boundary Plant	*Yucca aloifolia*
Bowstring Hemp	*Sanseveria*
Box, common	*Buxus sempervirens*
Brazilian Eidelweiss	*Sinningia lencotricha*
Brazilian Plume	*Jacobinia carnea*
Brazilian Tree Fern	*Blechnum brasiliense*
Buddhist Pine	*Podocarpus macrophyllus*
Buffalo Grass	*Stenotaphrum secundatum*
Bunny Ears	*Opuntia microdasys*
Burmese Fishtail Palm	*Caryota mitys*
Bush Violets	*Browallia*
Busy Lizzie	*Impatiens*
Butterfly Orchid	*Oncidium papilio*
Butterfly Palm	*Chrysalidocarpus lutesceus*
Butterwort	*Pinguicula*
Button Fern	*Rotundifolis*
Buttons-on-a-String	*Cotyledon rupestris*
Cabbage Tree	*Cordyline australis*
Calamondin Orange	*Citrus mitis*
Calico Plant	*Aristolochia elegans*
Californian Pitcher Plant	
	Darlingtonia californica
Calla Lily	*Zantedeschia*
Canary Date Palm	*Phoenix dactylifera*
Canary Island Banana	
	Musa acuminata cavendishii
Canary Island Ivy	*Hedera canariensis*
Candelabra Plant	*Aloe arboresceus*
*Candle Plant	*Senecio articulata*
*Candle Plant	*Plectranthus certendalii*
Candy Corn Plant	*Manettia bicolor*
*Cape Cowslip	*Lachenalia aloides*
*Cape Cowslip	*Streptocarpus*
*Cape Grape	*Rhoicissus capensis*
*Cape Grape	*Medinilla magnifico*
Cape Ivy	*Senecio macroglossa*
Cape Jasmine	*Gardenia jasminoides*
Cape Leadwort	*Plumbago*
Cape Primrose	*Streptocarpus*
Capsicum	*Solanum*
Cardinal Flower	*Sinningia cardinalis*
Cardamom	*Elettaria cardamomum*
Carpet Plant	*Episcia*
Carrion Flowers	*Stapelia*
Cartwheel Plant	*Neoregelia carolinae*
Cast Iron Plant	*Aspidistra*
*Castor Oil Plant	*Fatsia*
*Castor Oil Plant	*Ricinus*
Cathedral Bells	*Cobaea scandens*
Cathedral Windows	*Calathea makoyana*
Catherine Wheel	*Haemanthus katherinae*
Cat's Jaws	*Fatsia felina*
Century Plant	*Agave*
*Chandelier Plant	*Kalanchoe tubiflora*
*Chandelier Plant	*Bryophyllum tubiflorum*

Chenille Plant	Acalypha hispida
Cherry Pie	Heliotropium
Chestnut Vine	Tetrastigma voinieranum
Chicken Gizzard	Iresine
Chilean Bell Flower	Lapageria rosea
Chin Cactus	Gymnocalycium
Chinese Evergreens	Aglaonema
Chinese Jade	Crassula arborescens
Chinese Lantern	Abutilon hybridum
Chinese Primrose	Primula sinensis
Christ Plant	Euphorbia milii
Christmas Cactus	Schlumbergia
Christmas Cheer	Sedum rubrotinctum
Christmas Cherry	Solanum pseudocapsicum
Christmas Heather	Erica caniculata
Christmas Kalanchoe	Kalanchoe blossfeldiana
Christmas Orchid	Cattleya triannaei
Christmas Pepper	Capsicum anuun
Christmas Star	Euphorbia pulcherrima
Cider Gum	Eucalyptus gunnii
Cigar Flower	Cuphea platycentra
Cinderella Slippers	Sinningia regina
Climbing Fig	Ficus pumila
Climbing Lily	Gloriosa
Climbing Pepper	Piper crocatum
Clock Vine	Thunbergia
Clown Orchid	Odontoglossum grande
Club Foot	Pachypodium
Club Moss	Selaginella kraussiana
Cluster Cattleya	Cattleya bowningiana
Cob Cactus	Lobivia hertrichiana
Cobra Lily	Darlingtonia californica
Cockscomb	Cetosia argentia
Cocktail Orchid	Cattleya intermedia
Coffee	Coffea
Common Maidenhair	
	Adiantum capillus-veneris
Cone Plant	Conophytum
Copihue	Lapageria rosea
Copperleaf	Acalypha wilkesiana
Coralberry	Ardisia crispa/crenata
Coral Berry	Aechman fulgens
Coral Moss	Nertera granadensis
Coral Vine	Antigon leptopus
Corn Plant	Dracaena fragrans
Cornstalk Plant	Dracaena fragrans
Crab Cactus	Schlumbergia truncata
Crane Lily	Strelitzia reginae
Creeping Charlie	Pilea nummulariifolia
Creeping Fig	Ficus pumila
Creeping Sailor	Saxifraga
Cretan Brake	Pteris cretica
Croton	Codiaeum variegatum pictum
Crown Cacti	Rebutia
Crown of Thorns	Euphorbia milii
Crystal Anthurium	Anthurium crystallinum
Cup and Saucer Vine	Cobaea scandens
Cupid's Bower	Achimenes
Curly Sentry Palm	Howea belmoreana
Cushion Aloe	Haworthia alternata/maughanii
Dagger Plant	Yucca aloifolia
Daffodil	Narcissus
Dancing-Lady Orchid	Oncidium
Deersfoot Fern	Davallia canariensis
Delta Maidenhair	Adiantum raddianum
Desert Privet	Peperomia magnoliifolia
Desert Rose	Adenium obesum 'multiflorum'
*Devil's Backbone	Kalanchoe daigremontiana
*Devil's Backbone	Pedilanthus

*Devil's Backbone	
	Bryophyllum daigremontianum
Devil's Ivy	Scindapsus aureus
*Devil's Tongue (Cactus)	Ferocactus latispinus
*Devil's Tongue	Sanseveria
*Devil's Tongue	Amorphophallus rivieri
Dinner Plant Aralia	Polyscias balfouriana
Donkey's Tail	Sedum morganium
Dragon Tree	Dracaena draco
Dumb Cane	Dieffenbachia
Dutchman's Pipe	Aristolochia
Dutch Wings	Gasteria
Dwarf Aloe	Aloe jacunda
Dwarf Bamboo	Arundinaria
Dwarf Fan Palm	Chamaerops humilis
Dwarf Myrtle	Myrtus communis
Dwarf Pomegranate	Punica granatum
Earth Star	Cryptanthus
Easter Cactus	Rhipsalidopsis
Egyptian Paper Plant	Cyperus papyrus
Egyptian Star Cluster	Pentas lanceolata
Elephant Ears	Caladium hortulanum
Elephant Foot Tree	Beaucarnea recurvata
Elephant's Ear, Giant	Alocasia macrorrhiza
Elfin Herb	Cuphea hyssopifolia
Emerald Fern	Asparagus densiflorus
Emerald Ripple	Peperomia caperata
English Ivy	Hedera helix
Erect Swordfern	Nephrolepsis cordifolia
Eucharist Lily	Eucharis grandiflora
European Fan Palm	Chamaerops humilis
Eyelash Begonia	Begonia boweri
Fairy Primrose	Primula malacoides
False African Violet	Streptocarpus saxorum
False Aralia	Dizygothica elegantissima
False Heather	Cuphea hyssopifolia
False Holly	Osmanthus heterophyllus
False Jerusalem Cherry	Solanum capistratum
Feather Palm	Phoenix roebelenii
Fiddleleaf Fig	Ficus lyrata
Fiddleleaf Philodendron	
	Philodendron bipennifolium
Fig	Ficus
Fingernail Plant	Neoregelia spectabilis
Finger Tree	Euphorbia tirncalli
Firebush	Streptosolen Jamesonii
Firecracker Flower	Crossandra infundibuliformis
Firecracker Plant	Cuphea
Firecracker Vine	Manettia bicolor
Fire Crown	Rebutia sinilis
Firewheel Tree	Stenocarpus sinuatus
Fish-Tail Fern	Cyrtomium falcatum
Fish-Tail Palms	Caryota
Five Fingers	Syngonium auritum
Flame Nettle	Coleus
Flame of the Woods	Ixora coccinea
Flame Violet	Episcia cupreata
Flamingo Flower	
	Anthurium andreanum/scherzeranum
Flaming Katy	Kalanchoe blossfeldiana
Flaming Sword	Vriesia splendens
Flat Palm	Howea forsteriana
Floradora	Stephanotis
Florist's Gloxinia	Sinningia speciosa
Flowering Maple	Abutilon
Forest Lily	Veltheimia
Foxtail Fern	Asparagus densiflorus
*Foxtail Orchid	Aerides

*Foxtail Orchid	Rhinostylus retusa
Frangipani	Plumeria
Freckle-Face	Hypoestes phyllostachya
Free-Flowering Orchid	Aerides fieldingii
French Heather	Erica hyemanalis
Friendship Plant	Pilea involucrata
Funkia	Hosta
Geranium	Pelargonium
Geranium Leaf Aralia	Polyscias guilfoylei
German Ivy	Senecio milkanoides
German Primrose	Primula obconica
Ghost Plant	Graptopetalum paraguayense
Giant Dracaena	Cordyline australis
Giant Pineapple Flower	Eucomis pole-evansii
Giant Toad Plant	Stapelia nobilis
Ginger Lily	Hedychium
Gingham Golf Ball	Euphorbia obesa
Glory Bower	Clerodendron thompsonae
Glory Lily	Gloriosa rothschildiana
Gloxinias	Sinningia
Gold-Dust Dracaenas	Dracaena succulosa
*Golden Ball Cactus	Notocactus leninghausii
*Golden Ball Cactus	Echinocactus grusonii
Golden Calla	Zantedeschia elliottiana
Golden-Rayed Lily	Lilium auratum
Golden Sedum	Sedum adolphi
Golden Tom Thumb	Parodia aureispina
Golden Trumpet	Allamanda cathartica
Goldfish Plant	Hypocyrta glabra
Goldfish Vine	Columnea
*Good-Luck Plant	Kalanchoe daigremontiana
*Good-Luck Plant	Cordyline terminalis
Goosefoot Plant	Syngonium auritum
Grape Ivy	Rhoicissus rhomboidea
Grey Beard	Tillandsia usneoides
Gum Tree	Eucalyptus
Hair Palm	Chamaerops humilis
*Haresfoot Fern	Polypodium aureum
*Haresfoot Fern	Davallia canariensis
Hart's Tongue Fern	Phyllitis scolopendrium
Heartleaf Philodendron	Philodendron scandens
Hearts Entangled	Ceropegia woodi
Hearts-on-a-String	Ceropegia woodi
Heath, Heather	Erica
Hedge Wattle	Acacia armata
Hedgehog Cactus	Echinocereus
Helmet Flower	Sinningia cardinalis
Hen and Chicken Fern	Asplenium bulbiferum
Herald's Trumpet	Beaumontia grandiflora
Holly Fern	Cyrtomium falcatum
Honey Plant	Hoya carnosa
Horse-Head Philodendron	
	Philodendron bipennifolium
Hotdog Plant	Senecio articulata
Hot Water Plant	Achimenes
Hottentot Fig	Carpobrotus
House Pine	Araucaria excelsa
Impala Lily	Adenium obesum 'multiflorum'
Inch Plant	Tradescantia
Indian Azalea	Rhododendron simsii
Indian Jasmine	Ixora
Indian Shot	Canna hybrida
Indoor Lime	Sparmannia africana
Indoor Linden	Sparmannia africana
Indoor Oats	Billbergia nutans
Iron-Bark Tree	Eucalyptus
Iron Cross Begonia	Begonia masonica

Italian Bellflower	Campanula isophylla
Ivy	Hedera
Ivy Tree	Fatshedera
Jacobean Lily	Sprekelia formosissima
Jacob's Ladder	Pedilanthus
Jade Plant	Cotyledon argentes
Jaggery Palm	Caryota uris
Japanese Fatsia	Fatsia japonica
Japanese Hibiscus	Hibiscus schizopetalus
Japanese Lantern	Hibiscus schizopetalus
Japanese Laurel	Aucuba japonica
Japanese Maple	Acer
Japanese Pittosporum	Pittosporum tobira
Japanese Sedge Grass	Carex morrowii
Japanese Spindle Tree	Euonymus japonica
Japanese Yew	Podocarpus macrophyllus
Jasmine, Jessamine	Jasminum
Javan Grape	Tetrastigma
Jelly Beans	Sedum rubrotinctum
Jerusalem Cherry	
	Solanum/Solanum pseudocapsicum
Joseph's Coat	Codiaeum variegatum pictum
Jungle Geranium	Ixora coccinea
Kaffir Lily	Clivia miniata
Kahili Ginger	Hedychium
Kangaroo Paw	Anigozanthos manglesii
Kangaroo Thorn	Acacia armata
Kangaroo Vine	Cissus antarctica
King of Bromelliads	Vriesia hieroglyphica
King's Crown	Jacobinia carnea
Kohuhu	Pittosporum tenuifolium
Kris Plant	Alocasia sanderiana
Kumquat	Fortunella
Lace Aloe	Aloe aristata
Lace Flower	Episcia dianthiflora
Ladder Fern	Nephrolepis exaltata
Lady Palm	Rhapis
Lady's Slipper	Paphiopedilum
Lawyer's Tongue	Gasteria
Lemon	Citrus limon
Lily-of-the-Valley Orchid	
	Odontoglossum pulchellum
Lipstick Plant	Aeschynanthus lobbianus
Living Stones	Lithops
Lizard Plant	Tetrastigma voinieranum
Lollipop Plant	Pachystachys lutea
Love Plant	Medinilla magnifica
Madagascar Dragon Tree	Dracaena marginata
Madagascar Jasmine	Stephanotis
Madagascar Periwinkle	Catharanthus roseus
Magic Flower	Achimenes
Maidenhair Fern	Adiantum
Marmalade Bush	Streptosolen jamesonii
Measles Plant	Hypoestes phyllostachya
Mexican Breadfruit	Monstera deliciosa
Mexican Firecracker	Echeveria setosa
*Mexican Hat	Bryophyllum daigremontianum
*Mexican Hat Plant	Kalanchoe daigremontiana
Milkbush	Euphorbia tirncalli
Mimicry Plant	Lithops
Mind-your-own-Business	Helxine soleirolii
Miniature Date Palm	Phoenix roebelanii
Miniature Grape Ivy	Cissus striatus
Miniature Wax Plant	Hoya bella
Mistletoe Cactus	Rhipsalis
Mistletoe Fig	Ficus deltoides

Monkey Plant	Ruellia makoyana
Monk's Hood	Astrophytum myriostigma
Moonstones	Pachyphytum oviferum
Morning Glory	Ipomea
Mosaic Leaf	Fittonia verschaffeltii
Moses-in-the-Cradle	Rhoeo discolor
Moss Crassula	Cotyledon lycopodioides
Moss Fern	Selaginella emelliana
Mother-in-Law's Tongue	Sanseveria
Mother-of-Pearl Plant	Graptopetalum paraguayense
*Mother-of-Thousands	Saxifraga stolonifera
*Mother-of-Thousands	Tolmiea menziesii
Mother Spleenwort	Asplenium bulbiferum
Mountain Cabbage Tree	Cordyline indivisa
Myrtle	Myrtus
Netted Vriesia	Vriesia fenestralis
Never-Never Plant	Ctenanthe oppenheimiana
Norfolk Island Pine	Araucaria excelsa
October Plant	Sedum sieboldii
Oilcloth Plant	Anthurium andreanum
Old Lady Cactus	Mamillaria hahniana
Old Maid	Catharanthus roseus
Old Man Cactus	Cephalocereus senilis
Oleander	Nerium
Orange Star	Guzmania lingulata
Orchid Cactus	Epiphyllum
Ornamental Yam	Dioscorea discolor
Ox-Tongue	Gasteria
Ox-Tongue Lily	Haemanthus coccineus
Painted Lady	Echeveria serenbergii
Painted Leaf Begonia	Begonia Rex
Painted Leaves	Coleus
Painted Netleaf	Fittonia verschaffeltii
Painter's Palette	Anthurium andreanum
Panama Orange	Citrus mitis
Panamiga	Pilea involucrata
Panda Plant	Kalanchoe tomentosa
Paper Flower	Bougainvillaea glabra
Papyrus	Cyperus papyrus
Paradise Palm	Howea forsteriana
Parasol Plant	Heptapleurum
Parchment Bark	Pittosporum tenuifolium
Parlour Maple	Abutilon
Parlour Palm	Chamaedorea elegans
Parrot Leaf	Alternanthera amoena
Partridge-Breasted Aloe	Aloe variegata
Passion Flower	Passiflora
Patience Plant	Impatiens
Peace Lily	Spathiphyllum
*Peacock Plant	Calathea makoyana
*Peacock Plant	Stromanthe amabilis
Peanut Cactus	Chamaecereus silvestrii
Pearl Plant	Haworthia margaretifolia
Pencil Tree	Euphorbia tirncalli
Pen Wiper	Kalanchoe somaliensis
Pepper, Christmas	Capsicum annun
Pepper, Red	Capsicum anuun
Persian Shield	Strobilanthes dyerianus
Persian Violet	Exacum affine
Pheasant Leaf	Cryptanthus fosterianus/zonatus
Piggy-Back Plant	Tolmiea menziesii
Pigtail Plant	Anthurium scherzeranum
Pineapple	Ananas
Pineapple Flower	Eucomis
Pineapple Lily	Eucomis zambesiaca
Pineapple, Red	Ananas brachatus 'striatus'
Pineapple, Variegated	Ananus comosus
Pink Acanthus	Jacobinia carnea
Pink Calla	Zantedeschia rehmanii
Pink Quill	Tillandsia cyanea
Pin-Wheel	Aeonium haworthii
Pitcher Plant	Sarracenia
Plantain Lily	Hosta
Poinsettia	Euphorbia pulcherrima
Polka-Dot Plant	Hypoestes phyllostachya
Polynesian Ti Plant	Cordyline terminalis
Ponytail Plant	Beaucarnea recurvata
Porcelain Flower	Hoya australis
Pothos Vine	Scindapsus aureus
Pouch Flower	Calceolaria herbeohybrida
Powder-Puff Cactus	Mamillaria bocasana
Prayer Plant	Maranta/Maranta leuconeura
Prickly Pear	Opuntia
Purple False Eranthemum	Pseuderanthemum
Purple Heart	Setcreasia purpura
Purple Orchid Tree	Bauhinia variegata
Purple Passion Vine	Gynura scandens
Purple Velvet Plant	Gynura aurantiaca
*Pussy's Ears	Kolanchoe tomentosa
*Pussy's Ears	Cyanotis somaliensis
Queen of Bromelliads	Aechmea chantinii
Queen-of-the-Night	Selenicereus
Queensland Umbrella Tree	Schefflera actinophylla
Queen's Spiderwort	Dichorisandra
Queen's Tears	Billbergia nutane
Rabbit Tracks	Maranta leuconeura
Rainbow Star	Cryptanthus bromeloides
Rainbow Vine	Pellionia pulchra
Rat Tail Cactus	Aporocactus
Rattlesnake Plant	Calathea insignia
Red Banana	Musa coccinea
Red Crown	Rebutia miniscula
Red-Hot Cat's Tail	Acalypha hispida
Red Pepper	Capsicum anuun
Red-White-and-Blue Flower	Cuphea ignea
Regal Elk-Horn Fern	Platysperium grande
Rex-Begonia Vine	Cissus Discolor
Ribbon Cactus	Pedilanthus
Ribbon Grass	Oplismenus hirtellus
*Ribbon Plant	Chlorophytum comosum
*Ribbon Plant	Dracaena sanderana
Rib Fern	Blechnum brasiliense
*Rock Lily	Arthropodium cirrhatum
*Rock Lily	Dendrobium
Rooting Fig	Ficus radicans
Rosary Plant	Cotyledon rupestris
Rosary Vine	Ceropegia woodi
Rose Bay	Nerium oleander
Rose Grape	Medinilla magnifica
Rose Mallow	Hibiscus rosa-sinensis
Rose of China	Hibiscus rosa-sinensis
Rose of Smyrna	Hibiscus rosa-sinensis
Rose Periwinkle	Catharanthus roseus
Rose Pincushion	Mamillaria zeilmanniana
Rose Tuna	Opuntia basilaris
Rouge Plant	Rivina humilis
Royal Velvet Plant	Gynura aurantiaca
Rubber Plant	Ficus elastica
St Augustine's Grass	Stenotaphrum
St Bernard's Lily	Chlorophytum comosum
Saffron Spike	Aphelandra
*Sago Palm	Cycas revoluta